Million Dollar AGENTS

How Top Real Estate Agents
Really Create HIGH INCOME,
WEALTH, AND INDEPENDENCE

Phil Hollander & Dan Lok

INTERNATIONAL BEST SELLING AUTHORS

ISBN-13: 978-1-7771598-4-9 (Hardcover)

ISBN-13: 978-1-7771598-5-6 (Paperback)

ISBN-13: 978-1-7771598-3-2 (eBook)

This publication is designed to provide accurate and authoritative information in regard to the subject matter covered. It is sold with the understanding that the publisher is not engaged in rendering medical, legal, accounting, or other professional services.

Published by: Dan Lok Education, Inc.
www.DanLok.com

Address:
3318 - 1055 Dunsmuir Street
Vancouver, BC, Canada
V7X 1L2

"A rare and insightful view into how highly successful Real Estate Professionals create a balanced and prosperous lifestyle out of what can be a chaotic and highly unpredictable business. Written in a refreshing interview format that brings to life the unique systems and strategies of Agents that have truly made it in the Real Estate Industry."

Jillian Dobson
Broker
RE/MAX Realtron Realty Inc., Brokerage

This book is dedicated to all those realtors that I have met throughout the years who have taught me invaluable lessons not only about what really works in terms of creating a hugely successful real estate practice but also about what doesn't work.

I wish to thank all those who provided valuable insights and contributions to the creation of this book which include first and foremost the agents that I have interviewed and the agents, managers, brokers, and owners that I have met and worked with over the years, and my friends and colleagues at Morris Real Estate Marketing Group. A very special thank you to Bob Reaume who did an absolutely tremendous job of editing this book. I also wish to thank my beautiful wife Lisa and two amazing children, Sydney and Ryan, who have been very understanding as I have travelled throughout North America doing my work over the past decade and a half. I also dedicate this book to the loving memory of my mother, Carole Hollander, who has always been a great inspiration in how she courageously lived her life.

"People are always looking for the magic bullet. I really want to make clear in this book through these interviews that there is no magic bullet. If you look at the best athletes, the best musicians, the best business people, they really do the fundamentals well consistently over and over and over again."

"Since you can't be everything to everyone all the time, it is critical to have systems of communication that leverage both your time and relationships."

-Phil Hollander

Contents

Introduction 1

1. RICHARD ROBBINS:
    Helping You Build a Business You'll Love 3

2. PETER GAIN:
    Moving From Me to We 34

3. COLIN BLAND:
    Focus on Your Clients' Needs. 64

4. LEE YULE:
    The King of I Am 84

5. FRANCIS MACDONALD:
    Fire in the Belly 114

6. BILL PARNABY:
    Always Do the Right Thing 154

7. NOAH DOBSON:
    Well-Taken-Care-of Clients 183

8. GRETA TORLEN:
    Offices like Ours, Working with Companies like Yours . . . 208

9. WADE WEBB:
    One No Closer to a Yes 236

EPILOGUE 261

Introduction

THIS BOOK IS the result of over fifteen years of travelling throughout both Canada and the United States and meeting, speaking and working with literally thousands of real estate agents. After working with some of the top agents in North America, there is a clear and definitive common thread that defines them. If you really take a close look at what we would refer to as the "top 10% of realtors" who are successful and prosperous, while there are differences, there are many profound similarities:

- **In how they structure their business,**

- **Their strategies,**

- **Their overall mindset and how they approach what they do.**

This stands in stark contrast to the vast majority of agents who are struggling or just getting by barely making a living.

We have often said that "we have never met the five year old that decided they want to be a realtor when they grow up." Most come to real estate as a second or third profession and usually from vastly different backgrounds. Most agents start off in the same place with lots of unanticipated startup expenses and little or no business at the beginning. The ones who actually build a prosperous and successful real estate career with consistent income and a great lifestyle for their families have done so by discovering a few simple truths about the real estate business. Simple truths like how to manage themselves and their relationships.

They have done so in such a way as to navigate the journey from being a transactional agent perpetuating the feast-to-famine cycle, always being at the whim of the economy and competing with every other agent in their market, to creating a systems-based business and taking back control over their business and their lives.

Ultimately, this book is about the journey from being a transactional agent to becoming a prosperous systems-based one where it is all about the lifestyle. What these agents interviewed in this book have done is make the real estate business work for them rather than the majority of agents who can be at the whim of what can be a wildly unpredictable and tumultuous business.

In writing this book, we interviewed a broad cross section of the most successful agents and allowed them to tell their story with the ultimate goal of uncovering and sharing some of their "golden nuggets" of wisdom.

One of our favorite sayings is that "*all the great truths in life are simple for if they were complex everyone would understand them.*" It is our intent to share some of these simple truths with you so that you too will have a rich and rewarding real estate career.

Phil Hollander & Dan Lok
February 2017

RICHARD ROBBINS:
Helping You Build a Business You'll Love

RICHARD ENTHUSIASTICALLY BEGAN a career in real estate sales at the age of 24. After four record-breaking years including hitting a six figure income in his first year and every year after that, Richard decided it was time for a change. In 1989, Richard opened his own real estate brokerage some 90 miles from his small home town of Peterborough, Ontario and amidst one of the worst real estate recessions the country had ever seen.

Richard was undeterred by the enormous obstacles and in just 3 years he successfully ranked among the top 1% of all realtors in his marketplace and grew a powerhouse brokerage that captured 12% market share. Richard's extraordinary leadership and innate ability to inspire peak performance in his fellow agents also lead his successful brokerage of only 20 agents to achieve the "highest production per agent" of any brokerage within its trading area. It was here that Richard discovered a profound passion for speaking and helping others to achieve goals they never thought possible.

Today, Richard is an author, business mentor and sought-after expert in the field of personal and professional performance. He is best described by his audiences as the epitome of a true integrity-powered leader, and considers it his greatest honour to have had the opportunity to ignite the lives of over 250,000 audience members thus far.

On a personal note, Richard believes life is to be experienced at every opportunity. From flying a fighter jet through the mountains of South Africa to heli-skiing at the peaks of Whistler, racing NASCAR with his brothers and dad, and coming face-to-face with sharks some 80 feet below sea level – Richard seizes each and every opportunity to live life BIG.

Richard and his wife, Sue, Co-founder and Managing Director at Richard Robbins International (RRI), reside in Markham, Ontario, with their two extraordinary children, Jaimie and Tanner. The Robbins' are avid readers, fitness/health enthusiasts and personal development junkies who truly believe there's no place like home.

RICHARD ROBBINS IS a great example of an agent who like so many, start off with very humble beginnings. Initially selling firewood outside a car dealership as a young man he not only managed to build a hugely successful real estate practice, started his own brokerage and then created a world- class international real estate training and coaching company. In this interview he not only shares his personal journey to success, he also provides invaluable insights into how realtors can create a life for themselves and their families from the real estate business, rather than have the business control them. As you will read, he provides insights into the critical strategies and mindset a realtor needs to have to truly make it in this business.

Phil/Dan: We are here with Richard Robbins - the iconic real estate trainer, coach, mentor, and founder of the incredibly successful Richard Robbins International (RRI). For the last two decades, Richard has literally worked with hundreds of thousands of agents not only throughout North America but worldwide, helping them take their businesses to the next level. Rich, we really appreciate you taking time with us today, thank you so much.

Richard: My pleasure.

Phil/Dan: You are a great example. So many people come into the real estate business, as you know, and don't make it. You're an example of somebody who has come into the real estate business, been here for a long time, and you've been incredibly successful, but that's not typical. What did you do before real estate? How did you kind of find yourself in the real estate business?

Richard: First, I went to college but I left after a couple of months and not because I graduated early. I was never really good in school. I didn't enjoy studying subjects I didn't want to study. So, what I started to do, believe it or not, was order firewood by the transport truckload. I rented space in Peterborough behind an auto dealership, had the wood dropped off then I hired people to come and split it. Then I sold it.

I also worked with my dad. He was a local business person in Peterborough. He had three service stations, including the highest volume service station in Peterborough. It had lube shops and merchandise. I worked there for a number of years, and then I took over my own station. I was working then for Shell Canada, but I didn't enjoy the business concept. There are people that we meet as we move through life, and these people can influence our lives in a very positive or negative way. I think all of us are influenced by people, but the question is, do we do anything with the influence?

I used to play squash with a guy by the name of Terry Windrem, who is still a very good friend of mine. He is four years older than me and he was in the insurance business, insurance sales. And here I am in this old rickety old car, you know, in my early 20s, and he's driving a BMW. And I go, "What's the deal here man?"

I got really curious and found out what he was doing. He invited me to his house for dinner – oh, and he's got a nice house. I said, "Wow, this looks pretty good," and I started asking about sales. He said, "Well, if you're good at it there's a lot of money in it." I was always ambitious, and when you're in your 20s you're thinking mostly about money. It's not something that drives me now but back then I was a little egotistical.

After our meeting I thought to myself, well, I would like to sell. I was driving by a Century 21 office in Peterborough and I remember seeing really nice cars in the parking lot. The people I could see through the glass were actually dressed in suits! I thought, "Well, that's really cool." I decided to meet with the manager which led to getting my real estate license.

There was no obvious master plan. It was just, Oh, I'm going to sell something, and I want to sell something that I enjoy. When I look out my window, right here in my office, I see all of these houses, and all of these roofs. And they have to be bought and sold. It's something tangible. So, that's how I got into real estate.

Phil/Dan: So, here you are, you are in a brand new profession, a young man at 24 years old. What would you say was your biggest challenge starting out? Your story is significant because a lot of people don't make it in real estate, many don't last beyond their first year. What was your biggest challenge back then?

Richard: My age - because I looked young. I had trouble gaining people's confidence, for which I don't blame them. I did look very young. So, what I had to do was outwork everybody. I had to generate more leads than everybody else because I wasn't terribly experienced.

If I generated a lot of leads then I could get a few people to deal with me while I gained some experience. My biggest challenge when I started was my immaturity. The advantage I had was that my dad was a very successful businessman. When I was very, very young I used to go to work with him on weekends.

As a result, I had a certain amount of business savvy because I was always listening to my dad. I still to this day remember counting money. He worked for the Telegram Newspaper which used to be the main competitor with the Toronto Star, although they are no longer around. I remember my dad was a district manager and used to manage all of these carriers and the regional managers. I remember sitting at our table counting all of the coins that everybody had dropped off, then my dad counted them and put them in the bank. I used to go to the bank with him and he'd be putting all this money in.

I spent a lot of time with my dad when I was young. But I also had business savvy and I was also very interested in success. I knew that what my dad was doing wasn't necessarily what I wanted to do because I had already done it.

Phil/Dan: *So, looking back over your career, your incredible career, not only as a realtor but as an incredibly successful training and development company for realtors, among the top today, what do you say has been the biggest challenge?*

Richard: You've got to keep reinventing yourself. The world is changing so fast now, and it's changing so much quicker than it used to. And of course it's not going to slow down - technology is going to pick up the speed of change.

So, I think for real estate agents, we've got to keep reinventing ourselves. If you look at the average consumer today in the real estate industry, they

Million Dollar Agent Key Idea #1
"To be successful in the real estate business you have to keep reinventing yourself."

know so much more. They're so much more educated than they were back in 1985, when I started. In 1985, the real estate agent was a gatekeeper of information. Today the consumer has all the information that at one time it had to go to an agent to get.

You have to ask yourself, "Okay, how do I keep bringing different value in the marketplace as a business?" I don't care whether it's your business, my business, or a real estate business. Ask, "How do I keep bringing new value that the people will value?" I remember Jim Rohn, he was one of my great mentors, and he said, "If we would wake up every day, and we would spend as much time thinking about how to deliver value to the marketplaces as we do thinking about how to make money, we'd soon find ourselves rich beyond belief."

Phil/Dan: *What a powerful statement that is.*

Richard: Business people and salespeople are often thinking about the deal and making money, which is necessary. We've got to do that, there's rent to pay, food to eat, things like that. But I think the big question we've got to ask ourselves on a regular basis is, what am I doing today that is providing tremendous value to the marketplace? And if what you are doing is not, then you've got to say, "Okay, how do I change, how do I evolve, how do I reinvent myself so that I'm always relevant?" So, I think that's probably the ongoing challenge for me, how can we remain relevant to our customers?

Million Dollar Agent Key Idea #2

"Today, realtors are no longer the gatekeepers of information, so the question is how do I keep bringing value to the marketplace?"

Phil/Dan: *No matter what profession you are in - even if it's medicine - people skills can become obsolete if you don't make continuous changes, and real estate is no different. With the proliferation of information available today, people think they know as much as the realtors do, so realtors have to constantly find ways to create value. How would you describe your lifestyle now versus when you first started? I know my lifestyle was vastly different when I started out professionally many, many years ago.*

Richard: In the early days, what I did was outwork the competition. Most times, I would be the first one in the office and the last to leave. I was single, I had lots of energy, lots of enthusiasm, and I didn't mind working. So, I just put in the time. And then, over time what happened, and I think this happens to all business people is when you first start a new business you're excited, you want to give everything you've got to it.

But then what happens after a few years is, I am not saying you're not excited, you're still excited, but you lose some of that enthusiasm, and all of a sudden you don't want to be giving the business that much energy. So you have to change the way you function. I think real estate people should read the book *E—myth* by Michael Gerber. In it he says:

"Your business should be a vehicle to enrich your life, not one that drains the life out of you."

I was driving my business – I was having so much fun, it was so great. And then, all of a sudden I reached a point of reflection. "Well, just a minute here, Rich. If I want to keep doing more, that means I've got to keep working more. Instead of working harder, I needed to figure out how to work a little bit smarter." I've got to start to analyze everything I do, and ask myself, "Is everything I'm doing every day moving me towards the goal that I want?" And what I discovered when I was about 27, was that the goal that I wanted was a lifestyle goal. "Well, how do I want my life to be?"

And I was always a big goal setter. My mom still tells the story about me on New Year's Day, sitting down with everybody having dinner. I was a teenager and said to everyone, "Okay, I got pads and bring me pencils. Let's all set some goals for next year." I was always a goal setter and I asked myself, "Isn't the purpose of being in business – yes, you want to bring value to the marketplace – but that you serve your customers well?" Yeah, now we want to enjoy it, I get it. But at the end of the day you want to say to yourself, "I want something that is such a cool business that it has allowed me to build a life that I love." And I would say, really that's become our new tagline "helping you build a business you'll love," we haven't even publicized it yet.

> **Million Dollar Agent Key Idea #3**
> *"With the proliferation of information available today, people think they know as much as the realtors do, so realtors have to constantly find ways to create value."*

Phil/Dan: *What a fabulous tagline.*

Richard: Yes, because that's what it's all about. So, I look at my life and most of the time I do everything all day that I love to do. My life is very well-balanced now. I spend a lot of time with my wife; I get the opportunity to read a lot, to play golf as much as I want. But I still work really hard. Now the difference is, I find that I'm highly productive. I get a lot done in a short period of time, when I first started I wasn't as highly productive - I was high energy.

Phil/Dan: *A metaphor comes to mind: They say it takes the most fuel for the plane to take off but once it's in flight, it's a question of efficiency. So, that's very fascinating, you are a great example of that. You reversed engineered that - You say, "Well, what do I want to create here, and then what's the best way to do it as opposed to it's all about the money?"*

And the other thing you said that I think was so powerful is that, in order to be successful you need the passion, you need a kind of positive

*energy but you can't sustain all that youthful energy when you're 45 and
older. You need to find ways to rejuvenate yourself. And that's really what
you've done and it's pretty amazing, and quite an inspiration. So, here
you are, you know, many, many years later, had such tremendous success.
What drives you today to take things to the next level? I know you could
retire today if you wanted to, not that you should, but you could.*

Million Dollar Agent Key Idea #4
*"It takes the most fuel for the plane
to take off, but once it's in flight it's
a question of efficiency."*

Richard: I think retirement is almost a punishment. I don't look at retirement as something I want to do. Maybe that will change in the future, I don't know. But right now, I can't imagine retiring; I don't know what I'd do!

I have a really well-balanced life, and that doesn't mean that I don't work a lot, I do work a lot. It means I get to do almost everything else I want to do. I don't feel like I'm missing anything. I feel like my life is very, very good. Well, if I really enjoy what I do, what would I retire to? I really love what I do - I enjoy the process, speaking, working with the coaches and helping them get better. I enjoy putting on the multi-day events that we do. I'm developing a new RRI On Demand, which is a new training program that's been a lot of fun.

Well, here's an analogy I think about: people will get together on the weekends and play games - they play cards or they play monopoly, they play video games, they play different types of games. I look at them and say, why on earth would somebody play a game because a game is nothing but problems? Think about a game, when you're playing a video game they keep presenting you with problems and your objective is to try to overcome that problem so you can get to the next level.

So, you're sitting there the whole time trying to solve a problem, solve a problem, solve a problem. Oh blast, start again. And people say they like playing these games. Why do they like playing games? Human beings need to be stimulated, human beings need challenge.

I don't play videogames. Why wouldn't I play a video game? I'm playing the game of life. And a lot of people go to work and say, "Oh, boy I have lot of problems today." What do you think you've got when you're playing cards? What do you think you get when you are playing a video game? You get problems. Why are you so excited about solving those problems? You know why? Because at the end if you lose it doesn't matter, you get to start all over again. There's no fear of loss, there's no fear of failure, because it's just a game. Why not take that attitude towards life and look at your business and your life as the big game?

Phil/Dan: That's fascinating. That's the true spirit of entrepreneurialism. What stops people from being successful in real estate, or in any business, is the fear of failure. Some people are afraid to fail when they are playing a card game on the weekend or a videogame or what have you. I think growth and challenge is how we grow.

As you said, we're either growing or deteriorating - there's no in between. It's healthier for us to be stimulated in that way. So, I hope you never retire Richard. Let me ask you this: What do you like most about being in real estate? Given the principles you teach, you could take this to any business but real estate is the area that you've become iconic in. What do you like most about being in this business?

Million Dollar Agent Key Idea #5
"If you look at life and your business like playing a game it makes solving problems fun and enjoyable."

Richard: Well, first of all, I've been in here since I was 24. So, it's pretty well all I've ever done.

Phil/Dan: It's the water you're swimming in.

Richard: Yeah, it's the water. But it's the coolest business in the world. A plane takes off and I look down and what do I see? Houses, I see houses everywhere. This is incredible! Those people have to buy and sell homes. I love the idea that its tangible. I love the idea that they are everywhere. I love the idea that somebody's home is generally the most valuable asset. I love the idea that somebody's home is where they have their biggest net worth. A home is where somebody raises their family and you get to help them. A real estate agent is pure entrepreneurship because you don't have to go to school for four years.

Now, some people would argue. I look at that and say, it's so cool that somebody can go to school for whatever period of time they go school, and if they're committed to being really good, they're going to go out there and get trained, they're going to get coached, and they're going to learn, and they're going to learn the best practices then they can make themselves six and seven figure incomes. The number one agent in Canada last year, probably made around six or six and a half million dollars. Think about that number. Where can you go? Where can you go?

Phil/Dan: *There's no other profession in the world where with that entry threshold you can do that well.*

Million Dollar Agent Key Idea #6
"There are few other professions in the world with such a low entry threshold where you can do so well financially."

Richard: Right, and as soon as you get licensed, guess where the product is? It's sitting – it's not like you're going to make anything. Think about it. You get in some business and you've got to lease space. You want to open up a restaurant? Think about the amount of money you got to invest to open up a restaurant. That's entrepreneurship. You think, "But okay, I'm going to go out and I'm going to start building furniture." Well, think about the amount of money you've got to spend to start building. You've got to build it, you've got to sell it, and it goes on, and on, and on. Real estate is get a license, walk across the street and there are homes.

Million Dollar Agent Key Idea #7
"Real estate is such a great profession because as soon as you get licensed the product you are selling is right in front of you."

Phil/Dan: *Precisely.*

Richard: How good is that?

Phil/Dan: *You know the irony, Rich, is that you've got a low entry threshold; you've got virtually unlimited income. The irony is so many people fail. I think you said 90% of people who are entering this business are not enjoying life and they're struggling. Only 10% are really making it. Why? As you've often said, it's because they're not willing to invest in learning the skills. They don't teach you anything in real estate when you get your license about how to sell anything. They don't teach business skills, they don't teach you how to put in systems and run your business. It's such a big upside yet so few people make it; maybe that's the way it's supposed to be, but it doesn't have to be that way.*

Richard: Well, yeah, because of the low entry level and minimum time and money investment, a lot of people get in. And a lot of people get in and say, "I'm going to give it a try." And that's the biggest mistake you'll ever make. Trying real estate? No, real estate will try you, and it will beat you up and you won't last.

Phil/Dan: *You know, it's funny you should say that. We went on vacation with one of our neighbors who had gone into real estate because she had young children. And the thought was I'll have more time to spend with my kids. The irony is that she had to hire a nanny because people* wanted to see her when her kids wanted her most. There are some fundamental principles to be successful in this business. What makes you the best at what you do? I mean there are only a handful that have gone to the place you've gone. How did you do it?

Million Dollar Agent Key Idea #8

"To be successful in real estate you can't just 'try real estate' because real estate will try you."

Richard: Well, I think first of all it's very difficult. The price you pay to be great at anything is very, very high. And I would suggest that most people aren't willing to pay the price. So, the price for them is very, very high. The second component - who is your customer? You've got to know clearly who your customer is and we know who our customer is. Our customer is the top 10% of the industry. Our coaching isn't the most inexpensive, our events aren't the most inexpensive nor will they ever be, because our teaching is very businesslike.

A lot of people look at you and say, "real estate agents generally see themselves as salespeople." I don't see them as salespeople. I see them as business people. So, what we do is help transform somebody from being a salesperson into becoming a business person. They are entrepreneurs.

Phil/Dan: And that's a mindset shift, Rich?

Million Dollar Agent Key Idea #9

"The most successful real estate agents see themselves as business people and entrepreneurs, not just as salespeople."

Richard: Mindset totally. Most people wake up every day and they're thinking, okay I've got to do it. You'll do it, you'll do it, you'll do it, you'll do it, finally realizing, No, you've got to figure out how to build a business. And first of all, you've got to decide what do you want this business to provide? What? Why are you doing it? What it is you're doing? Let's paint a picture as to what sort of life you want to have - How many hours do you want to work, how much money do you want to make? We get really clear on that. We've got to know what we're trying to build, right? Now we know what we're trying to build. So, I get an idea. How many deals you want to do? Do you want to work more for listing buyers? Or sellers? That's what business people do.

Then we say, "Okay, now how are we going to build a business that will provide that to you? How are we going to build you a business that will fully support and serve the life that you want to live? Lots of different mindsets come with the people in this industry. So, if they're just trying to do deals every day, we're not for them, we know that. I look at it and say, "Our." I always say that working with our company is like getting your masters in real estate. If you're just going to high school in real estate, we are not the company for you. But if you really want to take it to the next level, and you want to build something that's really cool, that doesn't necessarily mean you want to make 100s of 1000s of dollars a year. Somebody could make $150,000 a year and build a great business.

Phil/Dan: So, would you say that RRI is a company that helps you even if you may not be the top 10% yet. But if that's your aspiration, you would do a whole lot better than what you're doing now, and that's the vehicle to take you there?

Richard: Yeah.

Phil/Dan: And so, you don't have to be the elite but you have to have the want to get there. Or at least evolve significantly from where you are, right?

Richard: Right. And that starts with, are you willing to make a significant investment in your own personal evolvement? Most agents aren't which is unfortunate. You get out there and you say, "Okay, now I want to do whole bunch of sales and build a business." So okay, well, what training do you have to do that? You don't have any. And you think you're going to walk out into the world and be a real success against people that have all kinds of great training and know how to do listing presentations, know how to handle incoming calls, know how to convert internet leads into appointments, know how to negotiate offers, know how to get buyers to work exclusively with them. You're going to go competing against people that know how to do that, and you have no training, and you think you're going to be able to compete? No, no.

Phil/Dan: It's amazing, and that's the way it is though. People don't realize that the best are the best for a reason, or the people that are successful are prosperous for a reason. And they're skilled, they have invested in themselves. And that's a good thing. There is a Mark Twain quote that says, "Talent alone is useless without training." And then, the other part of that quote is, "Thank God." Because if it's ultimately talent, then no matter how much training you've got, it wouldn't really matter.

And I think this is so powerful, because many realtors go into this business with dollar signs in their eyes and they don't realize that it's a business and they try and reinvent the wheel. And when I speak with younger realtors, they think, Well, I'm going to do real estate differently, I'm going to reinvent real estate. So, as you indicated it's important to be an entrepreneur and reinvent things, but there are fundamental laws that are like the law of gravity that you have to organize your business in a certain way. And you need to model the best, because if you're not modeling the best, who are you modeling? I think that's still very, very important.

Million Dollar Agent Key Idea #10
"There are a lot of people who may not have the requisite talent but they recognize that they can get to where they want to go, there is a pathway."

Phil/Dan: *What are the key qualities or attributes that make the top 10%?*

Richard: They have great planning, so they have business plans, right. They have great lead generating systems in place. You've got to generate a lot of leads in real estate, and you've got to do that systematically.

All great producers have leads coming in every day. Well, you better know how to qualify these leads. Real estate is an interesting topic to everybody; everybody wants to talk about it.

Million Dollar Agent Key Idea #11
"Being successful in real estate all starts with your willingness to make an investment in your own personal evolvement."

So, do you have the ability to quickly, in a conversation that might only be three or four minutes long, ask some questions to discover if there is really true motivation there and choose whether you can be of service to those people or not? Doctors only work with sick people. Shouldn't we be working with people that want to buy and sell real estate? One of the greatest wastes of time is working with people that don't have to buy real estate.

Phil/Dan: *Oh, isn't that true. Often times, I tell a 20-something realtor - emailers and texters - that you can't run your business on the internet. I mean you can do well with your leads perhaps, but it needs an escalation process where you want to meet someone face-to-face, because that's where in-person contact is made and that is very, very powerful. Let me ask you this Rich - The real estate business is what? How would you complete that sentence?*

Richard: So cool, right?

Phil/Dan: That's amazing after all these years. I think you've created that excitement because it's not something that comes from within that it's very cool. From a mindset perspective, how do the top realtors look at the world differently? How are they thinking differently? Yes, they're doing business planning, they've got their business. When people look at the same thing, they see different things. What would you say about the top realtors?

Million Dollar Agent Key Idea #12
"The key to success in real estate sales is to get face-to-face, face-to-face, and face-to-face. If you can't get face-to-face you're not going to make any money."

Richard: They love it, and they see this amazing opportunity. Think about this. You've got to love what you do if you want to be a great success in the world. I don't think there is a professional athlete in the world that wakes up in the morning and hates what they do. Could you be that good if you hated it, even if you're the most talented in the world? There's no way you're going to put in the time, you're not going to put in the practice.

You've got to be passionate about it. Passion to me is some form of love for what it is you get to do every day.

Can you help somebody become passionate? The answer is yes, because that's an outlook. Can you change somebody's outlook about something? One hundred percent - because some people just look at everything in the wrong way. Some people look at the industry and they can see everything that's wrong and other people look at the industry and they can see everything that's right. Some people can look at the industry and they can see the problems that come in sales. "Buyers and sellers are liars," they say all the time. Or there is no loyalty anymore. You want to know something? I can find lots of problems in any business, but I can also find opportunity.

So, when you look at the world, it's what you choose to look at. Wayne Dyer said, "When you change the way you look at things, the things you look at change." So, I can look at my business and I could wake up in the morning and say what a crazy business I'm in. Or you wake up and say, Wow, there are houses everywhere, there are agents out there that are trying to do well, and they really need our help and we want to help them if we can. When I look at a top producer and we work with some of the elite, they are making millions of dollars. We work with some that are making $100,000. The ones who are making millions, they're passionate, they're always thinking about it, they're always trying to figure how to be better -- it's not a means to an end.

Phil/Dan: *In preparing for this book I did a number of interviews of some really successful realtors and they didn't always think that way. There was this -- I call it the walk in the park moments when they realized that what they were doing wasn't working. And they came to this epiphany moment where they said, "I've got to change. I've got to shift my way of thinking first and then of course my strategy and the behavioral practice is second." Look at the trajectory of a lot of the most successful realtors. They didn't always start out that way. It wasn't a linear route from where they started right to the top. Often times they had a moment where they realized they were working so hard, they wondered what would be a better way than working 80 hours a week. Would you say that's a common theme?*

Richard: Well, what happens I think is you move from a place of where you are just out there doing it every day, earning a living, and the business starts to wane a little bit. That will break some people, obviously. They just decide, "Okay, I'm already here, I'll move on to something else," because maybe they're not spending enough time with their kids. Other people will go the other way and say, "I get to figure out a better way to do this."

So, once they choose to figure out a better way to do it, and if they look inside of themselves and say, if Joe is doing it this way and he is doing pretty good, Mary is already here and she is doing that, and she is doing pretty good, you'll look at all these other people, and you'll say, "Well, maybe what I've got to do is exclusive, maybe I should be finding it with some of the other people." Or maybe it's training or coaching or going and talking with some people that have already figured it out, modeling their businesses as you said. But I do think as you move through life, in all fairness, it's not always great. I remember because I've had terrible difficulties in my life, with health issues and business issues and financial issues. God knows everybody has it, right? Someone once said:

> *"If everything is really, really good in your life, just wait. And if everything is really tough right now, just wait. Everything changes."*

Phil/Dan: *It's true and very interesting. I think you could only get that perspective once you've been through a few ups and downs on the roller coaster.*

Richard: Yeah, and everybody does, right? Like you think they're going to build you, they're going to break you.

Phil/Dan: I think that one of the mitigating factors to become more skilled and to learn the lessons that are presented along the way is that you're able to circumnavigate them. On a really practical level, the top 10% think differently. They certainly have a business mindset, they certainly act differently. What are the keys if you want to really define the key daily practices that the best realtors do, if you have to crystallize them down to just a handful, what would you say they are?

Richard: Successful realtors don't ever take their eyes off their goals and dreams. Think about it, what are they working for? They see a lifestyle they want to create for themselves. They see something they want to build; they look at it as being fun. So, that's the big one. I think the second one is that a lot of the top producers that we work with, at least what we teach them is that you must be really good at lead generation and marketing. It's the number one thing in real estate. A lot of people can service business but few can market and lead generate. A lot of people focus so much on service that they're not spending enough time in marketing and lead generation.

Million Dollar Agent Key Idea #13

"Successful realtors first must focus on their goals and dreams and be really good at lead generation and marketing."

Another thing is, they're unbelievably curious. You can live in a state of judgment. My dad actually taught me this - you can either be judgmental or you can be curious. When you're judgmental, that's all based on fear, and you think you know it all and you're always judging everybody else. When you're in state of curiosity, you're always questioning everything. You say "Boy, that's really interesting, how did you do that?" Well, something really interesting is when I first started doing events, promotional events for an upcoming multi-day event, at the end, after I'd set it up, I'd offer the opportunity to purchase a ticket.

The people that were coming up very first and buying were the most successful agents. And I always found that interesting. And at first I thought, why they're buying is because they have the money. What I discovered later was they were the ones even buying when they didn't have the money. Where are the unsuccessful people? They're judging what's happening out in their environment, thinking somebody is trying to sell me something and I don't need that. I'll figure it on my own. I remember a guy said to me, "You know, Rich, I'm trying to make a decision between buying a new van and getting involved in your coaching program. Which one do you think I should do?"

And I said, "Well, if you buy a new van, how much more money is that going to make you?" He said, "Well, not very much." I said, "If you get involved in our coaching

Million Dollar Agent Key Idea #14

"Being in a state of curiosity will serve you better than always being in a state of judgment."

program, you can probably buy two, or three, or four vans. Can you see the difference?" The more unsuccessful agents look at all the money they're making as their personal money, they don't separate it. If I've got to create a personal life and a business life, I've got to spend X number of dollars in my business life to continually grow to reinvent myself to get better, to discover what the top people are doing because they're always trying to figure it out.

Phil/Dan: *That's why lottery winners are often more poor than before they won the lottery. There are some real lessons there. You had mentioned that as a key, when people wake up, you call that the hour of power.*

Richard: Yes, what we call R&R.

Phil/Dan: *That's a powerful concept, how you start your day. At a practical level, the best is to really set them up to win, right from the time they wake up in the morning. You said there are three key things, what would you define them as?*

Richard: One of our teachings is R&R time, review and reflection time. So, my theory is this: we wake up in the morning and what we do is get physically ready. We have a shower, we brush our teeth, we eat some food to give ourselves energy, but how many of people get mentally ready? Very few. And what's interesting if you think about it is that, your brain, your mind is software that drives the hardware. Your body is hardware, right. Some people, they think differently. They think differently and they feel differently so they act differently.

In other words if we can learn to manage the software better, it will drive the

Million Dollar Agent Key Idea #15

"To start your day well it is important to prepare yourself both mentally and physically."

hardware better which gets us to do the things in life that causes us to be successful. So, my theory is, for the first hour of the day, we focus on the mental side. We get ourselves a coffee or tea, whatever, and you go somewhere and sit and review all of your goals, the most important goals to you. If you think about a perfect day, shouldn't a perfect day be set up in a way that everything you do that day is moving you in the direction of your dream?

In other words, if I want to have a great relationship with my wife, shouldn't part of my day be one-on-one time with her? If I want to have a really successful business, shouldn't some point in my day be committed to some formal marketing and lead generation? Probably. If I want to be in good shape and have lots of energy, shouldn't there be something in my day that cause me to get some exercise, whether it's going for run, going for a walk, whatever somebody chooses to do? So, if you look at the most successful life, success isn't the destination but the journey. If we look at the most successful life, the most productive people, everything they do every day is moving them in the direction of their goals and dreams. I call it purposeful - purposeful production.

Million Dollar Agent Key Idea #16
"You control your day; do not let anyone else control your day."

Purposeful production means that everything I do all day is moving me in the direction that I want to go. So, why wouldn't I get up, first thing in the morning, review the most important goals, not just business goals, the things that are important to me? So, for instance in my life I've been learning to play the guitar for last couple of years. This means I've got to commit an hour of the day to that. So, I get to put that into my schedule. You get up in the morning and review your goals, create your schedule for the day, get really clear on what your day is going to look like. You control your day, don't allow everybody else to control your day.

Brian Tracy said, "You've got your one or two choices every day." One, you decide what you're going to do in the day to move towards your goal because if you don't have goals, you're going to be helping everybody else achieve theirs all day. Maybe meditate, maybe a prayer, maybe read something inspirational, something positive - get yourself into a great place first thing in the morning. All you're trying to do is put good stuff into the software because good stuff in equals good stuff out; or conversely, crap in, crap out. So, get this baby ready. And then the second thing I say, let's get ready physically. Go for a walk, a little exercise, run, whatever you do in terms of exercise. When we exercise in the morning, we have more energy that day, right?

So, the second thing is energy. And then after that, commit the rest of your work day to work and your evenings for whatever you want to do in your personal life and you decide how you're going to manage that. So, to me it's just saying, "Okay, if I've got a life, and if I have roughly 800,000 hours or whatever the number is in my life, if I want to be more successful, the way I'm going to be more successful is by doing things every day that are moving in the direction of my dreams and goals because I know that when I have a hugely productive day I feel really good at the end of the day. When I have a wasteful day, I feel terrible at the end of the day. And the only difference was what I did."

Well, that tells me that if I want to feel good as a human being, that I need to do everything every day that moves me in the direction I want to go, because that's being productive. And then I can be a success. Success isn't about me getting somewhere. So many people are waiting. They say, once I get there then I'll be happy. No, no. Success is saying, hey, I woke up this morning, I did my R&R, and I did my exercise, which by the way I've done both of those things today already then I went to that appointment, and that appointment was important, because it's moving me in the direction I want to go.

Then I did an hour of prospecting, because I need to phone some of the most important people in my life. I did that. And you follow all the

Million Dollar Agent Key Idea #17
"Define your goals and dreams first and then figure out how you're going to turn them into reality."

way through, and then hey, guess what I'm leaving at 5 o'clock today, and I'm going to go home and I'm going to sit for two hours with my wife and my kids, and have a really cool dinner. And then I'm going to go practice the guitar. Then I'm going to read for an hour, I am going to be in bed, and then I'm going to plan a really cool holiday. I know one guy that every October, he plans eight weeks off the next year. And he is one of the most successful realtors I know. Most people plan their holiday when they've got the money. I say bad plan.

Phil/Dan: *Because there is no motivation to make it?*

Richard: No, they have no money. It's like people say I'll save money when I have more. It's a bad plan. You start saving now, even if it's only 1%. You decide what you want your life to be now, and then do everything that day to make that come to reality.

Phil/Dan: This is so, so, powerful. It's all about taking back responsible control over the process, as opposed to being totally reactive to the ebb and flow with whatever happens, but that's why the 10% are at the 10%. That's right, that's so, so powerful. Boy, if there is one thing that people get out of this, if they get that, it will change their life significantly. Let's think about the areas of your life that generated business over the years. Well, let's think about this in the context of a realtor.

There are so many ways to generate business and I guess it's really subjective in a way, but you observe the realtors that do really well. What is their strategy? Is it not just one? And when we're talking about lead generation, you mentioned that that's so important. You have farming, and FSBO's (For-Sale-By-Owners), and expired listings and specialty referrals, referral repeat, website lead generation, we're living in this. We have so many different ways of communicating. What would you say is the key here?

Richard: Well, it's really simple. The foundation of your business should be built on repeat and referral business. That is going to be business coming from people you already know. If you're a brand new agent, you know people. And if you know people, they know people who want to buy and sell real estate. And 80% of the time, somebody is going to find an agent through a referral. That's the deal.

Million Dollar Agent Key Idea #18
"The foundation of your business should be repeat and a referral business."

So, if I knew 40 people and I was brand new to the business, first thing I would do is phone all 40 people, and let them know what I'm doing, let them know I'm committed to servicing, see if they have any interest. But most importantly, I would let them know that if they know of anybody that I'd love to work with those people, then what I would do is put a system in place, a very strategic system. We call it the lifetime referral system. Obviously, you send your preferred client updates that can go out to people, and start to bring value to those people because giving starts the receiving process. We must give before we expect to receive.

So, how can you bring value to those people? So, that's number one right there. And then obviously you want to grow that every year. We've got all kinds of our coaching members, but one coaching member in particular has 200 people in his database and that gets him 40 deals every year. That's 20% of his database turning into deals. Forty deals at an average commission of 8 grand, that's coming to $320,000. He's 33 years old. What a beautiful thing.

When he started with us, he had some 60 people in his database and now it's up to 200. That's where it starts.

Million Dollar Agent Key Idea #19
"It is so important that you give before you expect to receive."

But then if you don't have enough business there, you should be able to get 20% of the number of people in your database in transactions from that database if you follow the lifetime referral system which we teach. But if they're not going to get enough deals there, then you have to code all the other ways, which are for expiries, internet leads and all those sort of things. Farming is one, open house another. Now, will they all work? They will all work. However, what you've got to do is pick the ones that you think you can do really, really well. When I was brand new to the business, I was thinking I need business right now. I decided I was not going to start by farming, because farming is a 12, 18, 24-months process before you receive your returns, and it's really expensive. So, what am I going to do?

I'm going to go knock on the doors of those people because it doesn't cost me anything. I'd spend all morning on the telephone; I'd spend all afternoon door-knocking when I first started in real estate. Everybody goes, you mean prospecting for six or seven hours? I didn't have anything else to do. I got started, I'd walk into the office, I didn't have a buyer or seller, I've got to go find buyers and sellers and that's what I did. Mornings on the phone, afternoons meeting people. I did two open houses on Saturday, two open houses on Sunday. I chose that method when I was 24 years old because I had no money. The only thing I had was time. So, I said, I'm going to go and use my time. Now, as your business grows you want to stop exchanging time for money, because that's what I was doing.

Now, I want to start investing and start exchanging value for money. So,

Million Dollar Agent Key Idea #20
"You want to stop exchanging time for money and start exchanging value for money."

then I'm going to start to look at my databases growing. Now I might get involved in geographical farming, now I might get involved in internet leads, but understand that if you can convert 3% to 4% of internet leads, you're a hero. So, think about how many internet leads you've got to generate to convert. And everybody goes, "No, internet leads isn't the way." Yeah, it's great. But your conversion rate is going to be very, very low. Plus with internet leads, most of them don't buy in the next month. They're six, eight, nine months away from buying because they start looking on the internet. They don't finish there, they start there.

So, what you've got to do is look at all the ways of generating business. Your foundation is built on your repeat referrals then you choose what you want to do based on your budget, based on your energy, based on what's best for you. There are about 20 different ways and then you choose and you take three and as your business grows, get it to five or six revenue streams. But when you first start, repeat referral is number one and two others. So, think about when I started. I didn't figure my database for a couple years. I wish I had started with my database because I knew all kinds of people, but I didn't start there.

Million Dollar Agent Key Idea #21

"Having a very good real estate specific database is so important and the foundation of your business."

I had door knocking, cold calling, open houses. That's how I started in the real estate business. And if you look at my very, very first year I don't say this to brag or anything, but in 1985, I made just over a $100,000 in my very first year, and my average house price was 50 grand. So, they work. However, remember I said I outworked the competition seven days a week? Ten to twelve hours a day, that's what it took. But I couldn't do that forever, because you run out of energy. So, when it comes to lead generation, they all work.

Phil/Dan: *That is so powerful, Rich. I speak to lot of realtors who say they would rather die than door knock. So, if it's not door knocking, what you're saying is you pick one or two areas that you can be passionate about. The other thing is that I speak to lot of realtors that get in and get caught up because they're unbalanced. Basically, they've mastered, say, door knocking, they're crazed door knockers, but they're 20-30 years into it and they haven't managed the database, the referral and repeat. They haven't created that residual business that comes from their database. So,* *it's really having multiple streams of income, knowing where the core is. I call it, creating an annuity-based business, ultimately based on referral and repeat, and also to create the leads like you said. If you're not getting this done, you are not really growing and you also have to do the lead generation, but it's all about really working all sides of the equation. That is really phenomenal advice.*

From your perspective, I know this is very subjective and we live in a different time today than we did when you started, and when I started as well, but there are so many different ways you're communicating with leads in the lead conversion process. You've got internet, you've got email, or you've got social media, you've got direct mail, you've got face-to-face, you've got telephone. What's your dominant way of communicating or conversion really?

Richard: Think about this. Sales is influence, right?

Phil/Dan: It's the ultimate form of influence.

Richard: Then you say, okay, if I'm going to choose my path of communication,

> **Million Dollar Agent Key Idea #22**
> *"Don't do a little bit of everything; do a lot of a few, and get really, really, really good at it."*

would it not make sense that I choose my best way of influencing somebody? So, if I gave you all of these, and I said, we've got the telephone, we've got meeting in person, we've got email, we've got text, we've got communication through social media. They're very general. Which way do you think is going to be the strongest influence? If I want to really influence somebody, what's the best way to do it? Face-to-face?

Phil/Dan: Face-to-face because it's multisensory.

Richard: If I want to really negotiate or really do a presentation, I want to get face-to-face. So, what is the second best way to influence a human being? It's voice, it's telephone. We keep going down the list. Text should be three because people respond to text quicker than they do emails. Then I'd say we move communication to email. And you know, email really is just another form of social media to some degree. Email me and Facebook. So, they go down the list from there but understand that the lower you get, the more is going to take to produce a result because your ability to influence is weaker. And chances are, they're not just talking to you. Think about the internet, they're probably talking to a whole bunch of people and if I'm sitting face-to-face, guess who they're talking to? Me. So, you always want to go to the best way to influence.

If you have an internet lead, the first thing you can do is qualify them. I got to find out. Where are you moving, when do you want to move, and why are you moving? Three questions: where, when, why. Now, you can ask them in any way you want but discover that every time you talk. If you're in an open house and they walk in that open house, before they leave the open house know if they have a where, know if they have a when and know if they have a why. And if they don't say goodbye, it's over. That's fine; they're nice people, hangout with them. First thing I've got to do is qualify. The minute I discover they're qualified is the minute I discover that they have a when, where, and why. My next objective is very simple, it moves from prospecting to trying to find if they're motivated. If yes, now I have a lead.

So, now I move from prospecting to lead follow up. The minute I have a lead, I have one objective and that is get face-to-face, that minute. Not to say, oh yeah I'll call you next week, or I'll send you all this information, no. Everything I do should be leading to one place because the best way I can influence those people is face-to-face. So, if they're a new buyer, first time buyer or if they're an old buyer, if they are somebody that has seen a listing, or if there is somebody who wants the price of their home then I've got to get face-to-face either in my office or at the house. Or maybe I've got to just get them to go see a house so I can at least get face-to-face, and then maybe I can bring them to the office to do it. It needs analysis with a new buyer. But somehow, someway if you know they're motivated, get face-to-face. It's the most powerful way to influence a human being.

Million Dollar Agent Key Idea #23

"The first goal is to qualify the lead. Once you actually have a legitimate lead the next goal is to get a face-to-face meeting. The ultimate goal is to get face-to-face with a motivated lead."

Phil/Dan: *So, it's an escalation process. Your ultimate objective, really, is to get in front of them.*

Richard: You look at every source of communication to achieve one objective: get face-to-face with a motivated lead.

Phil/Dan: *And the key here is the motivated lead. How do you turn your prospects into leads? And that's really a process of influence. It's a process of* *escalating the relationship based on qualification. What marketing strategies do you currently use in your business? I mean you're obviously using a highly successful training, coaching strategy.*

Richard: You're using all of it, all of the main marketing strategies.

Phil/Dan: *From the perspective of realtor, what would you advise about the main marketing strategies you use for real estate agents today?*

Richard: The number one thing is your referral and repeat business, that's the foundation. It's like when you're building a house, you need a strong foundation. If you're going to build a strong business, you got to build a strong foundation. Your foundation is to build from repeat referral from people you know, that's where it starts. And okay, you may say, well, you're not getting a lot of repeat because you're a brand new agent. But those people you know can refer business. But the only way they're going to refer business is by you going out and bringing value to them. We've got 50 ways of how you can bring value to them. So, that's a large conversation. But that's what you've got to do and understand that giving always starts the receiving. Again, just going back to Jim Rohn because Jim Rohn was a great mentor of mine, and had an amazing influence on my life, and unfortunately he died in '09.

Phil/Dan: *In '09, yes, you're so lucky to have seen him in person.*

Richard: Yeah, I've seen him probably six times. But he was amazing, right? And he said, "If you're willing to go out and do more than you get paid, the day will come when you get paid more than you do." I remember when he said that, I said, yeah. When I was in my early 20s so many of us said the same thing - all I want to do is go make money. But I had to realize that if I want to make money, then I better provide value to the marketplace. So, I can't just go to people all day as somebody who wants to sell? The question is what am I doing for you? Let's say I offered you in the spring a complimentary market evaluation of your home. Would you find that valuable?

Phil/Dan: *Sure.*

Richard: This is worth it, right? So, I provide you with the complimentary market evaluation. I follow up a week later to see if you've got any questions. Now, I am giving you something like that. Then, I send you out a preferred client update every single month, and you get this really nice newsletter that gives you valuable information that a homeowner, not a buyer or seller, is interested in. If I am going to send something to homeowners and bring value, I can't be bragging to them about how many homes I sold. I can't be bragging to them about what's going on in my life. And then if you get that all time, you read it, and say, "Oh, well that's really good stuff. Well, that was nice to send that to us."

I am building something in you. I am building what Steven Covey called, the emotional bank account. Reciprocity - there's something natural in all human beings, and we can't help it. If you read Robert Cialdini's book on influence, one of the six influencers is reciprocity. Well, reciprocity is that as human beings when somebody does something for us, we feel obligated to do something in return, right? Guys, you walked in here to do an interview with me and what did you bring?

Phil/Dan: *A bottle of red wine.*

Richard: It's used in cultures all over the world. If you go to a lot of cultures, show up in their country, they have a gift for you, right? It works the same way. If you're willing to go out and do more than you get paid, the day will come when you get paid more than you do. Let me tell you about one of our coaching clients. We had a terrible, terrible winter last year. We had this shortage of salt. You couldn't find salt to pour on ice anywhere.

Phil/Dan: *I remember that they were lining up outside the stores.*

Richard: Guess what he did. He went and found all the salt he could get his hands on, he put it in the back of a van, and he went out with one of his friends and dropped it off to all his best clients.

Million Dollar Agent Key Idea #24
"If you're willing to go out and do more than you get paid, the day will come when you get paid more than you do."

Phil/Dan: *Unbelievable.*

Richard: This was in the early spring when there was a lot of cold, hard snow on the ground. He just went out and if they weren't home, he just put a yellow sticky on it, a little note. I know how hard it is to find salt. I hope you find this useful, his name was Adeel. He put Adeel on it, signed it. Now you imagine me coming home and seeing that. That is what you've got to be thinking about - the value. Money is an exchange of value. But people that provide the most value in the world make the most amount of money. Apple has more money in the bank than the US treasury right now. A very rich company is only rich for one reason, because they provide a lot of value.

Phil/Dan: And, that's the entire premise of your book 'Delivering the Unexpected.' That's it in a nutshell – they call that the elusive obvious Rich. It's so simple, and so powerful. My favorite quote is - All the great truths in life are simple. If they were complex, everyone would understand them. If we would only get that one thing, it would transform a struggling realtor into a highly successful, prosperous one. Thank you so much for sharing that.

We're almost at the end of our interview and I have to ask this, because I know this is a question that gets asked so often. If you were asked by someone considering going into the real estate business today, what advice would you give them? What are the key things they need to do in order to be successful? To really crystallize it, what would you say they are?

Million Dollar Agent Key Idea #25

"Money is an exchange of value. People who provide the most value in the world make the most money."

Richard: Be very committed to the value you're going to bring and the people you're going to serve. Once you become licensed, what you've got to do is you must develop your skills. It takes mindset, and it takes skill development. So, get in the business with the right mindset, be committed to the business, don't give it a try, you're going to get in and say, "I'm going to make it, man." And the only way you're going to make it is by doing an unbelievable job for the people you serve. It's the way the world works. We live in a transparent society today. You can't get away with being no good at something. Think about a hotel, you've got Yelp, people reading these reviews of hotels all the time. If you're not great today, you're going to suffer in business.

Second of all, once you get in, then you say, "Okay, I've got to develop my skills," because buyers and sellers do not want to work with unskilled sales people. They want to work with skilled sales people.

Phil/Dan: And that's due in part because of the degree of knowledge and sophistication the average consumer has today?

Million Dollar Agent Key Idea #26

"Don't get in the business to make a lot of money. Get in the business to do an unbelievable job for people."

Richard: Sure, right. Commit to personal development and becoming really, really, really good in what it is you do. And you'll be a success, there's no doubt that it won't happen.

Phil/Dan: *What do you think are the key challenges facing the real estate business today? I mean it's changed a lot since 1984-85 when you entered the business; the world has changed in that period of time. I heard a quote recently that* 95% of the information today did not exist prior to 1963.

Richard: Right.

Phil/Dan: *The knowledge we know, that's exponential growth in knowledge and information. And real estate certainly is no different than any other industry, but what do you say are the key challenges faced by this business as we move forward in this ever changing world?*

Richard: I think the biggest - biggest challenge that the real estate industry is going to be faced with - is the evolution of bringing relevant value to the marketplace. Because of consumers today, they say, "Hey, I can list my home on the website, I can list my home on Craigslist, I can list my home on Kijiji, and all agents do the same thing. If I just get my home in the market it's going to sell, my home's better than everybody else's," - that's what the consumer thinks.

> **Million Dollar Agent Key Idea #27**
> *"The consumer today is having trouble justifying the value of a real estate agent. They think they know as much or more than a real estate agent."*

Now, saying that whenever there's a huge challenge, there's a huge what? There's a huge opportunity. Because most people will not face that challenge, right? And they won't deal with it properly. They'll try to get away with it. So, that's why I'm saying become really skilled, become really good, become really knowledgeable.

So, that's the biggest challenge we're faced with, and I think that will continue to be the biggest challenge we're faced with, and that's just technology driven. Real estate agents are always going to be needed. I have no doubt about that. Technology is not going to eliminate real estate agents, however it's going to force them to become better, and better, and better at what it is they do. And for those who don't, it will be a struggle.

Phil/Dan: *One last question and thank you so much for your time. What in your view is the future of real estate?*

Richard: I mean when you look into the future you're always on the cutting edge. One of the reasons why I think RRI has been so successful is we're able to look at the emerging trends in real estate, and then chunk them down for realtors - the really key behavioral practices, things they need to do today in order to succeed and prosper in the business.

Phil/Dan: When you look to the future, what is the future of real estate in terms of all this technology? Do you see any emerging trends?

Richard: I think the future of real estate is

> **Million Dollar Agent Key Idea #28**
> *"So, the best job security is to get really damn good at what you do and get skilled and trained and be the best. Because if that's your intention and your commitment, you will be successful no matter what."*

exciting and because you still get all of these houses that people need to buy and sell regardless of market conditions. If all the market's bad, change your skill set. Now you've got to focus on being really good at pricing homes, right? That's the difference because fewer are going to sell, but listing some are still going to sell.

So, make sure yours are the ones that are going to sell. When the market is really bad you better be a good negotiator because buyers are going to negotiate harder, right? When the market is really-really good, well of course you're going to sell easily, so you better be able to communicate to a seller why they need you. You know, you've got to talk to a buyer when there are multiple offers and you've got to help the buyer understand why they need to make a better offer. Because if not they're going to lose it.

I think the future of real estate is really, really, bright, it's exciting. However, I do think that less people are really committed to being so good at what it is they do. And I do think we've got to learn to specialize more. Own something. Pick your niche; pick a niche, own it. I don't care if it's a geographical niche, a price range niche, tight condos, whatever you've got, choose but pick a niche and be more knowledgeable in that niche than anybody else.

> **Million Dollar Agent Key Idea #29**
> *"When you're knowledgeable, when you're perceived as an expert in the world, the world will seek you out."*

Phil/Dan: What a wonderful note to end the interview. And Rich, I can't thank you enough for your time. And this has been a real privilege and I know the advice you've given will be so beneficial to anyone who's smart enough to take it. Thank you so much.

Richard: Thank you. Appreciate it, man.

Million Dollar Agent Key Ideas Summary

$ To be successful in the real estate business you have to keep reinventing yourself.

$ Today, realtors are no longer the gatekeepers of information, so the question is how to keep bringing value to the market-place.

$ Your business should be a vehicle to enrich your life, not one that drains the life out of you.

$ With the proliferation of information available today, people think they know as much as realtors do, so realtors have to constantly find ways to create value.

$ If you look at life and your business like playing a game it makes solving problems fun and enjoyable.

$ There are few other professions in the world with such a low entry threshold where you can do so well financially.

$ Real estate is such a great profession because as soon as you get licensed the product you are selling is right in front of you.

$ The most successful real estate agents see themselves as business people and entrepreneurs, not just as salespeople.

$ Being successful in real estate all starts with your willingness to make an investment in your own personal evolvement.

$ The key to success in real estate sales is to get face-to-face, face-to-face, and face-to-face. If you can't get face-to-face you're not going to make any money.

$ Successful realtors first must focus on their goals and dreams and be really good at lead generation and marketing.

$ You control your day; do not let anyone else control your day.

$ Define your goals and dreams first and then figure out how you're going to turn them into reality.

$ The foundation of your business should be repeat and a referral business.

$ You want to stop exchanging time for money and start exchanging value for money.

$ Having a very good real estate specific database is so important and the foundation of your business.

$ Don't do a little bit of everything; do a lot of a few, and get really, really, really good at it.

$ The first goal is to qualify the lead. Once you actually have a legitimate lead the next goal is to get a face-to-face meeting. The ultimate goal is to get face-to-face with a motivated lead.

$ If you're willing to go out and do more than you get paid, the day will come when you get paid more than you do.

$ Money is an exchange of value. People who provide the most value in the world make the most money.

$ Don't get in the business to make a lot of money. Get in the business to do an unbelievable job for people.

$ The best job security is to get really damn good at what you do and get skilled and trained and be the best. Because if that's your intention and your commitment, you will be successful no matter what.

$ When you're knowledgeable, when you're perceived as an expert in the world, the world will seek you out.

PETER GAIN:
Moving From Me to We

PETER HAS BEEN helping families successfully meet their real estate goals for 29 years.

A lifelong resident of 51 years, Peter was born and raised in Coquitlam, B.C. with strong roots and an extraordinary sense of value to the community. Peter has made lifetime friendships and business associates through sports teams, charities, and his real estate practice.

Peter started at an early age in 1986 with NRS Block Bros. Although now licensed for 29 years, the early days had many challenges. Through hard work, determination, continuous learning, and coaching, Peter's drive to improve has created a business model that has received an array of impressive awards such as continuously in the top 3% Prudential in North America, and a Life Member Medallion through GVREB.

Peter still feels that the greatest measure of success is what the client says about the experience after the deal is closed.

Peter continues to surround himself with like-minded people to grow his team with the goal of superseding expectations. With core values and a hands-on approach of face-to-face representation, Peter has gained respect from clients, associates, and his community.

In this interview, Peter Gain, a highly successful realtor from British Columbia, underscores the need for incorporating systems into your real estate practice consistently doing the key activities each day that lead to present and future success. In doing so, Peter is a great example of someone who has truly taken control of the real estate business, not only creating great financial prosperity for his family, his team members, and himself, but also managed to do so while creating a great lifestyle.

Phil/Dan: Well, good afternoon, Peter. Thank you very much for doing this interview.

We are here with Peter Gain who has been a client for eight years. He epitomizes what we would say is the top 10%, though, more realistically, the top 5% of realtors, if not in the top 1%. Peter gets it. We often talk about Peter to other clients as an example of a realtor that understands systems and who applies this consistently in his business. And his results reflect that. So Peter, thank you so much for taking the time to do this.

Peter: Oh, my pleasure.

Phil/Dan: Now, I often joke that I haven't met the five year old that decided they wanted to be a realtor when they grow up unless their family was in the business. People come to real estate having done something else professionally. I don't know if I've ever asked you this, what did you do prior to going into real estate?

Peter: Golf.

Phil/Dan: You were a professional golfer?

Peter: I was working on it.

Phil/Dan: So you were working on becoming a professional golfer. Why did you choose, and how did you come into real estate? You could have done anything, you could have been in athletics, anything. But why real estate?

Peter: I went back to school and was between jobs, so I was just trying to figure out what to do. And I actually started selling vacuums door to door. Well, I sold three vacuums in three days. One of the ladies I did the presentation to was a realtor. She phoned my father and said, "Kid needs to be in real estate."

Phil/Dan: Really?

Peter: I didn't really want to do it, but my dad said, "I'll tell you what, I'll pay for the course, you go do the course. We'll see how it goes." And when I got finished, I was coming into the business at 21, which was a tough go.

Phil/Dan: By the way, given the average age of real estate agents today is 57, I'm sure it was a little bit younger back then. That's pretty young for real estate.

Peter: Yeah. The challenge to that was if you haven't bought or sold real estate, and you're going into somebody's house, you're asking them to put all their confidence in you for their business.

Phil/Dan: That would be a challenge.

Peter: I'd heard on several occasions, "You're too young to do the business; you're too young to do the business."

Phil/Dan: So that didn't stop you obviously, the age factor. You obviously believed in yourself and your capability, and I'm sure the results started speaking for themselves. So let me ask you this, what was your greatest challenge back then? Of course, you're 21 years old, brand new business. It's kind of a quantum leap from vacuum cleaners to selling whole homes, right?

Peter: The biggest challenge was trying to figure out how to do it. I started with NRS Block Brothers. And they said, "Okay, here's your area, go door knock, go cold call, go do that." One of the most entertaining things I ever did when I first went out to door knock was walked up to a gentleman who was just getting ready to mow his lawn. I said, "Hi, I'm Peter Gain with NRS Block Brothers." And I handed him a slip with my card on it, all proud of myself. And he put it on the ground, started the lawnmower, and ran it over.

Phil/Dan: Really?

Peter: Yeah. He did it to me a second time probably about three months later. Here's the best part. I sold his house five years ago.

Phil/Dan: Talk about poetic justice, really.

Did he know that you were the guy that he cut up his business card?

Peter: Yeah, he did. He did because I'd talk to him, and he'd say, "Do you remember what I did to you the first time?" and I'd say, "Oh yeah. I remember what you did the second time too."

Phil/Dan: The third time, here's twelve thousand bucks, right?

Peter: Well, we sold his house and he bought a place down in the Prince's Gate. And you know, that took -- God that would have been 25 years into it.

Phil/Dan: That is amazing.

Peter: Yeah, I just kept on talking to him. I thought it was entertaining.

Phil/Dan: And this is for those of you who think that tenacity isn't an important thing. A lot of people would be devastated by that and go into a different profession.

Looking back over your career, you've been in real estate 30 years now?

Peter: Thirty years this year.

Phil/Dan: Isn't that amazing? Well, that's an important anniversary, 30 years in business. Looking back, what would you say has been your biggest challenge over all the years? You know, obviously it's evolved, but what would you say is your biggest challenge over others?

Peter: The biggest challenge was remaining consistent and doing the things that you need to do. I think that's where RRI systems really kicked into place. Consistency is everything, you can't do it all on your own. I think the year that I started with RRI I tripled my business in one year.

Phil/Dan: That is impressive.

Peter: Literally.

Phil/Dan: That's pretty amazing. So that's focusing on your sphere of influence.

Peter: That's mostly on the

Million Dollar Agent Key Idea #30

"In real estate, consistency is everything; it is consistently doing what you need to do in order to be successful."

sphere of influence. And I always thought you had to go and beat your head against the wall, and you had to get new business all the time, you had to do this, you had to do that. There is no way I could have continued in this business for as long as I have and remained the same, trying to do the buying side and trying to do the selling side, and then trying to keep everybody happy. So when I actually broke it down and looked at it and said, "Okay, I need to bring an assistant in, I need to bring a buyer's agent in. I need to have this so systematic that it's a business, not a run-around." And typically most realtors now are a run-around.

Phil/Dan: *They're transactional. They're trying to do everything themselves. They're not free; they're not freeing themselves to do the high income producing activities - what they do best.*

Million Dollar Agent Key Idea #31
"You cannot truly succeed if you are a transactional realtor; you need to be freed up to do more high-income activities, and this involves becoming systems-based."

Peter: You go from me to we. And the second you do that everything changes.

Phil/Dan: It's a synergistic effect.

Peter: Yup. It takes off, right?

Phil/Dan: And I think what's so important is that you've evolved operating your business like a business as opposed to a one-person show. And so many people in real estate, even with the best of intentions, try to do it all by themselves. And by default, it's kind of like the law of gravity, they end up becoming transactional based and burning themselves out.

Peter: I would say eight/nine years ago I was definitely at a decision point. I couldn't continue the way I was going, only because you can't work that way. If you're going to go transactional, you can beat your head against the wall and you'll do X amount of business, but then you're going to have your ups and your downs, you're going to have your pitfalls. I'd rather do work on a system where you're going to have your ups and downs but those are little blips. Those aren't big.

Phil/Dan: Right.

Million Dollar Agent Key Idea #32
"You can work extremely hard and burn yourself out as a transactional realtor; or you can incorporate systems, work less hard and create a life for yourself."

Peter: As far as challenges go, when you look back at that sort of stuff, it probably was my biggest challenge.

Phil/Dan: So you've evolved beyond the feast and famine to a large extent, right?

Peter: Well, the other part of that was I had two kids in hockey, I was a single dad.

Phil/Dan: You had lot on your plate.

Peter: I didn't want to work every night and I don't typically work every night. The way it is now, I've got Nicola, who does some of the buyers, and Emma, who does the buyers. Rene, who's my wife, now does the phones. Heidi, she does all the admin.

Phil/Dan: *All the admin; keeps it running.*

Peter: The way it's set up now, I've got my office in the morning and for the first four hours, I'm on the phone. I'm talking to the people I need to talk to. My daily goal is to hit X amount of calls per day which could be forty calls - whether that's past client referral, people that are going to be doing business. And from there, once my goal is done for the day, the day is mine. I'm done.

Phil/Dan: *So you can go golfing?*

Peter: I can go do whatever I want, right?

Phil/Dan: *That's so great.*

Peter: But of course, you're going to have the other days where you've got to present offers, you've got to do some presentations and stuff like that. But for the majority, I'm home every night for dinner. I was able to watch my kids play hockey. I was able to do the things that I wanted to do.

Phil/Dan: *Interesting. I just want to highlight this because the transactional realtor doesn't have this luxury because they have not taken control of their time and business.*

Peter: Can't do that.

Phil/Dan: *A transactional realtor is at the behest of whatever reactionary circumstance they have to attend to. They're working days and nights.*

Peter: You know what's really cool, and one of the neatest things I've ever learned with the coaching was that we return calls. We don't answer them. And all my voicemail, if you listen to it every day: "You've reached Peter Gain, thank you for your call. I'm returning calls today between 11:00 and 12:00, 3:00 and 4:00, and again between 7:00 and 8:00." That way, people know I'm going to call them back at a certain time. And when they leave a message, they say call me between 3:00 and 4:00 at this number. It takes a lot of the waste of time out of it.

Million Dollar Agent Key Idea #33
"You do not need to answer calls; you return them. Doing this you control the process, not the process controlling you."

Phil/Dan: *And it also shows that you respect yourself, your time, and people respect this.*

Peter: Well, that makes it easy. I have had people say, "Geez, that's a really long message." Guess what? It works.

Phil/Dan: *What is your greatest challenge today? Now that you're 30 years into it, I'm sure it's a lot different than it was when you were 21 and starting it?*

Peter: I like the business, I like the systems, I like how we do it. The challenge now is that a lot of realtors out there don't understand the business. We have to deal with realtors who aren't prepared. As I would say 'prepared'. If I'm representing somebody, I'm making sure every rock's turned over down at city hall. I'm touching all that stuff and making sure that there are no hiccups down the road. The biggest challenge nowadays is dealing with people or realtors that are so-called representing people that don't have a clue what they're doing.

Phil/Dan: *So, then you almost have to do two jobs.*

Peter: Basically, what we end up doing is ours plus theirs to make sure our clients stay safe. That's probably the biggest challenge. The way my business is set-up now, I can do this until I'm 65 if I really want to. I don't want to but I could because of the system. It runs, right? Over the last eight years our system does a deal a week. How cool is that? I've had the same employees working for me now... I've had Emma with me for twelve years. So, we're obviously doing something right.

Phil/Dan: *Obviously, yes.*

Million Dollar Agent Key Idea #34
"Over the last eight years our system does a deal a week."

Peter: The challenge that we all face right now within the industry is education with all the agents, would be my thought.

Phil/Dan: *Is it partly due to low entry threshold of getting into the business?*

Peter: As soon as they made it part-time.

Phil/Dan: *I think that's very significant. I often have the conversation with a realtor saying, "Well, I'm doing this job and I'm a realtor." So I'll say to them, "What's your goal?" And they say, "To be in real estate full time." So*

I say, "Quit your other job and commit to being full-time." That's the only way you're going be successful. Where you have one foot on the dock and one foot on the boat, you'll just be in this ambiguous situation and you won't thrive. Another consequence of that is the degree of professionalism.

Peter: Yes, exactly.

Phil/Dan: You can't get good at something unless you put in your hours, your dedication, and your focus. How would you describe your lifestyle now versus when you first started the business? Now this is kind of an interesting

> **Million Dollar Agent Key Idea #35**
> *"Being a realtor while working at another job is like having one foot on the dock and one on the boat. You can only truly be successful if you fully commit to be in real estate; otherwise you'll end up in the water."*

question for you because there's a vast lifestyle difference between 21 and 50-some odd years old.

Peter: I've reversed what I used to do. I know a lot of people would laugh when I say that. When I was 21, all my friends were hanging out, doing all fun stuff. I was working. Now a lot of my friends are not hanging out, they're working.

Phil/Dan: They're worried about their retirement.

Peter: And I'm doing fun stuff.

Phil/Dan: I love it. I'm taking notes, Peter, I'm taking notes.

Peter: When I come into the year now, I book four holidays in January. I say, "Okay, I'm going away in May, I'm going to be going away in June, I'm going away in August, I'm going to go away in usually about November, December." It's so much different now from chasing business to now having the business, and having reliable people working in the business. I can relax and do what I want to do.

Phil/Dan: And also by booking holidays, it kind gives you a light at end of the tunnel.

Peter: Absolutely.

Phil/Dan: Psychologically, that's it. You would never have done that five, ten years ago.

Peter: Exactly.

Phil/Dan: *And it was almost like you'd get to this point where you'd wait until you're completely burnt out, and it would be a reactionary holiday.*

Million Dollar Agent Key Idea #36

"Pre-plan your vacations at the beginning of the year; not only does this give you something to work for, it prevents burnout and having to take a reactionary holiday."

You wouldn't totally relax because by that time it'll take you twice as long. Now, you're working towards an end goal.

Peter: You have a big why all the time.

Phil/Dan: *Right.*

Peter: Why am I doing this? This is what we do to facilitate our life. We don't do it to facilitate real estate, right?

Phil/Dan: *To me real estate is about a means to an end, not an end in itself.*

Peter: If you really want to break it down, it's a job, we do our job and we do it well. But we're rewarded well, and we enjoy it. Now, I got a buddy in the office that said to me the other day, he says, "You've taken over from me now." I said to him, "In what way?" He says, "You're the king of holidays." But that's the big difference. I don't think there was clarity back then, and I think it was a lot of running around, whereas now there's clarity, there is no running around.

Phil/Dan: *Interesting. And there's more life enjoyment as a consequence.*

Peter: Absolutely. I'm getting married next May.

Phil/Dan: *Really? Congratulations.*

Peter: In terms of lifestyle, I do what I want. I get to do the things I want to do. This business doesn't drive me. I drive the business.

Phil/Dan: *It's no longer the tail wagging the dog.*

Peter: No, absolutely not.

Phil/Dan: *So here you are, you're a very successful guy, Peter. You're right at the top and you're the epitome of what I want to convey in this book. What drives you to take your business to the next level? You could probably say I could retire now, not that you want to do that. What drives you to take things to the next level?*

Peter: I am competitive.

Phil/Dan: Okay. Well, you're like a pro golfer.

Peter: Trying to be.

Phil/Dan: So it's in your blood, it's in your DNA.

Peter: I'm a pretty driven guy. The way we're set up now, myself and my brother, our real estate holdings are well diversified.

Phil/Dan: You have multiple sources of income.

Peter: And that came through the family, as well. There's too much to do in my eyes, there's too many people that we can -- if you want to call it serve. There are too many people we can help; there are too many people that I like represent. This isn't a have-to, have to do, which is a big difference.

Phil/Dan: A big difference.

Peter: Yeah. It's something that I like about the challenge; every deal is a different deal.

Million Dollar Agent Key Idea #37
"If you do not respect yourself and your time, why should anyone else?"

Every deal is a new deal. Nothing is ever the same. I like playing golf and I like hanging out with my friends, but you can't do that 24/7 either.

Phil/Dan: I once interviewed a guy who is pretty close to being a billionaire. And so I asked, "What drives you?" And he said, "You can only wear so many nice suits, and only eat so many nice meals, and only drive so many nice cars. You have to have the reason to wake up in the morning." And it was an interesting response. And his motivation, he had a company with thousands of employees, was feeding families. He was creating value for people on a different scale than you and I, but it made sense to me that it gave meaning and purpose to what he was doing.

Peter: He loved it.

Phil/Dan: He loved it. So, just sitting around the pool, you can only do that for so long, right?

Peter: Yeah.

Phil/Dan: There was another guy I spoke to who was just as interesting. Could you imagine this? He pulled up to the ocean and took his cell phone - he's a realtor - and flung it as far as he could into the ocean and then, got into his Jeep and drove down to South America and retired at 44 years old. And he met a bunch of other guys with grey hair that had retired, but they *were about 15 years older. And he said, they kept asking him what he was doing there, and he said he's retired. Well, after five years of doing that, he's now back to being a realtor. It's interesting, right? He said he was okay for a few years, but he had to come back to the land of the living at some point.*

Peter: You still have to have the reason, right?

Phil/Dan: *Yeah. I thought that was interesting because it is a fantasy of mine on some days, taking my cell phone, unplugging it and throwing it - in my case, into the Atlantic Ocean. I'm not even that close to an ocean so it would be more likely Lake Ontario.*

Peter: Yeah.

Phil/Dan: *So why do you do what you do?*

Peter: For me, it's the rush. You know what? Everybody's got a sweet spot. And this is going to be a long answer to your question. But everyone's got a sweet spot. Now Nicola and Emma both have a sweet spot that they love buyers. My rush is going out on a listing presentation, it's competing against other agents, and it's getting a listing on my conditions. That's probably the biggest rush I get, and then when we sell it. For me, that's one of my big commitments. If I wasn't doing that, I don't know what I would be doing because it's a rush. And I don't know if that makes sense to you.

Phil/Dan: *It makes total sense to me, believe me.*

Peter: I like the idea of sitting down in front of somebody. I like the idea of going through our marketing and I know it inside out. So that when I actually sit down and talk to them, I'm telling them stuff they don't actually know, stuff that other realtors can't tell them because they don't know. And to me, that's the big rush.

Phil/Dan: *You know, it's interesting you say that. I can only speak from my own experience. I do about 100, 110 presentations a year times thirteen years, that's thirteen hundred presentations, maybe more than that. Who knows, I've lost count. And I probably spoke to 50 - 100,000 people over that period of time. And here's the thing. I still get a rush by speaking, I still get that. I understand what you're saying because you can't do something as long as you and I have been doing it without getting something back, or else you just would be doing something else.*

Peter: Dude, it's the Super Bowl when you're going in. It's the real estate Super Bowl when you're going into someone's house.

Phil/Dan: Yeah, I get it. I get it. And so, if it ever becomes too easy, I guess, in a way it wouldn't be the same thing.

Peter: It's the whole rush of it, I think.

Phil/Dan: What makes you the best at what you do? You represent such a small percentage of realtors.

Peter: You know what? Here's the thing. I'm not the best.

Phil/Dan: For the record, it's humbleness.

Peter: There are lots of guys out there that are better. There are a lot of gals out there that are better. There are lots of realtors that are better. What makes me unique, I would say, is that I'm able to take that group of people I call my winning team, and take care of them.

Phil/Dan: You say winning team, just for clarification, that's your clients.

Peter: That's my clients. Those are my A's and some are my B's. Those are the people that I've done business with; I'll continue to do business with. They will refer me business, and I'll continue to be in touch with them.

Phil/Dan: Peter, for the record, how many people are on your database?

Peter: Right now, I'm just sitting at four hundred.

Phil/Dan: Okay. And that's after 30 years?

Peter: Yeah. And there are those that are weeded out.

Phil/Dan: Because you've probably done three times that amount of transactions.

Peter: We've done way more than that. But you get a lot of people you do a deal with, some move to Vancouver Island. We say, "Hey, I'd like to stay in touch with you." "Why would we stay in touch? I'm over on Vancouver Island."

Phil/Dan: Right.

Peter: Well, okay, if that's the mentality, there's no point in banging your head against the wall. So hit the delete button. You don't get rid of them but you keep them there.

Phil/Dan: I don't know if you heard me talking in the seminar today, I was saying that critical mass is about 100 rock solid people. You have 400, right?

Peter: Yeah.

Phil/Dan: *If every one of those is worth seven transactions over ten years, the average commission being nine grand, 9x7x100, you're sitting on many millions of dollars' worth of business just from your sphere.*

Million Dollar Agent Key Idea #38
"For most realtors, the engine that runs their business, where the bulk of their business comes from throughout their career, is their sphere of influence and past clients."

Peter: That's what we were just saying. We averaged basically 40 to 45 units a year for the last eight years.

Phil/Dan: *Average commission?*

Peter: Let's say you know, you could've gone -- eight years ago, your average commission was probably about seven grand. Now your average commission is probably about nine five. We're selling houses in Central BC for a million dollars right now. That's $18,000 or $16,000 a hit, right? If you're looking at 400k per year of doing just your guys' system, like the Morris system, it's good.

Phil/Dan: *And that's warm selling, we're talking. We're not talking cold selling.*

Peter: Well, that's warm selling, but here's the cool thing. There are people who like to go out and door knock. There's people who like to go out and phone call. There's people that like to farm. The coolest thing is you have these people getting a touch every month via Morris Marketing, or they're getting attached through an automated email program that sends them values in the area. And then quarterly, every three months, you just pick up the phones and say, "Hey, it's Peter Gain calling. Just want to touch base, say hello, and see how you're keeping." "Hey, Peter, I was thinking about you the other day, blah, blah, blah, I've got a friend – whatever". That's it. That's as simple as it is.

Phil/Dan: *It's so simple.*

Peter: That is as simple as it is. I used to walk around and go, "Man, what is that guy doing to get all of this business? I can remember about 15 years ago, I was walking around going, "How can that guy be getting more business than I am? I'm way smarter than he is, I'm way more likeable. But he is consistently staying in touch with the people.

Phil/Dan: *I call it the "elusive obvious" because people are looking for the magic bullet in this business. So it's the perpetuation of consistently doing certain fundamental things. An analogy I would use is it's like a professional golfer or a professional athlete of any sort. The best are doing the fundamentals well, consistently, consistently, consistently, over, and over, and over again. I bet when you're training to be a professional golfer, you're probably practicing the same swing thousands and thousands of times. But it's the guys that do that consistently who win, and the same is true, I think, with real estate.*

Peter: Well, it's 100% true with real estate. I mean, if I knew it was this simple -- seriously, if I knew it was this simple 20 years ago, man. I've had people come into my office and say, "Hey, you know what? You're doing this, you're doing that. What could I do?" First thing I always point to is here's what you need to do. You need to get a base, go through your people; you've got to figure out who is your biggest fan, who's not your biggest fan, sort those people out with those fans, and take them to next level. And if you can do that, there's no one stopping you because you know what? They're now going to refer you to everybody. That's the bottom line. And that's how simple it is. That's how simple this business is.

Phil/Dan: *It's amazing. Again, because it's so simple, it evades so many people. It's amazing. It is absolutely amazing to me. And again, that's why I call it the elusive*

Million Dollar Agent Key Idea #39
"The real estate business is very simple - it is about doing the fundamentals well consistently each and every day."

obvious. So here is a kind of an interesting question. There are 12,000 realtors in the greater Vancouver area, what separates you from the competition? I mean, you're a really likeable guy; you've got all the characteristics. But what's the why? Why should I do business with you? Why would anyone do business with you?

Peter: Why should people do business with me? Because I'm actually going to bring them knowledge of the marketplace that they can't get anywhere else. They're going to get it from me. Whether it's through a market snapshot, whether it's being able to convey what the listings are compared to what the solds are, what the other agents are doing, how many days my listings are on the market compared to other people's or the percentage of my list to sell ratio. These are all things that realtors should know about themselves or the marketplace, and they don't convey it. You've got to be able to bring something to the market or something to the individual that they don't already know. And if you can bring something to the individual that they don't already know, and you bring that to recall in a laidback tone.

Phil/Dan: That's powerful, and it's interesting. When there are a lot of realtors to choose from, people do business with whom they know, like, and trust. That's really important. But it's your knowledge and expertise that makes the difference. And I think we face a fundamental challenge in this business because of the proliferation of information by the internet. People think they're all budding realtors but unless you're doing what you just described - understanding, providing expertise, and understanding your value proposition and communicating it - you're just another bag of rice, basically.

Peter: Basically, yeah, you can compare yourself against other realtors.

Phil/Dan: They don't do that.

Peter: Most other realtors don't do that. If you can turn around and you can sell it, typically I'm on the market for twenty one days, I'm 97% list to sell, and the average in the real estate board is 35 days on the market and maybe its 94% list to sell.

Phil/Dan: And there's a cost associated with that.

Peter: There's a cost associated with that. If I can sell your house for more money in less time, which is always the biggest cliché, which people always say you know, people are going to want information and the more information they have, the stronger they are. The stronger they are, the easier it is for them to make a decision. You get people that go in and say, "Well, I'm with RE/MAX," or "I'm with Coldwell Banker, and we've got the newest and the best office." What does that mean to me? It doesn't mean anything. I want to know what you're going to do for me.

Million Dollar Agent Key Idea #40
"It is very important that a realtor understands their value proposition and what separates them from the competition."

Phil/Dan: Because you're the face that they're dealing with. You're not dealing with some amorphous brand.

Peter: Lots of people say to me, "How come you aren't over at RE/MAX? How come you aren't over at...?" You know, why would I be? I say, "People don't deal with me because of the company;

they deal with me because of me. They know I'm going to represent them, they know I'm going to treat them well, and they know that they can refer me with confidence. Simple."

Phil/Dan: If you went to the hospital and you wanted to see a doctor and you needed surgery, and they said, "Well, you know, I'm not a very good surgeon, but I'm associated with a hospital that's got a great reputation." How comfortable would you feel?

Peter: I'm out, I'm out.

Phil/Dan: That's right. People are buying you.

Peter: I'm a different brand.

Phil/Dan: You're a brand unto yourself.

Peter: Yeah. If the realtors are to look at one thing - find out who you are and what your brand is, and use your brand. I'm an individual. I'm different than the other agents that are out there.

Phil/Dan: So you make it so that if they are not dealing with you, they're not getting the same results.

Peter: They're missing out if they are not dealing with me.

Phil/Dan: That's right. They're missing out, and they're not getting the same level of service or the same quality. And you do that for a long enough time, then you really make it almost impossible for anyone to deal with anyone else.

Peter: I'll give you an idea. I've got a complex down in Citadel Heights, 1140 Castle Crescent. There are 111 units in that complex. I lived in that complex for one year in 1990. I've sold 57 of those units since then.

Phil/Dan: Since then, even though you haven't lived there since? Talk about leaving a lasting impression.

Million Dollar Agent Key Idea #41

"You are your own brand."

Peter: I've sold 50% of the units in that complex.

Phil/Dan: Wow. I have clients who are the exclusive realtor to anyone who buys and sells on some of the Islands off Vancouver Island, one example is Lasqueti Island.

Peter: They just did it.

Phil/Dan: *Yes, they are realtors that represent that island, and no other realtor can get in there. And they own the island literally, it's pretty amazing.*

Peter: You know, I love that they own the island.

Phil/Dan: *They own the island in a very similar way to you owning the condo complex. How do you think that the best of the best realtors look at the world differently? What is their mindset, how do they view things?*

Peter: From a non-judgmental point of view, it's easy to say this person is this, and this person is that. There's always a reason why people react the way they do. I think everyone deserves an opportunity to see who they are, before you can say who they are. I don't know if that make sense.

Phil/Dan: *It's so easy to pass judgment on someone. But if we're just curious enough, we understand that there is a larger context there. I think it makes you a better businessperson, a better realtor, and it opens you up to more effectively dealing with more different types of people.*

Peter: I think so.

Phil/Dan: *What makes the top 10% the top 10%? Key characteristics?*

Peter: Consistency. Absolutely; consistency. There are certain things that everyone who has a sweet spot will do. If you know your sweet spot, you hone your sweet spot, and you do it consistently, you'll be there. Consistency is everything.

Phil/Dan: *As you've consistently said.*

Peter: There are days I don't feel like doing some things. Someone came in the other day and said, "Why do you have all that crap on the wall?" And I go, "You know what? I didn't get all those awards by doing nothing." There is reason it's there, and for me, it's my wall of shame.

Phil/Dan: *That's pretty cool. Just for the record, those are all your awards and acclamations for excellence in business. There are days I go to the gym and I don't feel like being there but I know that if I don't, there's a consequence to it, so I get that.*

Peter: Absolutely.

Phil/Dan: *Answer this question however you want, it's sort of a verbal ink blot test. The real estate business is what?*

Peter: Digressing.

Phil/Dan: Digressing? I've got to tell you, of all the people I've spoken to I've never received that response.

Peter: The real estate business is good for people that are self-motivated; it's not good for anybody that's not.

Phil/Dan: So, for all those people reading this book that are sitting in cubicles, working 9 to 5 who think that it's their ticket to freedom in unlimited abundance you would say...

Million Dollar Agent Key Idea #42
"Be careful about being too judgmental of other people; it can hurt your business."

Peter: Pay your dues.

Phil/Dan: In other words, it is a business and the more disciplined and consistent you are the more successful you will be and it's still very hard work.

Peter: First year I was in the business, I made $5000.

Phil/Dan: Okay, boy, wow.

Peter: Five grand.

Phil/Dan: Wow, you would have made more selling vacuum cleaners, right?

Peter: And the second year, I had to split that because it was a 50/50 split. There was no holiday that year.

Phil/Dan: Talk about a kick in the teeth, right?

Peter: But then the second year was $27,000.

Phil/Dan: Okay.

Peter: And I started to figure it out. And then I went from there.

Phil/Dan: What made you stick it out from $5000 and $27,000? A lot of people would have given up knowing that they only made $2500. I mean you couldn't even buy a decent used car 30 years ago. It's still below the poverty line, if you think about it, right?

Peter: I had people that had told me I was too young for the business. I remember going out on a listing presentation, and I did a great presentation. I went tripping in there with my NRS Block Books; the whole bit, but did a great presentation. He said, "I love your stuff, but you're too young." And I went, "You're kidding me." I sold that house. I found a buyer and I sold that house.

Million Dollar Agent Key Idea #43
"The day you stop learning is the day you stop growing."

Phil/Dan: *Interesting.*

Peter: I proved him wrong. Determination. I like to be told that I can't.

Phil/Dan: *There are a lot of realtors starving out there. Eighty percent of them are just getting by - they're not making a living, they're not abundant. The 10% that are really enjoying the best of everything.*

Peter: There are 12,000 agents on our board, 5,000 of those agents don't do a deal this year.

Phil/Dan: *I'm from Toronto, and when you go to the Toronto Real Estate Board, there is a kiosk and people are lining up every day to get their license. Four percent of them will make a decent living. We're talking about a marketplace similar to Vancouver, where the average house price is $1,060,000. The commission on that can be $40,000 or so. The cream really does rise to the top.*

Peter: The day you stop learning is the day you stop growing. So you always have to grow and learn. I still listen to some of Richard Robbins' teachings. There are lots of different things I listen to and it goes back to super basic stuff. Everybody needs to ignite.

Phil/Dan: *If you look at the best, they are learning and developing themselves, their knowledge, skills and abilities. If you don't, you end up regressing. If you're not growing, you're regressing. You don't stay still.*

Peter: If you're not looking forward, you're moving backward.

Phil/Dan: *It seems to be a hallmark of those people who do very well. You'll see people at these seminars; they don't really need to be there, because they're financially doing okay. It's the ones that are starving that should be there but aren't there, and that is kind of ironic to me.*

Million Dollar Agent Key Idea #44
"If you look at the best they are learning and developing themselves, their knowledge, skills and abilities."

Peter: But you know what? Every seminar that I've gone to, something will click.

Phil/Dan: *You made that key distinction.*

Peter: There'll be another revenue stream that will make you go, "Hey, you know what"

Phil/Dan: *It will pay the price of admission a thousand-fold.*

Peter: Yeah, absolutely.

Phil/Dan: *You're in a different place than the first time you may have heard that, and now you're in a position to act on the information or it resonates differently.*

Peter: A lot easier, yes.

Phil/Dan: *Let's chunk it down a little bit. So, what are the key daily practices that lead to your success as a realtor? So you wake up in the morning and what?*

Peter: Typically, what I like to do is go to the gym. I like to do my treadmill, and then this is what every day looks like. Every day starts out with emails at 8:30 in the morning. Calls to folks from 10-12. Lunch - I've got my top producer put in there. Then I've got appointments after that. So, typically I come in here, I know I'm going to answer my emails first thing, second thing I'm going on the phone. Hence that door is shut, and I'm the only one in here. Hence, why my voicemail says, "I'll be returning calls between 11:00 and 12:00 and 3:00 and 4:00. During the other times, my phone is off, I'm not talking to anybody, and I'm doing my daily goal. My daily goal is to make those calls, whether it's past clients, farms, whatever. But I am going to make my 30-50 calls. Now typically if I make 50, I've had a really good day. 30 is about normal because if you hit a lot of past clients, it's, "Hey, how're ya doing?" They want to know what's going on; they want to know how you're doing.

Phil/Dan: *Right, so there are unanticipated delays.*

Peter: There are unanticipated delays. Heidi comes in now at one in the afternoon, and we have a team meeting every Tuesday now at 1:00. They come in, we all talk about what's in the pipeline, and we talk about what we're doing. Any appointments or anything that needs to be taken care of, Heidi takes care of it. If I have no appointments in the afternoon, and I've completed my goals, the rest of the day is mine, I'm out there. I'm not going to sit here and beat my head against the wall because I find if you sit here and try and do 100 today and maybe 10 tomorrow and 100 the next day, you'll burn out. So you get your goal, you complete your goal, and you get out of the office. Done.

Phil/Dan: *Beautiful.   And you feel like you've actually accomplished something.*

Peter: I walk out of here every day with my goal met, it creates a different mindset to you, you have a very positive mindset, compared with very negative.   Any time I've missed the gym for three, four days, I get this feeling, and I know, "I've got to be in the gym, I've got to be in the gym." Same thing with work. If I miss three or four days, I'm going, "Okay, this isn't good." I can't go home and relax, or I can't go to the golf course, I can't do whatever. If I've completed my goal for the day. Just one simple goal, that's it.

Phil/Dan: *You got the right order in sequence here. You accomplish something, and then you reward yourself when you accomplish that.*

Peter: Absolutely.

Phil/Dan: *As opposed to going golfing first and then feeling guilty.*

Peter: The thing I find if you go golfing first, you're going to come in here later and go, Wow, look at the work. I'm out. And it doesn't get done.

Million Dollar Agent Key Idea #45
"Complete your daily goal first, and then you can relax and feel good having accomplished something."

Phil/Dan: *That makes total sense to me. If you crystalize three things that you do consistently that lead to your success, what would they be?*

Peter: Phone, phone, and phone.

Phil/Dan: *Okay, so the phone is the big thing.*

Peter: Phone is my friend.

Phil/Dan: *I spend a lot of time on the phone as well, although I travel a lot with what I do. But when someone emails me a list of twelve questions, I pick up the phone and call them. In a one or two minute conversation, I can address the twelve questions and any supplemental questions that they have. I often joke that the e-mailers and texters don't do well in real estate if that's their only method. It's a people business.*

Peter: You have to have that personalized stuff, right?

Phil/Dan: *It's huge. In my seminar, I say, "If I texted you my seminar, would you read it?" And not one person says yes.*

Peter: That's how I get my twenty four touches on my clients every year. 24.

Phil/Dan: *It's a proactive CMA (comparative market analysis). What is it in terms of all the different areas of specialization: farming, FSBO's (for-sale-by-owners), expired listings, specialty referrals, client referrals, website lead regeneration? What are the areas that have generated the most business for you over the years?*

Peter: Repeat and referral. In the beginning, it was geographic farming.

Phil/Dan: *It was geographic farming, okay.*

Peter: I have had some pretty strong success with farms, but it's a lot of work.

Phil/Dan: *And expense.*

Peter: It's a lot of expense. When I came across you guys, Morris Marketing Group, I pay every month and I forget about it, but it goes out. It is bar none the best, easiest system. The return I get on my investment is incredible.

Phil/Dan: *In generating brand new clients, what works?*

Peter: Farms. Farms are basic, farms are easy. I deliver stuff out or send it out, but I also phone them.

Phil/Dan: *That's what's key because a lot of people treat it as passive.*

Peter: You can send out all the stuff you want, but you'll triple what you're going to get by picking up the phone and saying, "Hey, it's Peter Gain; I just dropped off some information for you today. I've just sold another home in your area, just calling to see if you have any questions regarding the real estate market, market trends, and if there is anything I can assist you with, let me know. Done. I'll either leave that or won't I leave it, but I get a call back.

Phil/Dan: *It's funny; some people call that process of just sending out paper without any calls carpet bombing, right?*

Peter: But if I do it in the same spot, and it's a consistent basis. Like that one on Castle - 111 units; sold 57 of them.

Phil/Dan: *Incredible.*

Peter: But that's all the same idea, I call it drop and talk. You can drop all you want, but until you pick up the phone, it means nothing.

Phil/Dan: *You've got to have face-to-face; you've got to have phone time. If you're not willing to door knock, if you're not willing to provide other information of follow-up then it's a very expensive passive way of marketing.*

Peter: Oh, absolutely.

Phil/Dan: *In terms of the areas of specialization, say it's farming or even direct mail, email, internet, all the areas that you communicate with, what are you using to convert people? So in your case, you're saying it's the phone, you follow-up with phone? When you say you drop, is it direct mail you're sending? This is to leads, mostly leads?*

Peter: I'm not thinking of selling right now, I'm thinking of selling maybe two, three years, which then goes into my system.

Phil/Dan: Right.

Million Dollar Agent Key Idea #46
"It all starts with my belief that they're a 'when' until they are not a when."

Peter: I've got 7,500 names in the system.   Literally, 7,500 names.

Phil/Dan: Incredible.

Peter: And I've got notes on everybody. So when I come in here, I go on my computer, who am I calling? Okay, the names come up, I start making calls. Now I don't have to remember the conversation I've had with you before, I've already made the notes, and the notes are already there.

Phil/Dan: It's just a prompt.

Peter: It is just a prompt. So, now I know that I talked to Dave five months ago and he was telling me his dog wasn't well. "Hey, Dave, how are you doing? Oh, good, blah, blah, blah. Hey, just wanted to touch base, how did your dog make out?" Something basic. Bang, door's open, right? Now, they may not be selling now, but you're the guy that asked him about something that was important to him. And a lot of the stuff I get now isn't stuff like, come and do an evaluation. It's come and list my house. Come and sell my house for me. I've already earned their business.

Phil/Dan: So it's a question of when?

Peter: It's a question of when. Everybody's a question of when until they prove themselves other than that.

Phil/Dan: That's very cool. And that speaks to your belief in what you do and how you do what you do. That's pretty cool, that's pretty cool. And how do you convert prospects into clients?

Peter: It all starts with my belief that they're a 'when' until they are not a when. And a lot of it will be through email programs or a drip campaign, whatever you want to call it, which goes out to them and they get information of just-listeds, just-solds in the area. But again, three months later, "Hey, it's Peter. I sent you a note with my card attached to it. Wanted to make sure first of all, you got that, and secondly, you're getting the information that I've sent out for you." "Yeah." "Do you understand it?" "Yeah." "Any questions?" "No, but when we have any, we'll call you." "Okay, thanks, bye." It's all no pressure. It's not like, "Are you going to sell? When are you going to sell?" It's all, "Hey, how you doing?" It's just coming from a very soft side.

Phil/Dan: And you're just planting seeds, planting seeds, and they eventually come back to harvest.

Peter: Yeah. It's just my way of doing it.

Phil/Dan: So the main marketing strategies you currently use are listed just-solds, referral and repeat, direct mail to past clients, email drip programs. What are the marketing strategies that have been the most effective for you?

Peter: I'm still going to go back to marketing repeat and referral.

Phil/Dan: Okay.

Peter: That's my bread and butter.

Phil/Dan: Okay.

Million Dollar Agent Key Idea #47
"The difference with having repeat marketing in place is being calm and knowing how history predicts the future."

Peter: The difference with having repeat marketing in place is being calm and knowing what I know and how history predicts the future. In the market is everything that I've done, and I've got eight years sitting right there that shows me that 70% of my business comes from repeat and referral. I don't worry anymore. I don't have to worry.

Phil/Dan: Because you've got a trust in the process?

Peter: It's a proven system. I didn't make the system...

Million Dollar Agent Key Idea #48

"If you want to be successful in real estate, model what successful people are doing. It's ok to be unique and different; however, you do not want to reinvent the business. There are certain fundamentals that have stood the test of time."

Phil/Dan: *But you've worked the system.*

Peter: But I use the system.

Phil/Dan: *That's a key point because a lot of people come into this business, Peter, and they try to reinvent the business. There are laws of nature that I could say, whether you and I believe in gravity or not, it's irrelevant. If we jumped off a building, we'd hit the ground. There's nothing wrong with being unique, but there are certain processes that are fundamental to the real estate business that cannot be ignored. And if you don't do them, there's a consequence associated with that.*

Peter: The simplest thing I ever heard from Richard was, "Do what the successful people are doing."

Phil/Dan: *Hence this book. No truer words spoken.*

Peter: Yeah.

Phil/Dan: *If you were asked by someone getting into the real estate business today, what are the key things they need to do in order to be successful and prosperous in the business? What are you going to tell them?*

Peter: What I have told the last ten I've talked to. The best way you can start is by making this pyramid a wide base. So a wide base has to start with the people you know, family, friends, and acquaintances, if you believe that acquaintance is somebody that is going to refer business to you.

Phil/Dan: *Sphere of influence.*

Peter: Sphere of influence, you get that going. On top of that, you've got to break it down, and you have to literally become a system person. And when I say system person - I have systems for everything. And when I say a system person, I know I'm going to be here at 9 in the morning. I know I'm going to make X amount of calls by 11:30. The thing that people have to do is they have to systemize what they're going to do, they have to look at it, and attack it the way that other people have, right? So, anyone starting out has to be out in front of people. They have to be meeting people, have to be talking to people, that's the whole premise.

Phil/Dan: You know it's interesting, I once had a session in Calgary, and after the seminar this guy pulled me into the office. And he had these three big giant computer screens on his desk, and he had this flip chart, and he said, "My whole strategy as a former VP of a tech company." He said, "I'm going to send out these automated postcards, and then they'd go to a website, and the website sends these automated emails. And if they're interested in step 12, then I'll have some human contact with them. So what do you think?" And I remember I looked at him and I said, "With all due respect, you're going to be out of the real estate business within a year." And he said, "What are you talking about? I spent so much money, this is so well organized." I said, "You've taken people out of the equation. You got to get in front of people." And especially in this business.

Peter: You have to be in front of people. And the thing is you know, don't be ashamed of what you do, ever. If you're in this business, you're in this business. And everybody you meet, you don't have to come out and say. "Hey, I'm a realtor, are you buying or selling?" But people need to know what you do. Don't be ashamed of it.

Phil/Dan: Be proud of it.

Peter: Be proud of it.

Phil/Dan: And rightly so. And the good realtors that I know, the ones who do it well are worth every penny and more. So what's changed for those getting into the real estate business today?

Million Dollar Agent Key Idea #49

*"Never be ashamed of telling people you are a realtor.
Tell everyone you know and be proud of it."*

Peter: It's a lot more complicated.

Phil/Dan: Legislatively or regulation-wise?

Peter: Regulation-wise. There have been some good things, and there have been some bad things. And I think when we originally did a contract before, it was you know, nine copies pressed hard, one page, right? Now it's nine pages, don't press hard, or I can just send it to you in an email. You know, everything is automated now. I used to walk around with a pocketful of quarters, my pager would go off and I'd run to dial it. "You called?" Back then when we used to do a deal, the deal would take two to three days to do. There were no copies, there were no photos, there were no faxes, and there was no email. You ran it from a point A to point B.

Phil/Dan: *Incredible.*

Peter: Look at it now.

Phil/Dan: *How many deals did you do when you went to Hawaii for the first time, just for the record?*

Peter: 12.

Phil/Dan: *Wow. There are people who'd like to do nine deals in a year, let alone twelve while they're vacationing in the Hawaii.*

Peter: There's something about making $80,000 when you're on vacation.

Phil/Dan: *Yeah. It makes you want to stay longer, doesn't it?*

Peter: Yeah. That's right; I'll convert up to first-class coming home.

Phil/Dan: *So what is the most significant difference in the real estate business today versus when you first started the business?*

Peter: Business is easier now than it used to be, but it's a lot less hands-on. If you're doing your business right, people will always need you.

However automated you make it, people will always need that person they need to talk to, to understand, to feel comfortable to go through a contract.

Phil/Dan: *So how do you think these changes will affect realtors who are successful and prosperous in this business?*

Peter: I think it will make it more difficult because there is way less of a connection. I've done three deals this year where I haven't even met the realtor, haven't even seen the buyer, and they haven't even shown the house.

Million Dollar Agent Key Idea #50
"However automated you make it, people will always need that person to talk to, to understand, to feel comfortable going through a contract."

Phil/Dan: *Amazing.*

Peter: So for me, I'm with my client, I sell the house, I'm with them. Closing, I'm in touch with them. It's not email, it's not texting, and it's a personal, one-on-one touch. And I think where a lot of these people are going to have difficulty is, they're doing one-off bang deals off email. There is no personal touch to it.

Phil/Dan: *And how do you create a relationship?*

Peter: Well, it's a one night stand is what it is. There is no relationship there, it's just I'm using that agent to do this deal. If the agent is that lazy to do the business that way, are they going to stay in touch with you? Are they going to keep you up-to-date with what the market's doing? Are they going to keep you up-to-date with you know with some cool things going on in your neighborhood, or here are some cool things that you can do with your house? Not a chance. So, where does it leave me? I'm going to still have a lot of pie over the next five years, whether the market is good or bad.

Phil/Dan: *What are your views of the future in the real estate business?*

Peter: The people who are doing the one-on-ones and they're dealing with their clients and their business right now, it's all customer-based. And if you don't have a customer base, you're going to be a transactional realtor. And you're dead.

Phil/Dan: *And they're a dime a dozen.*

Peter: They're a dime a dozen and you're done. Because the separation between the people that have a base and people that don't is going to get bigger, and bigger, and bigger. And the way I look at it is whether the market is good or bad, I'm taking your buy, because I'm going to get referrals.

Phil/Dan: *Isn't that amazing? And so, you know, it underscores the people that do well at what they do and by virtue of that, never have to worry about the future. They focus on their own excellence. I try and convey that to people, but they don't get it.*

Million Dollar Agent Key Idea #51

"Transactional realtors are a dime a dozen. Relational realtors are worth their weight in gold."

Peter: It's easy to quit.

Phil/Dan: *It's easy to quit. But look at the rewards if you stick it out.*

Peter: You know, I mean, I could have done it differently 20 years ago, I could've quit.

Phil/Dan: *Peter, you have been an absolute pleasure to interview, it's one of my most enjoyable interviews. You've been very generous with your time, and we've got some really great stuff here that is so fundamental. And I think any realtor who's smart enough to listen and take heed for these words of wisdom ought to do so. So thank you very much.*

Peter: Thank you; my pleasure.

Million Dollar Agent Key Ideas Summary

$ In real estate, consistency is everything; consistently doing what you need to do in order to be successful.

$ You cannot truly succeed if you are a transactional realtor; you need to be freed up to do more high-income activities, and this involves becoming systems-based.

$ You can work extremely hard and burn yourself out as a transactional realtor; or you can incorporate systems, work less hard and create a life for yourself.

$ You do not need to answer calls; you return them. Doing this you control the process; the process doesn't control you.

$ Being a realtor while working at another job is like having one foot on the dock and one on the boat. You can only truly be successful if you fully commit to be in real estate; otherwise you'll end up in the water.

$ Pre-plan your vacations at the beginning of the year; not only does this give you something to work for, it prevents burnout and having to take a reactionary holiday.

$ If you do not respect yourself and your time, why should anyone else?

$ For most realtors, the engine that runs their business, where the bulk of their business comes from throughout their career, is their sphere of influence and past clients.

$ The real estate business is very simple - it is about doing the fundamentals consistently well each and every day.

$ It is very important that a realtor understands their value proposition and what separates them from the competition.

$ Be careful about being too judgmental of other people; it can hurt your business.

$ The day you stop learning is the day you stop growing.

$ If you look at the best they are learning and developing themselves, their knowledge, skills and abilities.

$ Complete your daily goal first, and then you can relax and feel good having accomplished something.

$ It all starts with my belief that they're a 'when' until they are not a when.

$ The difference with having repeat marketing in place is being calm and knowing how history predicts the future.

$ If you want to be successful in real estate, model what successful people are doing. It's ok to be unique and different; however, you do not want to reinvent the business. There are certain fundamentals that have stood the test of time.

$ Never be ashamed of telling people you are a realtor. Tell everyone you know and be proud of it.

$ However automated you make it, people will always need that person to talk to, to understand, to feel comfortable going through a contract.

$ Transactional realtors are a dime a dozen. Relational realtors are worth their weight in gold.

COLIN BLAND:
Focus on Your Clients' Needs

COLIN BLAND (FROM the not so "bland" Bland family), has been creating raving fans for over 17 years in the Leduc/Edmonton market.

Growing up in a large family with 6 kids, Colin enjoyed scholastic and athletic achievements: hockey, boxing, lacrosse, volleyball, tennis, water skiing and more. He also studied and played guitar and sang.

He gave up on athletics going into high school and instead taught guitar and played rock & roll full-time for 10 years. His music career transitioned into sound engineering and stage lighting. Colin owned and managed his own company, Alberta Stage Lighting Ltd., for 15 years.

Throughout his life, Colin has always enjoyed his role as coach, teacher, mentor, trainer and motivator. This is true whether it's giving a powerful motivational speech to one of his hockey teams, working with a buyer or seller or encouraging a friend or client to move fearlessly forward in their life.

Colin never does anything half-heartedly. And the same applies for real estate. He always puts 110% of his enthusiasm, experience and skill into his profession.

Colin is a consistent top producer achieving Coldwell Banker's International President's Elite, Edmonton Real Estate Board Top 5% for 14 consecutive years, and has achieved Coldwell Banker's Ultimate Service Award for 16 consecutive years.

When he's not achieving his real estate commitment, Colin still enjoys an active lifestyle playing hockey, golf, water skiing and yes, he still plays guitar. He loves his time at his lake house in the summer.

COLIN BLAND IS a great example of a realtor who consistently translates his energy and passion into continuous success. Although he started his real estate career with considerable sales and business experience, he not only understands the importance of lifelong learning and personal and professional development, but also the need to on a daily basis apply what he has learned into creating results. Colin is a great example of how having a success mindset translates into phenomenal results which he is always striving to improve upon. There are many great lessons that can be learned from Colin.

Phil/Dan: We're honored to be here with Colin Bland who is really a superstar real estate agent out of Leduc, Alberta which is just south of Edmonton. Colin handles the greater Edmonton area and he exemplifies the type of agent that this book is based upon which is the top 10%, or more like the top 1% of agents in the country, and is always striving to get to the next level. With that in mind, thank you Colin, for taking the time to do this. It's an absolute honor to be speaking with you. We've got some questions for you.

Colin: Okay.

Phil/Dan: I often joke that I've never met the five year old that said they wanted to be a realtor when they grow up. Tell me what did you do prior to real estate?

Colin: Before real estate I owned a production company called Alberta Stage Lighting and we did rentals and sales, and designs and full production for numerous different types of clients. Churches, schools, theatres, musical shows, corporate presentations, whatever it was for, a pick up rental or a big concert, we did all of that and sales and rentals. And prior to that I was a salesman at Mother's Music in Edmonton and before that I was a musician, professional rock and roll musician from the time I was 15 to the time I was 25.

Phil/Dan: That's a very interesting background; surely you had a sales background, a business background; why did you choose real estate as a profession of all the things? You could have gone into the music industry. What got you into the real estate?

Colin: In my lighting company it was a very, very rewarding experience. I never had a rich Uncle Johnny or somebody to invest so you know it was pretty much me. I love to help people create a vision of their show or their installation and make that a reality. But there are so many moving parts, so many different components, staff and equipment and suppliers and trucking and so on. I knew that I really liked selling; I really liked helping somebody accomplish a goal. So I was coaching minor hockey at the time and I recruited a fellow by the name of Bob Buttar to be one of the assistant coaches because he was a very successful hockey player in his youth, he played Junior "A", and he was the manager of the Coldwell Banker office.

So when we would have a coffee or a beer after work, eventually the subject of sales would roll around and I would ask him different questions and he never really tried to recruit me, but I realized that this was a good opportunity. And so there was just me and the clients, it was a very straight-forward simple relationship. I can look after those people, the product was the product and I had no control over what a house would be or what it wouldn't be. So at an infamous lunch with Bob, I got in my car and a big switch went off in my head and the decision was made in that instance that I would get into real estate. And so I took the course, got in. It took me three years past that point to sell my lightning company. So until then, I was working two jobs, working very hard and so that's how it all began, fortunately. Bob and my mentor Del, they pointed me in the right direction and one of the things I did was to take Floyd Wickman's course.

Phil/Dan: That's a famous course. Floyd Wickman has been around for years, one of the foundational courses for realtors who have done very well. How many years have you been in the business?

Colin: Seventeen.

Phil/Dan: Okay, so that's quite a long time ago. When you started out your real estate career, what would you say was your greatest challenge?

Colin: Before I got into real estate I had asked a friend who was in real estate, "You know me quite well, what do you think the obstacles might be?" And he said, "For you, none." But to be honest the biggest challenge in the beginning was having two full time jobs. I literally did do two full time jobs at once. For a lot of people it's prospecting. For me, I just followed the training program and so I just did what they told me and it worked.

Phil/Dan: A lot of people go to these training programs but they don't feel really good about going through the programs. But that's like joining a gym and not working out; they don't actually follow the formulae. They don't implement the ideas. I think one of the keys that you mentioned is you didn't try and re-invent the real estate wheel, you followed the pathway presented to you by someone who's already done it, right? And I think that is a very key thing.

Colin: Yeah, absolutely. Whenever I speak in front of a group of real estate agents inevitably the question comes up - what do you think is the most important thing and what is that biggest secret of your success - and the answer is always the same: do what you are taught. You know there are all these courses out there that are phenomenal. In later years, I went to Richard Robbins seminars and I just grabbed on to everything. I could learn from him and utilized a lot of those tools and of course those tools worked, too. So I think the biggest problem that real estate agents have is they don't follow the training, they're too opinionated, and they are too judgmental about what the training tells them to do, instead of being curious of how it works rather than judging why it won't work.

Phil/Dan: You know that's an interesting thing you just said, I like that. I think curiosity and the willingness to learn without pre-conceived ideas is one of the keys to successes for those people who do well, not just in real estate but any industry.

Million Dollar Agent Key Idea #52
"So I think the biggest problem that real estate agents have is they don't follow the training. They're too opinionated, and too judgmental about what the training tells them to do, instead of being curious of how it works and not judging why it won't work."

Colin: Absolutely. You know if somebody is new in an industry, a job, a career, if they haven't done that before, they shouldn't have those opinions.

Phil/Dan: A lot of times people bring these biases and I see it with new agents who try to re-invent the wheel. The premise of this book is to model the strategies and the proven pathways by those who have already done it, who are already successful, like you, in the business. What would you say has been your greatest challenge over all the years? When you started out you were juggling two businesses. What is the one thing that stands out as your greatest challenge?

Colin: The biggest challenge is myself. The market's not a challenge, the competition is not a challenge, the sellers and buyers are not a challenge, it's myself, to be disciplined. I have to do the things that I'm supposed to do when I'm supposed to do them, whether I feel like it or not. That's the biggest challenge. I've developed all the necessary skills, so I need to constantly drive myself to be disciplined.

Phil/Dan: You had mentioned that it's kind of like winning the internal game because you know what to do - it's getting yourself to do it if I'm quoting you consistently.

Colin: Yeah. A high producing real estate agent doesn't necessarily do things differently. They just do things, whether it's a listing presentation or prospecting or whatever. They have a high level of skill but they just do it more. They're on their game more. I feel like I'm only on track 30% of the time, but fortunately for me, the rest of the competition is only on track 5% of the time.

Million Dollar Agent Key Idea #53

"The biggest challenge is myself. The market's not a challenge, the competition is not a challenge, the sellers and buyers are not a challenge; it's myself - to be disciplined."

Phil/Dan: That's very telling, so for you to get better, if you increase the amount you're on track by 5%, the economic returns from that alone to your business are phenomenal, if you think about it.

Colin: Absolutely. You've probably heard many great professional sports coaches say there is a fine line between winning and losing, like if one team beats the other team eight to one, they're not eight times better, they're just a little bit better and they're consistently above the other team. You're consistently above your competition. So for example one of the things that I always preach to my assistant is that all the different tasks we do, we want to be better and we want to be the best at each individual task. We're never going to be perfect but if we're always moving in that direction, then we'll succeed, we'll be the best of the best.

Phil/Dan: Interesting, so, it's not a linear equation. You're moving forward in that direction and you may have a setback but as long as you course correct and you get back on track and move forward, that's really essential for your long-term success. That's fascinating, Colin. Over the years, your greatest challenge in your words is doing what you need to do consistently, would you say that's your greatest challenge today?

Colin: Absolutely, but I guess another challenge would be, when I get a negative client, that I don't let their negativity distract me because I have so many great people that I work with that it's a real challenge with that negative matter, you get that? That person who is just – one of those people and I let them take up too much space in my brain. That would be the only other thing.

Phil/Dan: I can speak from personal experience, in that I think we all have that same challenge. Very often in my day, I meet that one person and rather than acknowledge all the great people and great things that have happened, they give a little bit too much

Million Dollar Agent Key Idea #54

"The key is not to focus and put too much energy on that one negative person or thing. Look at the big picture and all the other good things that are going well. This helps to put things into perspective."

energy to that one person that doesn't really deserve it. If we would all learn to shift our focus to the totality of things it would certainly help our perspective, I couldn't agree with you more. I'd like to know for you, what was the big reason for you to get into the business?

Colin: Well, I wanted to be able to excel more; I wanted to be able to pursue excellence and not have all the obstacles that came with the business I was in before. You know, always solving problems. The competition was always lowering prices and so on. It's the same in every industry but in real estate I would be in control of myself and be able to battle. I didn't have to rely on the other external forces to be in line. I could just go out there and battle myself.

Phil/Dan: There is a lot more freedom arguably if you're an entrepreneur on your own and you don't have the security of being in a large corporation. There is a lot to be said about defining your own destiny and not being restricted by the rules and procedures in the industry.

Colin: Absolutely. To be quite honest too, I wanted to make a lot more money.

Phil/Dan: Okay, I got it.

Colin: I was a on a path of self-improvement and I refer to myself as a self-improvement junkie.

Phil/Dan: And that's still the same today as it was 17 years ago, if not more so, right?

Colin: Yeah.

Phil/Dan: *A lot of the agents that I speak to that are really at the top of their game have never stopped that process. I've worked out for 35 years and I remember one of my neighbors saying to me, "Why do you keep working out, you're already in shape". And it's kind of a silly question to me. Why does a top person in their field keep developing themselves? Well, the reason that you're in the top of your field is because you developed yourself consistently and over the years and, you don't stop, right? And I think that is one of the keys to why you are being successful, is that you've always been a self-development junkie, you keep striving. Even though from the outside someone may say why does he need to?*

Colin: There's nothing special about special people, it's what they do, not who they are, that makes them special. That's the line that Floyd taught me. And what that really means is that other people have done it, other people have earned a million dollars in commission in one year. That means I can do it too, right? When it comes to sales or becoming a doctor, a lawyer or buying a place in Jamaica, whatever the other people have done, I can do it, too. I just have to figure out what it is that they do and how they do it and if I model that I can be successful too. As Richard Robbins said, if we are going to go to work every week, and try to make money, we might as well make bags of it and not stop.

Million Dollar Agent Key Idea #55
"There's nothing special about special people; it's what they do that makes them special."

Phil/Dan: Right. You know you are putting in the time anyway, right?

Colin: Yeah. So if I'm going to be there, I'm going to work 40 hours a week or 60 hours a week. I could make a little, I could make okay, or I could make a lot. Well, I choose to make a lot because I'm going to be there anyway. Different individuals have different motivations as to why they do something. Mine is pursuit of excellence, to be the best of the best and then in harmony with that I put myself in a position where I can help other people, whether it's my clients, give money to a charity or teach new realtors. I really want to be in that position so that I can help other people. I don't do that selflessly, I do it selfishly because I love to be in that position, I love to do those things.

Phil/Dan: I suppose that becomes part of the intrinsic motivation itself, right? I get it, believe me, I get it more than you know. How would you describe your lifestyle now from when you first started in the business 17 years ago?

Colin: On a day-to-day basis it's just a challenge to push myself to be efficient.

Phil/Dan: *In terms of your lifestyle, obviously you're established now.*

Colin: I have a very good lifestyle. I have a wonderful home with a wonderful lady. I have property; I have a really nice boat, rental properties. I look forward to the future of my business, and travelling. I've been teaching myself that, "If you set a goal, you can achieve it, it can be done. So carry on young man."

Phil/Dan: *So, what has been the biggest change in your lifestyle now from when you started out in the business? Obviously, you were doing well financially but how would you describe the biggest change now versus then?*

Colin: I have much more certainty in my success. When you start out, it can be quite scary and that's where you have to take the leap of faith and follow the training. There's a reason why they teach you what they teach you.

Phil/Dan: *And so there is a lot of trust and faith in the beginning and then after you establish a track record of success, you have some frame of reference in terms of having done it before, it gets easier I suppose.*

Colin: Yes. Repetition is the mother of skill, and when you continually do things the right way and have success, you get jazzed about it, right? And you want to do it again, right? Like Og Mandino, the greatest salesman in the world. He said "I will practice and improve and polish the words I utter to sell my goods. Because many have attained great wealth and success with only one sales talk delivered with excellence." And let people know that in the sales talk, ladies and gentlemen, in your listing presentation, right? " I will constantly seek to improve my manners and graces for those are the sugar that people are attracted to."

Phil/Dan: *Wow, I marvel at your ability to remember all these quotes, it's pretty amazing, Colin.*

Colin: Yes, they made a difference for me.

Phil/Dan: *You have a reputation, you've probably repeated them thousands and thousands of times or read them thousands and thousands of times, I'm sure.*

Colin: A lot of the quotes I use the first time I read them, they hit me so hard that I memorize them in the next day. Because it was so impactful to me.

Phil/Dan: *What do you like most about being in the real estate business?*

Colin: I love being in control of carving my own path. I love the challenge of another month, to do eight to ten transactions and be the best, beat my previous month or my previous year. I love the challenges of that and I love the thought of the lifestyle that provides for me. And I love the thank yous from my clients. You know, when you've done a good job and everything comes together, and they go, 'Gee Colin, that's a lot, that's awesome.' And that's probably the biggest reward - when you get that thank you letter from your client.

Phil/Dan: *Yeah, I guess it makes all that stress and all the stuff that goes along with all the hard work, all worth it. I know you're a humble guy but, what makes you the best in what you do? I know this may sound like some of the questions asked before but it's an important question.*

Colin: I think what makes me the best is, I follow what I've been taught. And get curious about why it works. Everything from sending out a thank you letter with a request for a letter of reference and filling out the survey to understanding why you delivered the house warming gift to their office rather than their home, understanding all the tracks techniques and dialogues, being honest and upfront with sellers about what I do, and what price is going to work and what price isn't going to work. You know and be honest with people, because too often agents tell people what they want to hear rather than what they need to hear so that they can achieve their goal.

Million Dollar Agent Key Idea #56
"It is important to be honest with people and tell them want they need to hear as opposed to what they want to hear."

Colin: Well, it would be skill and systems. There is a defined way that I'll do all the tasks that are involved, and the biggest set of skills that I have is selling, one-on-one selling. Whether that's making a presentation or doing a negotiation. What makes me better is my knowledge and my skills are always at my fingertips. I've studied and I've practiced, so that when those moments come up where I have to draw on those skills, they're right there.

Phil/Dan: Why would someone choose you over any other realtor in the Edmonton area?

Colin: I come prepared. I'm professional and there isn't anything that they can say to me that I don't know the answer to, when it comes to the marketing and then selling of the property.

Phil/Dan: I speak to a lot of realtors, Colin, and they're certainly not doing as well as you are. In your view, how do the best realtors look at the world differently than everyone else?

Colin: Well, I think the best realtors have the skill set and they have the confidence. They know how they're going to handle all the different situations that come up. So that frees them up to be able to focus on the clients, like, who is that client, and what are they all about, what makes them tick? And what do I need to do to help them? They're freed up because they're so skillful and they're so rehearsed.

Phil/Dan: So they're not worried about how to do what they're doing because they've mastered that. Their focus moves to, what are the client's needs? How can I relate to this person?

Colin: Richard Robbins said fear is selfish, it's self-centered. If you're fearful, you're worried about yourself. Are they going to listen to me? Are they going to like me? Can I get a paycheck, right? That fear is so cunning, and so you focus on the other people, and you say, "Well, I'm going to get to know these guys and figure out how they're thinking, this is going to be fun, you know. They might not even know what the hell is going on here, but I'm going to figure them out and I'm going to help them." And when you go on that perspective, you're not thinking of yourself and you can't be afraid. And fear, there's an acronym for fear, false evidence appearing real. As a matter of fact you can say that a coward dies a thousand deaths, a brave man only once, because when you're afraid, it rolls around in your mind and it eats at your guts and it gets that stress in your body, when you're afraid. But when you just go forth and you're focused on other people, you're not afraid, you're in the zone, man, you're in the zone.

Million Dollar Agent Key Idea #57

"One of the absolute keys to letting go of fear in business is to focus on the needs of the other person."

Phil/Dan: Colin you should have been a preacher.

Colin: No problem. I was at a funeral one time for my

aunt. I did, I actually sang a piece that I wanted to sing for her. It meant a lot for me, and I also spoke, and I was switching off between Og Mandino and the bible and the correlation between them. Anyway, afterwards I was sitting with my mom and we were having a little lunch and this lady comes up to me and she said, I can see that you're a man of the cloth.

Phil/Dan: *Well, as you're not, you ought to be. That's true.*

Colin: I said, "Well, ma'am, I am not, but thank you."

Phil/Dan: *Well, well, that's pretty amazing. So, generally speaking Colin, what makes you the top ten percent? I interviewed Richard Robbins himself and he said, you know, for 80 to 90% of realtors their life is terrible. They're struggling day-to-day just to get by, they're not making a good living, and then you have the top ten percent that just love it. They're successful, they're prosperous, and they're doing well. In your view, what makes the top ten percent, the top ten percent? What are the key things?*

Colin: You have to develop the skill; you have to know your scripts, the techniques, your dialogues. You need to have situation awareness, understand the situation that you're in. You have to read and react to the situation. If you get some real nasty person on the phone, you don't book an appointment; you get off the phone and move on to somebody that you want to work with.

You know, when somebody comes up with an objection, what's the situation?; what's going on? You just know how to handle it. Successful realtors, they're skillful, they're prepared, they have situation awareness, and they work hard. You play hard but you also you work hard, when you're at work, you work. Most top producers do more in a week than what most agents do in a month or two months. Before we started the interview, I mentioned I've taken about 16 listings in 40 days. Well, 16 listings for the average realtor is four years.

Phil/Dan: *Incredible.*

Colin: I'm not going to brag, I'm saying that is the difference with the top producing agents.

Phil/Dan: *If that doesn't speak volumes I don't know what does, Colin.*

Colin: Richard is absolutely right. I see the pain and the frustration in their eyes and you hear the uncertainty in their voice. Because when you are a low producing agent, every deal is such a big deal. That deal is the one or one of the two paychecks you're getting that month, right?   As a top producer, you've already got five, six or seven deals and you get in a situation where people are going to be rude or not understanding, you're going to attack the situation and you're going to win because you're not afraid of losing that deal. You're going to do what is right regardless of the obstacles.

Phil/Dan: Interesting. I speak to a lot of agents who say that you have two types of clients: you have the ones you enjoy working with and then you have the others. You should have two types of fees: a regular fee that you charge for those people that you enjoy working with and then you have an aggravation fee, which is 10 times the amount for people that give you the most grief. I guess you've also reached the point where you don't need to work with those high aggravation people at all.

Colin: And that's a key, sort of an advanced skill to develop, is to recognize if you got a difficult client and if you can fire them early enough great. If you get into it, you know how you're going to deal with them. If you mess with the kid, I'm going to close you, first opportunity. And that's a key component because like I said, with most top producing realtors when they get a nasty client it is really, really distracting.

Phil/Dan: So the key is to shift their focus from them, get out of the situation and take control of the situation as early as possible. How would you complete this sentence, Colin? The real estate business is what?

Colin: Very rewarding.

Phil/Dan: How so?

Colin: I've learnt the skill and I'm good at what I do. I can make a lot of money, if you figure out all those parameters, it's great. I make more money than most doctors and lawyers.

Phil/Dan: Probably most doctors and lawyers combined, based on what you're telling me, which is more than the premier of the province, that's for sure. You don't have to deal with all that grief. So what are the main ways that the best realtors think differently, how they look at the world differently?

Colin: I think good realtors are always moving forward in their thinking. A low producing realtor can really get depressed over a collapsed deal and drag that around with him for a long time.

Phil/Dan: High producers are on to the next deal because you know there's an unlimited abundance of them, anyway.

Colin: Yeah. And you mentioned the word abundance. That's something that I think most top producing agents see - there's an abundance of business out there, there is enough for everyone. If I go and I make a ton of money, that is like me going down to a lake and filling up a gallon pail. There's more than enough for everyone but you've got to go out and help people. The effectiveness of helping people is in direct proportion to your income. If you're not that good at helping people - it doesn't matter if you're selling beer and peanuts, doing real estate or as the coach of a hockey team, your effectiveness in how you can help people will determine your income. It's not a government job, it's not a position. You have to bring value to the market place.

Phil/Dan: Well said, Colin; well said. On a more sort of specific level, what are the essential key daily practices that lead to your success as a realtor? You mentioned earlier it is the application of your skill and knowledge on a consistent basis. If you were to chunk that down, when you're on the game, what are you doing, what are the key daily practices that you do that mostly lead to your success?

Colin: Your prospecting and follow up. Those are the two main things. Then I guess you just stay on track with all the other specific needs, your specific things that you need to do.

Phil/Dan: When you get up in the morning and you're planning your day, do you have a certain routine? How do you get prepared to go create those 17 listings?

Colin: Those seeds were sown a long time ago. My daily thing is pretty simple. I'm what they call an orange sky personality, where I'm bouncing off walls and I'm not a very pragmatic person, but I force myself to do this. I look at my day and I know what appointments I have, so those have to happen, and then I look at my to-do list and there are always a ton of things to do. I pick the top two or three things that I need to do and I focus on them first because if I focus on them there's a lot of little things that will take care of themselves. If I do it the opposite way I'll never get to the priorities, and the little things start to multiply and get complicated.

Phil/Dan: Interesting.

Colin: My coach that I have with Richard Robins told me about how he and Richard would think, where is my next listing coming from? Where is my next deal coming from? Every day I ask myself that question, where is my next listing, where is the next deal coming from? And the prospecting, the lead follow-up and asking those key questions, that is pro-active activity. Processing a listing is re-active and hopefully we use administrative people to help us with that. And if a buyer wants to see a property or they want to put up an offer on a property, we're reacting. Realtors who are good at doing those key pro-active activities will generate the income.

Phil/Dan: *What are the best realtors doing consistently better than anyone else? Of all that activity a professional realtor engages in on a daily, monthly, weekly basis and so forth what are the best doing consistently?*

Colin: If they don't have the skills, the tracks techniques and dialogues, they're working on those, rehearsing them, refining their systems - the way they post up the listing, the way they do their listing presentation, the objection handling techniques that they are going to use, are they going to do it different, next time? If they're not loaded up with those skills, they're refining that, they're prospecting, they're following up on leads, and they're following up on with their sellers on feedback and update market analysis. They have goals that they want to hit, whether it's a number of listings, whether it's the amount of gross commission they want to earn, the number of deals they want to do, the number of vacations they want to take. They're very focused, they're prepared to work hard, and they're prepared to work long because they know there's going to be some dry spells here and there. And so top producing real estate agents keep going and going. And right now, I'm numb because I've been working so much, but I know that it's by choice. Nobody forced me to do it.

Phil/Dan: *What are the top three things that you do consistently that lead most to your success?*

Colin: Well, following the systems.

Phil/Dan: *Okay, so you're working on the business as opposed to just being in it, right?*

Colin: Yes, and be focused. You have to have laser beam focus so that your mind is dwelling upon what it is that you want to achieve a large portion of the time. When I'm getting ready for work, I have this little, tiny book, it's four inches by four inches. It's a quote by Dr. Wayne Dyer and it says, "As you place more and more of your energy on what you intend to manifest, you'll start seeing those intentions materializing." Well, I can't just think about this a little bit here and a little bit there. I have to stay focused and dwell upon what I want to achieve, the tasks I want to do.

Phil/Dan: That's such great advice especially in the ADD world that we live in, where there are so many distractions whether it's the news, our cell phones going off, emails, texts, social media. I always have to remind myself, bring myself back to those key things that are my stated outcomes for the day. And it's so important to consistently do that because there are so many things that could pull you in so many directions.

Colin: In Dr. Wayne Dyer's book he says, "Give thanks for everything that you are, everything that you have, that's the first step towards discarding a scarcity mentality."

Phil/Dan: Just for the purpose of our readers it sounds like a great book, I love Wayne Dyer. What is the name of the book that you're reading?

Colin: It's Dr. Wayne Dyer, *Everyday Wisdom for Success*. It's intended that you read one of these pages every day, but I just left it on that one page for the last two years.

Phil/Dan: I admire your focus. What are the best realtors doing differently than the average realtors?

Colin: When you meet with the client, we do presentations, most realtors don't even have one. In addition to that, your presentation is the way you look, the way you sound and enthusiasm. Barry Hannah said that, "The most important characteristic that people want to see in a real estate agent is enthusiasm." Enthusiasm comes from a Greek word 'en Theos' which means God Within. So, when I go out on an appointment, I'm jazzed. I get animated and I'm not there to be elegant, I'm there to communicate and get to know them. You need that enthusiasm; you have to look like a professional. There are far, far, too many realtors in this industry who find reasons why they can dress down rather than dress up right? Looking your best, you should be sharp because people will judge you very quickly. And top producing agents they always look sharp, they talk sharp, they have a lot of enthusiasm.

Million Dollar Agent Key Idea #58
"The most important characteristic that people want to see in a real estate agent is enthusiasm."

Phil/Dan: I met a guy who had a landscaping business, and I asked him why are you so successful in landscaping? You seem to get all the accounts. He said he had so much positive energy that when he shook the person's hand at 7:00 am they had no choice but to hire him. He just overwhelmed them with enthusiasm because early in the morning the client was often not fully awake at the time. I remembered that and have used that in spades.

Colin: We're asking about what top producing real estate agents do that is different. Most top producers stay in touch with our past clients. Ideally I want to talk to my clients, to meet all my 'A' clients four times a year, but that doesn't happen on a regular basis. That's one of the things I struggle with.

Phil/Dan: *That's where systems come in.*

Colin: Thankfully I know this guy who got me hooked up with Morris Marketing Real Estate which is a professionally written newsletter with articles and information about real estate for people when they own a home, not just when they're buying and selling and it's a way to stay in touch with people. It's a good working way to remind them; here I am if you need me.

Phil/Dan: *And for our listening audience here this was an unsolicited endorsement of Morris Real Estate Marketing Group and the products and services that we offer.*

Colin: It's accurate though.

Phil/Dan: *Thank you, I appreciate that. Million dollar revenue streams. When you think about all the areas that have generated for you, what areas generate the most business for you? You have commodity-based strategies, you have relationship-based strategies, you have farming, fish boats, for those people who are not for-sale-by- owners, expiring listing specialty referrals. You just mentioned referral and repeat, website regeneration. What has been the economic engine for you over all the years?*

Colin: Oh, it's very much repeat and referral, it's relationships by far. Everything else pales in comparison.

Phil/Dan: *When I speak to the most involved and successful agents like you Colin, they will tell me that over and over again. You need the lead generation but a lot of times people spend so much time, energy and money on trying to market to people they don't know as opposed to just taking care of the people they do know. It's very interesting.*

Colin: When I started, I had no extra money to do any advertising or pay for postage for farming. I just said, "I've got to take really, really good care of these people so they'll come back to me and they'll send others to me." I was fortunate enough that I had the past experience of my other business where I would solicit letters of reference for my clients. I did that so much that I had packages with letters of reference that I would divide it into different types of clients. I had a stack of letters for fashion shows, from all the big malls that put on shows, from Ford models in New York because one of their people was out here choreographing a show. I had letters from the premier's office, from the prime minister's office, from corporate presentations, IBM, all the major festivals that happen in the Edmonton area.

And so when I gave a package to a prospect, not only did I give them letters of reference but I gave them letters of reference that were specific to the type of client they were. We have this thing called ultimate service and one of the perks of it is we send out a questionnaire. So, I would send out a questionnaire and I'd give a handwritten thank you note which is what Richard Robbins taught me and ask for a letter of reference. I stayed right on top of it and even more. I break down the letters of reference into first time home buyers, investors, people that try to use a for-sale-by-owner service, people that buy and sell, people that just sell, people new to the community. So, when they get a package of letters of reference it's for the people just like them. And that really, really helped me out, that was phenomenal.

Phil/Dan: What great advice that is. Thank you. When you think about new clients, people that don't know you, what is your area of expertise for generating brand new clients? Where do your new clients come from?

Colin: From the old clients. I get the odd ones who are new clients. They didn't know me, nobody referred them to me. So, it's a bit of a shock for them because you know I don't hold anything back. I've calculated all of my business in a given year; 84%-92% of it is from past clients and referrals from past clients.

Phil/Dan: You know, I asked this question to an agent one time and he said the most bizarre place he got a client was by inadvertently dropping his business card in a shopping mall parking lot. It was raining and the card got soaked and a guy who was walking through that parking lot picked up the card off the ground, soaking wet, and happened to need a realtor. So, he called him up and said, wow, I should be leaving my card inadvertently around shopping malls all over town!

Colin: Well, it's interesting that you say that because realtors have all sorts of ways they get clients and then they think it's like some sort of technique they should use.

Phil/Dan: Well, once you turn it into a technique and it never works, right?

Colin: Getting back to what top real estate agents do, we follow a system, we don't make exceptions of not being prepared, and we don't make exceptions for pricing things too high. Within reason, I mean are we going to take something a little high, maybe work them down later? Possibly, but we're always moving in the direction of our system.

Phil/Dan: You know it's interesting you're not dropping business cards on a deserted park or shopping mall parking lot hoping that someone will call you. You go back to the fundamentals by wisely applying what works in the system, that's interesting.

Colin: There are one out of 10 or one out of 30 guys that are successful that nobody can figure out what it is. You don't want to try to copy that guy - follow a system that works. I love to help people and everybody knows I like to help people. But what's interesting is the longer I'm in the business and the more successful I am, the less people come to me and ask me questions. It used to really bug me but then my broker told me, "You know Colin, you ought to forget about that. The reason that people don't come and ask for your advice is because you're going to tell them the truth and you're going to tune them in. Most people when they ask somebody for advice they just want the other person to agree with them."

Phil/Dan: You know your broker is a very wise man.

Colin: He really put my mind at ease.

Phil/Dan: If they truly wanted your advice they would actually watch you and do what you do as opposed to just ask you and not follow your opinion. Another topic - lead generation and communication strategies. For your area of specialization which is referral and repeat using internet, email, social media, direct mail, in person, face-to-face, telephone. What are you using to communicate with your dominant lead generation?

Colin: Well, that lead generation once again, that comes from past clients' referrals.

Phil/Dan: *Okay.*

Colin: Mass marketing newsletters.

Phil/Dan: *Okay, so direct mail.*

Colin: Taking the "A" clients out for lunches.

Phil/Dan: *So, personal, face-to-face.*

Colin: In person or to go for a beer or a breakfast, could be a lunch, a drink after work or handwritten thank you notes. What's interesting is when you get good at what you do, you have a certain level of business that keeps coming in so that you're struggling to find time to prospect because your current customers are keeping you busy!

Phil/Dan: *This is where systems come in because it's the balance between working on execution versus succeeding for the future, administering your current business versus creating business for the future, balancing the here and now versus creating business for tomorrow. The answer is in having systems that leverage both your time and relationships, and that is key and I think you do that quite well, Colin. How many listings do you have?*

Million Dollar Agent Key Idea #59
"Having a systems-based business is about balancing your business here and now and creating business for the future. It is essential that you do both and having systems in place is key to doing this."

Colin: I think it's 16 in 40 days.

Phil/Dan: *Wow! That ought to be the title of my book.*

Colin: I think three of them are from this spec builder. This guy's been building homes for over 20 years. I met with this individual and thought I would do my presentation and just lay it all out there, even though I know builders can be tough to negotiate with. We met in this vacant home so I had my laptop on the island and he was standing there, and because I was standing I could be a lot more animated and use a lot more big body movements. And I went through my presentation and I listed the property above average commission. And he told me that he's been building houses for over 20 years, then he said, "You know Colin, I have to thank you. You're the first person who's ever explained to me why I should pay a full commission."

Phil/Dan: *You explained to him and showed him as well. Beautiful, thanks Colin. I can't thank you enough for this.*

Million Dollar Agent Key Ideas Summary

$ So I think the biggest problem that real estate agents have is they don't follow the training. They're too opinionated, and too judgmental about what the training tells them to do, instead of being curious of how it works and not judging why it won't work.

$ The biggest challenge is myself. The market's not a challenge, the competition is not a challenge, the sellers and buyers are not a challenge; it's myself - to be disciplined.

$ The key is not to focus and put too much energy on that one negative person or thing. Look at the big picture and all the other good things that are going well. This helps to put things into perspective.

$ There's nothing special about special people; it's what they do, not who they are, that makes them special.

$ It is important to be honest with people and tell them want, not who they are, need to hear as opposed to what they want to hear.

$ One of the absolute keys to letting go of fear in business is to focus on the needs of the other person.

$ The most important characteristic that people want to see in a real estate agent is enthusiasm.

$ Having a systems-based business is about balancing your business here and now and creating business for the future. It is essential that you do both and having systems in place is key to doing this.

LEE YULE:
The King of I Am

BORN AND RAISED in Edmonton's south side, Lee went to Hardisty Jr. High and McNalley Composite High before attending the University of Alberta. To provide an income during that time he says he had the world's best part-time job - playing in a rock band on weekends. If you can imagine the decision-making process of the very young adult mind during the late 70's, he decided to follow that career path, and during the following 15 years was a musician, comedian, children's entertainer, actor and talent agent.

Tiring of the road, limited pay and the arrival of his first child, Lee decided that a change was in the stars. After a little soul searching and urging from his buddy, Danny Hooper (already in the biz), he embarked on a new career in real estate in 1992.

Now, with three adult children and many more years under his belt, Lee finds he has much life experience to draw upon. He has learned that people are real estate, not houses, condos and land; that clients want information, not pressure, and the only way to succeed at anything is with the constant application of effort, integrity and to never stop learning.

Now, Lee skis, plays hockey, cuts the grass, compulsively renovates and looks for a purpose ("now that my kids don't need anything from me but money"). Lee's kids tell him they are going to inscribe "He thought he was funny" on his headstone.

LEE YULE IS a great example of a realtor who has successfully made the journey from ego-based/transactional realtor, working extremely hard at great expense to sustain the infrastructure of a business, to a systems-based realtor where it is all about lifestyle. Lee now does very well financially by defining the real estate business on his own terms. Lee has so many valuable lessons to share not only on how to create a successful and prosperous real estate practice but also on how to avoid the many pitfalls that many realtors fall prey to and are so common in a business that can be all-consuming. Lee is frequently sought out as a real estate speaker by his peers who greatly appreciate his vast knowledge, expertise and wisdom.

Phil/Dan: Well, good morning Lee. We are here with Lee Yule and he is one of Alberta's, if not all of Western Canada's, best realtors for a number of reasons. He probably wouldn't say that himself, being humble, but that is why I've included him in this book. We've known each other for well over a decade, Lee, which is kind of amazing. And you're a realtor that I've watched who gets it. You understand how this works. You've evolved in your careers and I really appreciate you taking the time to do this because I know how busy you are. So thank you.

Lee: No problem; my pleasure.

Phil/Dan: Okay. So, let's get right down to it because your time is very valuable. What did you do before going to the real estate business?

Lee: I was in the entertainment business.

Phil/Dan: What were you doing specifically? How did your career evolve and how did you come to the decision of wanting to go into real estate?

Lee: I was in the entertainment business, specifically music and comedy. Within university that was the world's best part-time job. All my buddies had these terrible jobs trying to get through school and I was playing as a musician in a rock band which was a big novelty because Disco was king. University just didn't seem to sparkle and the things that I was doing in the university didn't seem to have much shine. So what I did was just straight ahead went and kept playing music because it was going so well at the time. And that continued on until I was in my 30's and of course it changed, it evolved. I eventually ended up in the entertainment business including being a comedian. And then I was a talent agent and I was doing a lot of things and eventually I had a client that I was booking named was Danny Hooper. He was just getting out of real estate and back into the entertainment business.

Phil/Dan: It's like you traded positions or something, right?

Lee: Right. We did, we did a switch essentially is what we did. And I went into real estate and of course my kids were all being born and I was tired because being in music is sort of like being in sports. If you're in the minors, kids ride in the bus and it's not comfortable and it's certainly not very profitable and it just takes its toll on you. It was time to do something else so I went into real estate.

Phil/Dan: Let's be clear, you're also a pretty damn good musician, you may describe yourself as being in the minors but you were pretty up there from what I understand.

Lee: It's true. I did well for myself and I was wildly successful because I had a really crappy old house which I had a mortgage on and a 69 Plymouth Mod Top. And so in my business I was pretty successful.

Phil/Dan: So, you had someone in the music business who had recommended you go into real estate because he saw your potential for being good at that.

Lee: He did, he said, "Lee, if you're going to take your skills to the next level, why not sell something that has a much better potential to make a good living?"

Phil/Dan: That's a pretty dramatic switch because you knew the music industry very well and here you're going in a completely new profession. So when you started real estate, what would you say was your greatest challenge?

Lee: Well, it's funny you know, I don't think of it as a challenge. What happened to me was just an unbelievable growth curve. It was like somebody switched on a set of 500 watt lights right in front of me. I just couldn't believe all the opportunities that presented themselves for personal growth, because I had pretty much settled into what I was doing. In fact I knew what I was doing but in this moment I started going to self-improvement seminars. And the funniest thing is, it didn't seem like I was challenged. I felt that it was just an incredible opportunity to grow and I did unbelievably so.

Phil/Dan: *You entered in this total world of opportunity which probably was very refreshing on a number of different levels. How long have you been in real estate?*

Lee: Twenty three years.

Phil/Dan: *Obviously you've evolved considerably and we're going to get to that in a moment but over the years if you had to crystallize what has been the one largest challenge that you've had to face professionally in the real estate business what would you say it is?*

Lee: Well, the biggest thing is to come up with a reason to do what you do and you come up against this a number of times. Early in the game, I learned about setting goals because I never really had done that. I did but I didn't realize what it was. So, during the process of learning about self-improvement, I came across the concept of goals and how you attain goals. But one of the worst things that happened was I realized that goals in themselves are very material. You go blowing by them and you look at them in your rearview mirror because you visualize them. It caught me by surprise that it was such a downer, because I'd already seen the goal and I was looking at it as I went by and in my rearview mirror. It really took me a while to figure that out - it wasn't the goal. It was the process of getting to the goal that was important. In fact, the goal was really nothing. It was about what you did in the meantime and that was the biggest challenge just to come up with that and always coming up with something new to head towards so you didn't start feeling hopeless and going in circles which happens at various times in your career when you hit watershed moments in your life.

Phil/Dan: *That is so profound. I just want to focus on it. I know from personal experience that if you're always going for the attainment of a*

> **Million Dollar Agent Key Idea #60**
> *"It is not the goal; it is the process of obtaining the goal that is important."*

goal and you don't have a new goal but you blow by it, you don't enjoy the process. It's a bit of a letdown because you work so hard and when you've got it, it's the 'now what?' phenomena.

Lee: Oh, terribly so. So what I came up with was as a result of those experiences was the concept that it's not where you're going but it's what you're doing. You have to develop a process that you like and you enjoy getting up and doing every day. That makes the goals easy – not only easy to attain but it's no problem to go by because it has an automatic reset on it.

Phil/Dan: Right. So the goal is in effect the natural by-product of living the life that you want as opposed to an end in itself.

Million Dollar Agent Key Idea #61
"Your goal is the natural by-product of living the life that you want as opposed to an end in and of itself."

Lee: Right, exactly. I want to be rich, repeat it a million times, is not a goal. And I see this in my business all the time. You know exactly what it is. You see these young guys, in 5 years they work all the time. They don't see their family and they make a lot of money but they walk around with this glazed look on their face, thinking maybe I should hire another assistant. You know they already make more money than they can spend; maybe what they should do is come up with a reason to get up in the morning.

Phil/Dan: It's like a reengineering what's important for one's life. I guess in real estate given the economic potential and the upside, this can be a vortex that can suck people in and they get caught in that trap all too often. Looking back over your career, you can see how that would be a reoccurring motif until you evolve beyond it to redefine things in such a way that you made it work for you as opposed to being a victim of it.

Lee: Exactly. Realizing it, looking at it and seeing it, because I see people in my business that are older than I am, that are on the hamster wheel going round and round and round and they're number one. They believe their own advertising instead of reorienting and saying, you know, I'm doing this to have a full life, I'm not doing this to be number one. As long as my cat loves me when I get home and everyone's fine, what else do you need? We need a certain amount of money but a lot of realtors make far more money and have a far larger financial footprint than is totally necessary but they don't see it and they just keep going for more and more and more. You look at these guys; a lot of them get pretty empty. You know, it's social carnage. When you look at guys that are wildly successful in the real estate business, or any business for that matter, it does not mean that they know how to do anything else including having a balanced existence. Now, I don't really believe in balance, I think we're always going somewhere but it's sort of a goal unto itself, right? It's the fine balance.

Phil/Dan: *It's being conscious of it and it's a mitigation process at best. You're always course correcting on some level, believe me.*

Lee: Oh, that's right, you bet.

Phil/Dan: *Most people do it unconsciously and they get so removed from what's important that they lose their compass.*

Lee: Oh no, I get it, totally. It's because you start believing you're own advertising, it's one of the worst problems in real estate if you're successful. And there are a couple of different kinds of people in real estate. There are the ones that go on and they do an okay living but they sort of piggy-back off of other realtors but you also get the people that are usually very successful, what they call generators. A generator generates enough business to support 4 or 5 realtors.

Phil/Dan: *So, they're sort of the catalyst; the rainmaker, if you will.*

Lee: They are the rainmaker, absolutely, and the guys call them the generator but exactly. They create, they generate business and unfortunately there's a good part and a bad part. The generator will always have lots of business but he will also be seduced by the sirens of the success that it brings.

Phil/Dan: *So the message is you have to find yourself amidst all of this success and be humble.*

Lee: And be willing to leave your ego at the door. The hardest part I found is that I reached a fairly high level of success and I was in the top 4 or 5 in my office, year after year and in the process of getting bigger spaces and more equipment, the problem is you can become wrapped up, your ego becomes your identity and at the end of the day we are not our job. That's easy to say but it's far easier to go up than it is to go down. It's the same thing for people to downsize their houses, we see it. You have a million dollar house, so basically you're going to have to buy a million dollar condo to make yourself happy. The best is sideways but we sure don't like to downsize career wise. You get to a point where you've paid for a lot of things, you know your kids have their education, they are all starting to leave home, you had your divorce, whatever is going on in life, you have to say to yourself, 'I really don't need to make $900,000 a year. Maybe I should back off and do something and spend more time doing other things that aren't necessarily about spending money and making money.' But that's very hard to do when you spend 20 years of your life doing nothing but that.

Phil/Dan: *And your whole ego, your whole identification is based upon that. Well, that's like a revolution of consciousness, right? That's such great advice and I would say it's a little bit of a warning for those young realtors that are reading this from an elder statesman. You're not that old but I mean now somebody has lived through it to tell a cautionary tale because you know and I see it a lot.*

Lee: You know, one of the problems I find is you sit and try to discuss it with them and unfortunately until they walk a mile in your shoes, they don't know what you're talking about.

Phil/Dan: *They're blinded by the dollar signs right?*

Lee: Or they're blinded by the all the work they put in and they can't figure out why anybody would do what I'm suggesting, to park your ego at the door, especially when you've always been some kind of peon. And now you're self-important and you're self-employed and you're making money and you're this guy in a suit that shows up and has the esteem of all these people. He has so much respect for you and you're really responsible for some very important things in their lives. If you're in the middle of that and you've never had that all your life, and suddenly you've got that, it's pretty hard to leave that at the door. Or even listen to somebody who does it. Many times I've had guys come to me later and go, oh I know, I think I get what you mean, now.

Million Dollar Agent Key Idea #62
"It is so important for your long term success in the real estate business to check your ego at the door."

Phil/Dan: *But they hadn't had an experience or journey to discover that, right?*

Lee: Absolutely.

Phil/Dan: *Well, that's profound. If there's one thing in this interview that I can really underline is what you've just shared. This has been amazing in terms of that one insight alone. I remember when we first met, I was interviewing you and you called yourself the king of – what did you call it?*

Lee: Oh, I don't know. The King of I Am.

Phil/Dan: *The King of I Am. I think that's what it was, I loved that term. Having evolved beyond the King of I Am to where you are, what is your greatest challenge now, today, having gone through that journey?*

Lee: You know the hard part is that real estate tends to be an all or nothing kind of business. You're either rolling in it, working all the time or you're not. So, the hard part now is to cut and really put it in the places where I work. I don't work as much. I worked all my past clients and successes to the point where I don't have to work nearly as hard and I can do other things that I love to do that have nothing to do with making money. So you can transition into… retirement is probably not the right word for a realtor because you never do, but to transition into a two-thirds or one-third work week or 50% work week and still do well enough to accomplish your goals. Your ends, whatever they may be.

Phil/Dan: *That is a beautiful segway into the next question which has to do with lifestyle. You alluded to this just a moment ago. How would you describe your lifestyle now versus when you first started in real estate or when you were all about ego?*

Lee: In the beginning, you're trying to get a network, referrals, and you're trying to get your name up there and you're trying to keep the listing board full and you're trying to get all the money. So what happens when you first go, you're blown away by all the money you're making but you're working all the time - you're on, you're on, you're on, but you're spending more, spending more, spending more. At about the 5-year point, you realize that now everything costs 10 times as much as it used to, but you're living in a much nicer house, you've got a better car, everything is going so much better and you've got to put in the time, you're still working like a madman. Then, you transition into the point where you start getting other people to work for you and now you're becoming a people manager.

You're no longer a realtor. You're a manager. You're managing a bunch of people. And you get to that point and you're still

Million Dollar Agent Key Idea #63
"One of the greatest skills you can have in both business and in life is the ability to deal with ambiguity."

working, working, working. Now unless something happens to you, usually we have watershed moments in our life which can happen to us and artificially we'll say, alright, you have to take a reset which is a health event, a divorce, something. There are a lot of guys, they take themselves away too far and get too far and bite off too much and then have to chew on that and recover. So at those points you can then decide what it is you're going to do. Once those things happen to you a few times, then you learn the skill of reinventing yourself. And it's a skill and it's a learned skill to graciously reinvent and not fear it and that's one thing the music business did for me. You have to reinvent yourself and go to new projects all the time which may not be like the old ones. And some of them are failures, some of them are successes but you have to walk through those doors and keep walking through those doors until it gives us successes.

Phil/Dan: I often say that one of the greatest skills that one can have as a business person, an entrepreneur, is the ability to deal with ambiguity. Lots of people leave 9-to-5 jobs, their cubicle in downtown wherever they have relative "economic certainty" and a paycheck, to go into real estate where there's no paycheck and yet unlimited potential income, relatively speaking. What kills a lot of people and destroys them but makes it so difficult, is the dealing with the ambiguity and part of that is having the skill which you just described. You must develop the ability to deal with unpredictability but to reinvent yourself so that you continually learn, grow and survive and thrive amidst all that.

Lee: And thrive and also enjoy yourself. It's what happens to a lot of people who keep doing the same thing - you start to really hate your life.

In terms of an underlying negative tone, it takes a lot of courage to say, 'Even though things are going well on the surface or to the outer world, I need to change this because I'm not happy. I need to change this up and not be afraid of less money or not be afraid of a smaller house or people not bowing down.' You have to not be afraid of letting those things go.

Phil/Dan: That is so amazing. I often hear a lot of very wealthy people interviewed about their life and they say they enjoyed the process of acquiring the wealth but once they got it, they looked back with fond affection at those years. But what you're saying is that you can constantly recreate that if you're adaptable to change rather than becoming a slave to something that you're burnt out and bored with.

Lee: It's your ego man and it's the fear of change. Your ego is really important. It's important to be egocentric, not egotistical. It's good to have a strong center but you don't want to let it run you because your decisions can become superficial to say the least.

Phil/Dan: So the evolutionary journey is all about making the real estate business work for you and defining your life from that as opposed of being a slave to the business.

Lee: Yeah. Inside the business, I hate to work with an investor who has done nothing but make money. I like to work with guys who've taken a couple of serious body blows, lost the money, that have been hurt but they're still there because when you work with them, they're much more realistic. They're more grounded. They're aware of the negative and the positive of their actions and they're willing to accept them. There's an underlying arrogance that gets pounded off, what I'll say beats their corners off.

In my own case as a realtor, one of the positive aspects of having your life blow up in a horrific way is you can then rebuild it in any way you want according to the new knowledge that you gained from all your experiences.

Phil/Dan: *So you're no longer forced to repeat the past blindly. You're at the moment of choice and you can recreate it in any way you want. When you were talking about blowing the corners off, I was thinking metaphorically about a wheel moving so much more smoothly because it doesn't block.*

Lee: That's right. And there are some people in the business that have their share and they keep repeating it over and over but don't progress as an individual which is important. I know you're trying to write a book to help realtors become better mechanics, right? You know, the mechanics of real estate and making money I haven't really talked about all that. I suppose I could.

Phil/Dan: *Well, I've got some more specific question but you know the book is really about focusing on those realtors that have made it and the title is the 'Million Dollar Agents' but it's not about the money at all. It's about what does it mean to be at the top of your game? What does it mean to be beyond subsistence? As you know the majority of realtors do not make it in a way that they're economically prosperous. It's the lessons that I want to cut into steel that you've gleaned along the way, as you've gone through this.*

Lee: The idea is trench warfare, so you back off and you're seeing things in a larger picture which includes yourself in it.

Phil/Dan: *So you're more conscious of the process as well as the end result.*

Lee: The idea is to be aware enough of your choices, you know what's going to happen as a result of them and this is on many levels in terms of business as well. A guy will say for instance, I'm going to crack my budget;

I want to do a million dollars next year. Well, what they're not telling you is they're going to work five times as hard, have a budget assistant, and have blood squirting out of your ears to do so. So be careful what you wish for.

Phil/Dan: That's very powerful advice, Lee. But what makes you the best at what you do? However you want to define it.

Lee: Don't take yourself so seriously.

Phil/Dan: I want to really highlight that for the reader because there are many people who are so focused on the how and what I've learned is that once you've crystallized or defined the what, be open to the how, be open to the how manifesting in any number of ways by being responsive and flexible to changing circumstances that are totally unpredictable. That will lead you to the what.

Million Dollar Agent Key Idea #64
"If you want to be successful in real estate, don't take yourself so seriously."

Lee: There's something that I learned about dealing with specific instances, ethical issues. There are all sorts of things when you're dealing with people intimately with all this money, with this level of responsibility for the advice you give and the contracts you help them enter. So the idea is that if you ever come up against a conundrum, I would say you need to have a basic philosophy of what you're doing, and that includes an individual contract or whole business, it can go from very large to very small. And when you have a question or you don't know what to do or you don't know where to go, refer back to your basic philosophy. For instance, who signed the contract? It's not your pocketbook and it's not the other guy who is on the other side of the deal. It's the guy who signed the contract. It's just an example but if you have a basic philosophy and it does the same thing in your business, my business is going to support my lifestyle while still retaining its authenticity.

Phil/Dan: That's another powerful point because you can get lost in the goal and lose your bearing, your compass as to what's important and what's not important. If you haven't in advance found that overall philosophy, that guiding framework by which to conduct yourself it's very easy to kind of get caught up and then to forget who signed your paycheck at the end of the day.

Lee: Right. You know I talked about consequences, and I'll give you an example of an unintended consequence. You know you start making a lot more money because you're doing more transactions and you're farming out a lot of things to other people to do because you simply can't do it, you replicate yourself. What you don't realize is you're now going to be paying a lot more taxes. You have to hire someone to do nothing. I mean at one point I had somebody one day a week who was doing nothing, like your payroll.

I was paying somebody and it got bigger and bigger to the point where he became almost like a monster and when I tried to reduce my business I got audited, I got a GSG audit, a personal audit and a payroll audit because you're making that machine that suddenly builds expectations of everybody around you including the bureaucracy. So when you do try to change, there's going to be a lot of resistance, you create this monstrous bureaucracy and so all I can say is a lot of times when you're watching this stuff, be careful what you wish for because you don't realize that if you want to become the King of I Am, you're going to have border wars and insurrections and attempted assassination, you know it's really hard to be King.

Phil/Dan: *A very wise person once said it's very hard to turn an elephant, to make an elephant change direction.*

Lee: Like turning the corner, I used to call it. It's like when you develop and when you build something or build a development which is a business I was in for quite some time, planning is everything. That's how you stay and keep your budget on track. The

Million Dollar Agent Key Idea #65
"It is so important that you remember who you are working for, who signed the contract and pays for and supports your lifestyle. Integrity and having a moral compass is everything in business."

more defined your plans are the more detailed your plans get, then you only have to react to smaller things because you have a defined plan. Now, you also have to be careful with that because you can define your plan all you want but boy you better be able to be on the balls of your feet because things are going to be moving around on you and you've got to be able to accept that graciously.

Phil/Dan: *We often live at the point of infinite possibilities whether we're aware of it or not and anybody thinks that they can control everything just stop for a moment and think about all the things going on concurrently all at the same time. From planes taking off and landing to trains and cars driving and just everything happening concurrently. Really, we can only control ourselves, our mindset, our philosophy, and our individual choices.*

Million Dollar Agent Key Idea #66
"We can only ever control ourselves, our mindset, our philosophy, and our individual choices."

Lee: And our attitude towards what's happening to us. We are then a victim of our own personality and that's one of the things that I teach those who are new in the business. Find out who you are because one of the biggest problems I find is people try to follow a path. They say this guy is the best and loves what he does, even though they personally are nothing like this individual. You've got to be true to yourself so you have to know who you are and what you like to make those decisions. That's your first journey. Who are you?

Phil/Dan: There was a study; I think it was on Madison Avenue. One of the findings was that 90% of businesses are based on emulation. They emulate others, which is fine but unless you know who you are, it's hard to constantly copy someone because you not only lose yourself in the process but if the environment shifts, who are you? How do you adapt to that if you're not being yourself?

Million Dollar Agent Key Idea #67
"It is very important in real estate and in life to know who you are as a person. This allows you to respond and adapt to changing circumstances rather than get lost and make poor decisions."

Lee: You can become very unhappy. This is usually how you can tell you're doing something that isn't quite congruent with your insights, yourself, who you are. You become unhappy and you don't know why you're unhappy. It's funny I read something the other day that was very profound. Most people don't know how to be happy; will never know how to be happy. So what people do is try to avoid things or change things just enough. It's surprising that some people get up in the morning.

Lee: You and I both feel people that will usually make you raise one eyebrow and you wonder. Well, with all that negativity it's amazing that you don't just explode.

Phil/Dan: *I met a few of them along the way, Lee.*

Lee: Yeah.

Phil/Dan: *I know this is a bit of an amorphous question but Lee what separates you from the competition? You're in one of Alberta's largest cities Edmonton. There are a lot of realtors, at least several thousand. How many are in the Edmonton Real Estate Board?*

Lee: Somewhere around 3,500.

Phil/Dan: *That's a lot of realtors and the population is just about a million people. But what separates you? Why would someone choose to work with you, Lee, versus the competition?*

Lee: Right away, it's authenticity. When you show up, you're authentic. You're not just some goofy talking head that looks like some good dental work in great promo shots.

Phil/Dan: *Plastic fantastic as they say.*

Lee: What you're looking for is someone who you immediately feel is going to tell you the truth regardless of the good, bad or the otherwise and is not necessarily in it entirely for themselves. They're going to do what's right for you regardless and you presume that. It becomes your motto. The real you walks into it every time. You never worry about the money. You just do what is right and if that means telling someone not to do something, that's good, because that's the old pay it forward thing. You don't worry about it too much. You never worry about that. The money will come if you do the right thing.

Phil/Dan: *Another powerful point. One time I was delivering a seminar, I think it was in Langley, BC and I stopped and asked the audience, do you know what the one secret of all sales is? I said maybe 95 percent of salespeople including realtors wake up in the morning and ask, how much money can I make? How many deals can I do? The ones that are truly successful really ask themselves a different question - how much value can I create? How much service can I provide in the interest of my clients?*

Lee: And this is one of the big questions people have. How can I defend my commissions because they're

Million Dollar Agent Key Idea #68

"The really successful realtors ask the question how much value can I create and how much service can I provide in the interests of my clients."

under siege at all times and it comes right back to this. You see, you know this is about value, not cost.

Phil/Dan: *In the absence of value, price becomes an issue. People only have a question of price when they don't perceive they're getting value for what they're paying for.*

Lee: Exactly. And when you find someone that does not perceive you or perceive value in what you have to offer then go find somebody else. Because that's what you want. If you want valued transactions because they will turn into other transactions and other transactions, walk away from stuff that's not going to give you value. You walk away from that stuff and go to the swimming pool, go lift some weights, write poetry, learn interpretive dance, anything.

Million Dollar Agent Key Idea #69
"In the absence of value, price becomes an issue."

Phil/Dan: *Lee, in your view, how do the best realtors look at the world differently from everyone else? How would you categorize that succinctly?*

Lee: Well, I think the best realtors are not hungry. They're driven to be the best in what they do, try hard and do everything but they're not driven by hunger. They're more driven by providing a valuable service and the confidence that that is what's going to sustain them. They don't even think about it. They just get up every day, do what they do, create a process for themselves and just put themselves out in a most authentic way, as much as they can. Good realtors are great communicators. The personalities vary, the styles vary, the approaches vary but they're great communicators and they have a lot of energy and it's transferring to the people that need the service.

Phil/Dan: *Of course it's well said because you're a great communicator. What makes the top 10% if you had to give a laundry list? What makes the top 10% of the ones that are making an abundant living, the ones that are successful? What are the key things?*

Lee: Energy. They don't lose the intuitiveness that exists for these guys. They don't give up; they don't let anything get in their way. They get up every day with the ability to do the grind. It's like a successful marriage I suppose, the ability to grind, the kids will understand this. The kids all play videogames and I see my son doing videogames and make an art of this. The trick is to get to the next level, to do the grind. You grind, you grind, you grind and you get some success but there's a lot of grinding. You're down in the trenches and the ability to do that, I think that's really what makes the top 10%. It's what works and they're not afraid to change if it isn't but they're grinding and grinding. They just don't give up.

Phil/Dan: That's amazing. People are always looking for the magic bullet. I really want to make clear in this book through these interviews, that there is no magic bullet. If you look at the best athletes, the best musicians, the best business people, they really do the fundamentals well consistently over and over and over again. They love what they do. They have the bigger picture. They have drive and all those things but they also perpetuate their success by doing the fundamentals. They're not looking for the bright and shiny object all the time or the next big thing. They realize that the fundamentals have to be done and that's part of the growth.

Lee: There is no bright and shiny object. There never has been, never will be. Success is getting up in the day and feeling fulfilled and content with the fact that you're doing what you're supposed to be doing and you feel good about what you're doing until the next thing you do, right?

Phil/Dan: I couldn't have said it better myself.

Million Dollar Agent Key Idea #70
"Good realtors are great communicators."

Lee: Being in the moment, finding a way to create your process that enables you to be in the moment. The longer you live, you want to be more in the moment, instead of always living for the next thing, like when you're looking for the next goal, this or that, that's what's driving you. You're never you. You're always someone else.

Phil/Dan: You know if the readers get one thing out of reading this book, I hope they get that one point you just made. That goes back to enjoying the process as well as the destination. How would you complete the next sentence, Lee? The real estate business is blank, is what?

Lee: It's like swimming in the ocean. You can go any direction but you can also drown at any moment.

Phil/Dan: Okay, or eaten by sharks, if you want, instead.

Lee: Eaten by sharks, ending up on a tropical island, drinking too much salt water, you name it, because you touched on endless possibilities. It can be exactly what you want it to be. The only limitation is your attitude towards the thing. Never assume you know everything because you don't and you never will. That's what music taught me. The better a musician I became, the more I realized I did not know. That carries beautifully into real estate.

Phil/Dan: You just dovetail on that. Again another profound point Lee is that you're learning. When learning stops, so does change and evolution. If you're not learning, you're deteriorating; you're not growing as a person in your life.

Million Dollar Agent Key Idea #71
"When learning stops, so does change and evolution."

Lee: Right. We used to say this in the music biz years ago, up or down you never sustain yourself.

Phil/Dan: I just want to get a little bit more of a practical plan on a day-to-day basis, sharing with the reader what you do specifically. In your view, what does it take to be the best in your field?

Lee: Pay attention. Pay attention to what you're doing. Look at what's working, what's not working. You just be present, be present and always be questioning. Try to stay curious about what you're doing and be willing to make changes if it's not meeting your expectation.

Phil/Dan: What are the key daily practices, Lee, that you do that lead most of your success?

Lee: Okay, I can tell you very simply. Usually, you have a plan for your day. You have a plan for your week. You block off time - it's the oldest thing in the world - it's getting your day timer out and blocking in all the things that you need to do, starting with the most important things first. Your recreation time and your physical work out, for example, racquetball. Put all those things in, put time in with the family, put all those things in, put all your work times. Really break it down and get up early and get after that and do it. Spend the day being purposeful. Early in your career you say I need to prospect, okay. Well, get in three times a week and do it. Even if you hate it do it because in the process you make for yourself, you can't avoid things that you're not really happy with but you can avoid things that you really hate.

So think about that. Try to stay with things that you can tolerate. Some guys chase for-sale-by-owners, that's fine. I didn't do it very long because I found it brutally negative and the results, the positive aspects required are weighed by the negative aspects because I'm dealing with people that didn't value me. But it doesn't mean they shouldn't do it, that's all personality. The idea is to compartmentalize your time and with efficient use of your time you don't have to work as much. It's just more efficiently set up. You're not just meandering through your day like a bumper car.

Phil/Dan: *Because I suppose if that's the way you do things at the end of the day you're going to end up pretty well bumped and bruised, no pun intended.*

Lee: You'll have no idea where you are.

Phil/Dan: *True. I know a lot of people in that situation. If you identified the top three things that you do consistently for most of your success in real estate, what would you say those three things are? I know there are a thousand things you do and thousand things you do well, but of the top three things that you consistently do, what would those top three things be?*

Lee: The number 1, remain authentic, get up early in the morning so you're inserting your energy right and plan, planning your time as best you can.

Phil/Dan: *Okay. What would you say the best realtors do from your observation and what the average realtors do?*

Lee: You have to maintain a really high energy level, that's the one thing that becomes very difficult as you get older is trying to maintain this incredibly high energy level all the time.

Phil/Dan: *Yeah, that comes at the time when you need to generate the most amount of income to support the life-style.*

Million Dollar Agent Key Idea #72
"You can't avoid things that you're not really happy with but you can avoid things that you really hate."

Lee: I think personally that you don't, you don't need to as you get older, if you're planning your time then you can let your income drop and make your life simpler; the phase I am in. The Japanese, right? Traditionally the bulls are in full fight mode until 55 and so would live in the center of the compound. Your esteem goes up and everybody has prestige where they move to the outside of the compound and they're more of a valuable resource. Then the young bulls are all fighting and pounding in the middle again and you end up on the outside where you work a little less. You require less resources and the idea is to plan that. Don't look at it when you're 70 and you're energy is dropping, that seems like bad planning to me.

Phil/Dan: *I love that metaphor that a plane uses most of its fuel upon take off but once you're in flight, you can become pretty damn efficient. I think it's a nice way to sum up what you're suggesting, great advice. Obviously your career has involved considerably over the last 23 years or so but when you think of all the years you've generated business from, you alluded to the fact that you did for-sale-by-owners and you did really like that but what area has generated the most business for you? There's farming, there's FSBO's, there's expired listings, specialty referrals, referral in repeat, website lead generation. There are all these different areas where realtors to a greater or lesser extent generate business. For yourself Lee what has been the area that has generated the most business for you?*

Lee: Well, you know all these systems are all ancillary to the center. The center is to have personal contacts of as many people as possible and then remind them that you're there in a way that isn't really annoying. When you go for cold capture business which is very expensive because you're doing large institutional advertising and you get all this cold business, it's tough, it's a hard one. What the best thing is, to call the people you know, stay in touch with the people you know. They'll send you something. You stay in touch with them.

Phil/Dan: *How do you use social media?*

Lee: All the websites, Twitter and Facebook and all that stuff is just support for your main, your center which is your sphere of influence, your database which is your company. They beautifully help with making contact which your company helps with, that's your core. For me, everything comes off of that, and has for 23 years, that's most of my business. I think 95% of it is from that and staying with that is your core. It hasn't changed with all the technology; that has not changed. Everything else is just window dressing. Our core is people that we know and the people that they know and the people that they know and you make sure you do a good job, you remain authentic and it will travel. Just make sure they remember who you are.

Phil/Dan: *You summed it up so well. There's a great saying that all the roads in a city lead ultimately to the center of town. The center of town in real estate is to develop a certain modicum of business from relationships.*

Get to a critical mass point where you literally create a business where it's become self-perpetuating based on its own self.

Lee: You've got to keep what you have. I know how fast I want my wheel to go. Sort of like that the millstone, you just lean on it and give it a little shove, little shove, little shove. Believe me; you leave your business for

Million Dollar Agent Key Idea #73
"There's a great saying that all the roads in a city lead ultimately to the center of town. The center of town in real estate is to develop a certain modicum of business from relationships."

three months and that stone just about stops. It's like digging a hole in water; you just disappear in a big way. You have to remember – do something to keep, keep that stone moving at the speed that you want.

Phil/Dan: *And again to the earlier point that the more efficient you can make that, for the newer realtors, you've got to do it all. You've got to generate leads from open houses and expireds and FSBO's and whatever you like to do.*

Lee: You're putting 5 hard years in and really, really burning it. That should sustain you your entire career if you can put these systems in place.

Phil/Dan: *Because you're at that critical mass point where now you can leverage those relationships and sphere of influence.*

Lee: And you have transactions under your belt to ultimately keep the whole thing going, right?

Phil/Dan: *Let me just ask you, in terms of generating brand new business from strangers, what is your main source? Do you use the internet, email, social media, direct mail, in person, telephone?*

Lee: Brand new business? Interestingly enough, I still do it through social circles. For instance, if somebody would move home that didn't know anybody, what I would recommend to anybody is become part of the Rotary Club, join a soccer team, a rowing club or a knitting club, just passively let them know what you do because you become 'the guy', in their eyes because they get to know you, they know who are you but you practice that behavior and just make it part of your lifestyle. And so it also helps to make you a better-rounded individual if you're part of these folks. And you try not to be mercenaries like some 'mercenary guy'; you know that you've got to be part of these things, that's why. Socially, stay very active, because your job as a realtor is to find business. Doing business is no harm. Finding business is a bitch.

Phil/Dan: *Well said.*

Lee: And that's what makes a generator, what makes some people quick to business and to realize later that the business is nothing to do with houses or very, very little.

Phil/Dan: *I love it.*

Lee: In real estate houses are a technicality on a people problem. It's all about people problems, right? And if you make someone happy what happened between the beginning and the end of the transaction is sort of irrelevant, frankly. What you did was centre on satisfying their needs. When you do real estate, if you create success for someone they will refer you to everybody and if you have no success or just you didn't sell the property, they won't really call you back because you have to leverage your success. And the idea is when you do your efforts for marketing, you stay on that, you stay on your successful transactions, people that have been part of that and they will in turn help you out for a period of time, that also has a short life though.

Phil/Dan: *Without moving the grindstone or keeping in touch with them in a certain way or really enhancing that relationship continually, I often joke a lot of realtors date their clients.*

Lee: I know I'm being recorded but it's like a one night stand, all this intensity. It's also so torrid and with this massive consummation but the one difference is you want them to remain your good buddy after you're done. It's all rather torrid and all-consuming and it's the most important thing people do in their lives with the most money that they'll ever deal with.

Phil/Dan: *And if they don't hear from you for one month, two months, six months, what they think is all you cared about was the money.*

Lee: You don't want to maintain the intensity, you just want to be background, part of the background that says, yeah he's there, he's the guy, he's successful, he still cares if I refer him to somebody, and he'll care for them, too.

Phil/Dan: *Right. And so in other words, you're still appreciated and acknowledged even though physically you can't be there to the same degree as you were going through the transaction.*

Lee: Nor do they expect it. See, that's a real mistake to dive in too hard, right? Because people don't expect that. They don't expect you to be… it's a bit creepy. If you're right in the middle of a deal, they want to hear from you all the time and this is about some experienced sensitivity to what you're doing.

Phil/Dan: *That's a very important point because when you're dealing with people going through a real estate transaction, there's family issues, legal issues, financial issues and change all rolled into one. They tend to get closer with you, you're helping them.*

Lee: Right and you don't want to be friends with all your clients. It doesn't do them any service or you.

Phil/Dan: *That makes sense.*

Lee: You want to be professional. You want to be friendly. But you have to be careful. You can't fall in love with everybody because there are just not enough of you to go around.

Phil/Dan: *Hence the need for systems of communication which I want to touch on as well.*

Lee: Exactly, well, it's friendly. People call me after they move and for some reason I didn't change their address on the database or something and they'll call me and say, "Lee I'm not get-

> **Million Dollar Agent Key Idea #74**
> *"Since you can't be everything to everyone all the time, it is critical to have systems of communication that leverage both your time and relationships."*

ting your thing anymore, I don't think you changed my address, this is my address you remember, right?" And I'm going, "Yeah, I remember I sold you the house." It's really nice because they really want that and there's something about the contact that they really appreciate. Or they'll phone up and say, I read the newsletter about how to repair an appliance as opposed to replace it. So I have to be a little careful to make sure that I read the newsletter as soon as it shows up in my inbox.

Phil/Dan: *Your newsletter gives them useful advice on how to increase the value of their home and things like home safety, and so on.*

Lee: Exactly, and people will actually phone me and discuss some element of it.

Phil/Dan: This underscores the need for you to read your own marketing. So what are the marketing strategies you currently use? I know when you first started you had to do a bit of everything because it's all about priming the pump and driving it. But now you're marketing strategy is what?

Lee: Well, it centers on the database, basically. It's all the people that you know and that you've done a transaction with. First of all, make sure that you're using some system, some combination of direct mail and email because some people like direct mail and hate email and some people hate direct mail and vice versa, so you want to do that. Those will be your prime, database, number 1. That is the world which everything revolves around. From there, you would probably want to phone all those people, if you are looking to increase your business or keep your business going, up to three times a year. I would think that would be probably a good cycle, four is quite a bit. I'm not sure if I would recommend that. Twice a year is fine. Try to work your way through, have it diarized. Just phone and say, "Hi, how you're doing? I'm not really looking for anything but it's been a while since we've talked and you're on my database. Are you receiving the material? Do you like it?" And if they say, "No, my brother is in real estate." You say thank you kindly and then take them out of your database. It keeps your database clean. This is old school.

Phil/Dan: This is old school but it's interesting, I often say to realtors that real estate is a people business. Pick up the phone, call. I think of marketing today as diversification.

Lee: If you're not communicating with them, if you're not making calls, calls aren't coming back to you. If you're not generating, if you're not returning emails, emails are not going to come back to you. That's giving the shove to the stone ahead, right, a little push. That's what it is about. Every day, you have to make some calls, talk to some guys.

Million Dollar Agent Key Idea #75
"Every day you need to push the wheel of your business and this involves focussing on doing the fundamentals."

Phil/Dan: And again it goes down to the fundamentals. I was interviewing another realtor from Port Moody who does very, very well and he said he gets up in the morning and he has a certain amount of calls. He pushes that wheel every single day and then he goes golfing.

Lee: I don't have to push it very hard, just keep it moving at speed I like it. And I also know exactly how fast I like it to go because when it starts going too fast, I'm very aware of it, I look at it and go, this is a beef, it's going to chew me up. You're controlling it, it doesn't control you but you do that by staying engaged.

Phil/Dan: *You know it's interesting Lee, nothing is sadder than when I speak to realtors being in business as long as you have or longer, who haven't done those little things along the way. They are still perpetuating the feast or famine cycle, they're still living, they're still repeating their first year business over and over and over again to the point where 20 years in the business they're starting from scratch because they haven't maintained their database. They haven't created the annuity-based business for themselves based on referral and repeat business.*

Lee: Hunters and farmers. There's a hunter and there's a farmer. A hunter everyday has to get up and go chase something down and kill it and wrestle it to the ground and then hack it up and try to eat it. A farmer spends a few years dividing up his land, putting out fences and tilling the soil and putting nitrogen in and then he just has to go out and keep getting the wheel ahead. Now, we all do both but the idea is to learn to be a farmer, not a hunter. You can feed a village from a farm but when you're hunting you'll be lucky if you can feed yourself.

Phil/Dan: *If you look at the evolution of the human species, we've evolved from*

Million Dollar Agent Key Idea #76
"Learn to be a farmer, not a hunter."

hunters in packs fighting bison or whatever we're fighting, huge game animal to farmers. And that's how we've evolved and built cities and actually became economically prosperous.

Lee: Absolutely, and it's exactly the same for us as individuals. In real estate you want to develop great farming systems. In fact, if you're really good, you'll get other people, your buddies sending clients to you, so you're not even having to instigate.

Phil/Dan: *You create advocates.*

Lee: Right. It depends on where you are in the world. In Canada, we have to be a little more reserved or people will start ignoring you. So you have to know where it is for your marketing, your area, what works, right? Because it's different for everyone in every area. You know how much you're staying in touch and how much self-promotion you can do.

Phil/Dan: *That's socially or culturally acceptable. That's interesting.*

Lee: You look at RE/MAX, it's all over the world but can you imagine that diversity that you would have if you were in Sweden? What would be appropriate to advertise yourself as opposed to what would be in the Southern United States?

Phil/Dan: *It's funny you should say that Lee because I was just speaking to a realtor who had moved from Sweden to Edmonton, where you are. She was having a hell of a time because culturally business is done so differently there and in particular real estate is done very differently there. She had to reinvent herself and adapt to Canadian culture. I can imagine if you moved from Edmonton to Dallas, Texas or something like that it would be another quantum leap.*

Lee: For sure. All the American realtors you see at conventions from Texas wearing American sparkling flags and the rotary pumpkins and all the stuff. If you did that in Canada, you would be rejected because it's just not our cultural norm but if we did what we do here in Texas, people would wonder, well, he must not be very good because he's not blowing his horn hard enough. So, it's not a matter of what actually works, right? It's knowing what's going to work for the area.

Phil/Dan: *You're one of the guys that new realtors will go to; ask to buy lunch, dinner, coffee. They ask you what do they need to do to be successful and prosperous and what are the key things? What would you say they need to do to be successful from the get-go?*

Lee: I would say probably one of the biggest things to be successful is to know yourself, so you know the systems to put in play. That's number one. Number two, develop a database. Contact everybody and then every day create a contact habit or a culture within yourself, so that you're habitually contacting people. You're just habitually contacting people all the time because that's your job.

Phil/Dan: *Twenty three years ago was obviously a different time period than it is today. What has changed? What has been the biggest single change you've seen in the real estate business since you began?*

Lee: We're no longer gatekeepers, we're process experts. We used to be gatekeepers of the almighty MLS information so people had to come to us; they had to come to us to get the information. Now that information is readily available, all the time, everywhere. We're not gatekeepers of information any longer. It's now freely distributed. So what has happened if you have to become a value added in the pack, why would they call you? The reason they call you is they want to know what to do with this bloody information.

You not only translate the information for people but you also add other things.

I'll give you an example of another business that does this: everybody who is a renovator, renovators for anywhere from the simplest job all the way to incredibly expensive. And really great renovators charge tangy dollars and they may charge incredibly high numbers. But what they do is, they make sure that during the renovation, they do everything they said they were going to do and everything ends up well and there are no surprises. And if there is a surprise they come to you right away and say, "Oh, by the way I'd seen this coming, what would you like to do about it?" And so you're never surprised. A crappy renovator will repair and build it in standard, that's nothing like what you had in mind. So you can charge 10 times as much money and people will gladly pay it, if you guide them through the process and tell them ahead of time, here's what's going on, here's what's going to happen, here's what you're going to need to do.

Phil/Dan: *Whenever realtors ask me, should I just send people regurgitated statistics from the real estate boards or the association? I say, well, what value is in that? If your value proposition is in the interpretation of what that means specifically to that individual, it does, because otherwise people can glean that information from anywhere, the internet, radio, TV, newspaper. The reason why I'm hiring my financial planner or stockbroker or financial advisor is not as a transactional expert but to give me advisement, interpret what the markets are doing so I'm making wise decisions.*

Lee: What do these things mean to me or seem to me? I always tell people, the information I have is nothing that you can't learn easily. The problem is you don't do this every day, you don't want to do this every day, so what I'm going to do is guide you through it and make sure you know what you need to do to make this successful for you.

So you know because who wants to learn somebody else's whole job all the time. I don't know how the bond market works; I'm not even really interested in this. I'll hire somebody who does know and can explain it to me as it relates to me right now for what I need to do.

Phil/Dan: And hence the term Lee, wealth is packaged experience. I think the best realtors package their experience in such a way that makes it valuable for the recipient.

Million Dollar Agent Key Idea #77
"Wealth is packaged experience. I think the best realtors package their experience in such a way that makes it valuable for the recipient."

In a very expediting way, your clients hire you as a professional to do what they could learn themselves but certainly wouldn't do it as well and don't have the knowledge, expertise or experience.

Lee: And this goes out to those who really believe that they can do it themselves and I think that's great. I think there's absolutely nothing wrong with that. Please fill your boots, that's awesome.

Phil/Dan: There's a price to pay for that.

Lee: A large majority of people would just say, look I don't have the time nor the wherewithal to try to figure this all out. Could you please do this for me? And then of course you'll say, thank you very much, let's talk about what is needed and how we can make your journey be the least tumultuous that we can.

Phil/Dan: There lies your value proposition.

Lee: There is the added value. What can I offer? That's what I can offer and I can offer it well because I walked down that road so many times.

Phil/Dan: You know Lee, you're such a fascinating guy and so successful on so many different levels. I could do this interview for hours but in the interest of time, let me ask you one last question to finalize the interview. What in your view is the future of the real estate profession? You've seen it evolve over the last 23 years and you'll be long retired living the lifestyle you want in 23 years from now. In the future how do you see the real estate business evolving?

Lee: What I see is the tools that have occurred will just continue along the same line you can see. The realtor will have to become more of an expert in a lot more things. I'll give you an example. You have to understand renovations, you're going to have to understand decorating, you're going to have to understand how to deal with all these different things to help a client out because if you don't, you won't be able to help your client. What advice do I give them for renovating? These things require a lot of experience. And that's what the future of the business is. It's much more to do with TV; it actually started to do this. What's going to work? A lot of realtors don't know anything about what other work costs, the locality of a property or what's going to be high for something that's used. And the idea of what's going to happen is the client is going to become much more sophisticated as information gets more readily available. If you want to remain in real estate, you just have to know more and do more.

Lee: You never stop learning and every time a situation comes by you're going to make sure you're remembering, you're learning with the lesson. Every day that I don't learn something means I wasn't paying attention.

Phil/Dan: On that note Lee I want to thank you very, very much. This has been a

Million Dollar Agent Key Idea #78

"Every day that I don't learn something means I wasn't paying attention."

fabulous interview. And you've been very gracious with your time. I hope you don't bill me for all your time but the least I can do is dinner on me again.

Lee: We will, we'll definitely do that.

Phil/Dan: And thank you Lee, so much. It's quite self-evident why you are where you are.

Lee: It's also good when you do these kinds of things because you end up with more self-reflection. You think about what you know and what you don't know. These interviews actually end up being very valuable, don't they?

Phil/Dan: On multiple, multiple levels. Thank you Lee, very much.

Million Dollar Agent Key Ideas Summary

$ It is not the goal; it is the process of obtaining the goal that is important.

$ Your goal is the natural by-product of living the life that you want as opposed to an end in and of itself.

$ It is so important for your long term success in the real estate business to check your ego at the door.

$ One of the greatest skills you can have in both business and in life is the ability to deal with ambiguity.

$ If you want to be successful in real estate, don't take yourself so seriously.

$ It is so important that you remember who you are working for, who signed the contract and pays for and supports your lifestyle. Integrity and having a moral compass is everything in business.

$ We can only ever control ourselves, our mindset, our philosophy, and our individual choices.

$ It is very important in real estate and in life to know who you are as a person. This allows you to respond and adapt to changing circumstances rather than get lost and make poor decisions.

$ The really successful realtors ask the question how much value can I create and how much service can I provide in the interests of my clients.

$ In the absence of value, price becomes an issue.

$ You can't avoid things that you're not really happy with but you can avoid things that you really hate.

$ There's a great saying that all the roads in a city lead ultimately to the center of town. The center of town in real estate is to develop a certain modicum of business from relationships.

$ Since you can't be everything to everyone all the time, it is critical to have systems of communication that leverage both your time and relationships.

$ Every day you need to push the wheel of your business and this involves focussing on doing the fundamentals.

$ Learn to be a farmer, not a hunter.

$ Wealth is packaged experience. I think the best realtors package their experience in such a way that makes it valuable for the recipient.

FRANCIS MACDONALD:
Fire in the Belly

AFTER 35 YEARS of hard work and leadership, coaching others to prosper, and showing a strong passion toward the overall success of the Canadian real estate industry, Francis MacDonald has built a solid reputation amongst his peers.

Starting his real estate career in 1978, Francis has steadily pushed to build organizations offering the respect and training that salespeople desire—and the service the public deserves.

In the mid-1980's Francis built the real estate arm of Central Trust to 35 offices, employing over 350 salespeople and staff. Later, in the early 90's, he brought Prudential Real Estate into Canada, building the franchise to pronounced success.

Now, in 2015, Francis and his team have begun a new venture by starting their own real estate brand; with a new focus on supporting local. Press Realty was launched with an open attitude toward positive changes needed in today's marketplace.

Francis works day in and day out to ensure every member of his sales team is provided with continued care and support. They are his family – and it shows. But he also believes in tough love, setting a high standard for his real estate agents, strengthening his commitment to providing the public with quality, customized service that meets their needs.

It has always been—and always will be Francis' goal to run a business offering unrivaled service. It is this determination that has shaped Francis' professional accomplishments over the years.

FRANCIS MACDONALD IS a great managing broker-owner. He exemplifies what a Managing Broker should be and do to ensure his agents build a successful and prosperous real estate practice. From his over thirty years of industry experience he understand that if his brokerage is going to thrive and be successful he needs to do whatever it takes to provide his agents with the tools and resources they need for sustainable long-term success. In addition to providing his agents with the best knowledge, tools and resources required to succeed, he personally mentors and coaches his agents holding them accountable to ensure they do what they need to do to achieve their desired outcomes. An entire book could have been written based on the wisdom provided by Francis in this interview.

Phil/Dan: *Well, hello Francis. How are you doing? You know, it's so good to see you. We are absolutely honored to be here with one of our mentors. We would consider our mentor an inspirational leader, and that is Francis MacDonald.*

Over the years we've been involved in the real estate business, we've met many, many different agents and brokers. And I will tell you, Francis is quite special and quite unique for a number of different reasons. I know he's too humble to admit that, but he really gets it.

And he has a wonderful, wonderful track record. And not only in being in the trenches in this business but taking agents, no matter where they start, and helping them become successful and prosperous in this business and doing very well, redefining what they do like no one else. So Francis, we appreciate you taking the time to speak with us. And I'm very much looking forward to your answers to these questions in this interview. So thank you so much.

Francis: I appreciate you asking.

Phil/Dan: *So Francis, let me ask you, how many years have you been in business now?*

Francis: It'd be 36 years.

Phil/Dan: *Wow. And so when you work with a new agent – agents come into the real estate business, as you know, from so many different backgrounds, and they get their license and they're thrust into this world we call real estate. How do you take them and help them become successful? Where do you start?*

Francis: One of the first things that I do when I interview an agent that's thinking about getting into business, I truly interview them. What I find in the marketplace is a lot of companies will just hire people for the sake of hiring people. They play the numbers game. I prefer to go with quality versus quantity. Because not only am I going to, as a broker, spend a lot of time and effort with a new person, but that individual is going to spend a lot of time and effort in getting in the business.

In most provinces in Canada, it's fairly reasonable to get into the real estate business. It doesn't cost you a lot of money. But what it does cost you is a lot of time, if you're going to do it right. So I truly interview somebody that I'm talking to and make sure that they fully understand what it is that they have to do to be successful in the business. I think that's the start.

Phil/Dan: Before we get to that, I'm very curious as to what you think are the essential ingredients to be successful. Do you ever talk someone out of not becoming a realtor?

Francis: Absolutely.

Phil/Dan: A lot of people go into this business with dollar signs in their eyes. And they don't realize that it's a business. There's a reason why only a small percentage actually do extremely well in this business, whereas a lot of realtors struggle.

For 90% of realtors, this business is hell. But for 10% of this business, it's heaven, because they've created a business where they have a beautiful, well-balanced lifestyle that gives them everything. How do you determine who's going to be successful? What do you ask someone when they're getting in the business?

Francis: Well, first of all, I think it's crucial that they understand that it is a business. And you have to look at adapting systems. You have to make sure that you have the focus to be able to follow a system.

You have to want to and feel comfortable getting out of your comfort zone. Because let's face it, you're not brought up to be a salesperson. Usually, you're brought up and taught don't talk to strangers, don't do this, don't do that, you know.

So all of a sudden you're looking at an industry whereby it's all about

Million Dollar Agent Key Idea #79

"You have to want to feel comfortable getting out of your comfort zone."

talking to people. It's all about building relationships. So, first and fore-most, what I normally do with somebody is I'll get them to make some cold calls or some calls to friends of theirs and interview those friends, and say to those friends, "I'm thinking about getting into real estate. What do you think?"

Phil/Dan: *Interesting. So because they may have a perception of their own skill and ability that may not be how other people perceive them.*

Francis: It's also important to have a hiring package and a system that we give people and show people. And it basically lays out verbatim what they have to do to be successful.

Phil/Dan: *A roadmap.*

Francis: A roadmap. That's right.

Phil/Dan: *A lot of people have a 9-to-5 job. They're in a cubicle in some corporation. And they think, you know, "I want to leave the rat race. I want to go be my own boss." So they go get their license. As you said, it's a relatively low-entry threshold. It doesn't take a lot of money. But it's not five years of university; they're not going to medical school here. Then they get thrust into this world and it's very sink or swim; it's commission sales. They don't have the 9-to-5 paycheck anymore.*

Francis: And that's the biggest hurdle. For most people to make that switch over from having a steady weekly or bimonthly income to being on a cash flow basis where you don't get anything unless you earn and get a commission, that's a huge change for people.

And that's why it's important when somebody is looking at getting in the business or somebody is wondering why they may not do so well right now in the business. They should look at the environment they're in. They should look at the support that they are being provided because it is a tough business, and there are certain things that you must do on a regular basis. The successful people will do all of those things that the ordinary, everyday person or the not-so-successful agent doesn't want to do. We're tough.

Phil/Dan: *And I want to pick up on that concept. It's very profound. What's interesting is, it's a bit of a catch-22. Here you have all the freedom in the*

Million Dollar Agent Key Idea #80

"Successful people will do all of those things that the ordinary, everyday person or the not-so-successful agent doesn't want to do. We're tough."

world, and yet the freedom to hang yourself, to basically be unsuccessful as well as to be successful.

And when you don't have a boss breathing down your neck, how do you perform those disciplined things consistently to ensure your success? Having the freedom can be a curse to a lot of people, because they're hanging around a lot of coffee shops if they're not doing those critical tasks. Tricking themselves into doing busy work as opposed to the things they need to be truly successful.

Francis: Years ago when we implemented the independent contractor status for sales people, purely for the tax situation, that really hurt the industry as far as I'm concerned because a lot of brokers looked at that as an excuse to back off and say, "You're independent. You do your thing."

If you're looking at getting into business or if you're not happy where you are, you should find somebody that's going to make you accountable. You should find an environment that you can be comfortable in.

What I always recommend, I really never hire anyone until they attend one of our sales meetings, sit in on some of our training, until they understand what all the rules are and how we operate. They're agreeing that this is a structure they have to follow. You can't sugarcoat this business.

Whether anybody likes it or not, at the end of the day if somebody is not doing well in the business, if they've been in for a while – and this happens to lots of people – or if you're going in brand new, if you don't prospect, if you don't have a system to prospect, a system to contact people and to stay in touch with those people so that you can build that rapport and so that you can get business from them and then repeat and referral business from them. If you don't have that system and if you're not prepared to do the activities in talking to people – and there's many, many ways to do it, to fill that funnel in terms of potential leads and people that will help you – then don't go into business.

Phil/Dan: *Many brokers won't tell them. They won't tell people that's the reality. It's better they know at the outset what they're in for. There are a lot of good brokers that say that, but it's better that they know this is the reality.*

Francis: Agents should interview the broker. I interview people all the time. And I'll tell you the truth, many of them will say to me that this is the first time they really were interviewed.

Million Dollar Agent Key Idea #81
"Success in real estate has a structure."

Usually the broker just starts selling them on, "This is what we do," and on and on and on. Instead of asking them questions as to what are their expectations, what do they feel an agent has to do, how much do they think an agent should earn, what is their goal for what they want to earn. You know, what hours they want to work, how much time they want to put in. Those kinds of things.

What I always say to sales people is I encourage them to go talk to other brokers. I want them to make an informed decision. I want them to be comfortable, because there's a high turnover in this business. In the first couple of years, people get out.

And it's sad because there are a lot of people that get out that shouldn't be getting out. But unfortunately, they made the wrong decision. They decided to go with a broker that might pay them a higher commission split, thinking they would earn more money.

Phil/Dan: *But they didn't have the skill, the support, resources and mentorship.*

Francis: Right. If you pay too high a split, you haven't any money to provide the support and the training and the things that you need to provide support with the support staff - people who put the listings in for them, people to help them with writing ads, people to do their sales for them in terms of the processing. All of that stuff.

What I believe is if they can find a brokerage, like mine, for example. Our brokerage is continually working at providing services to the sales people that we can do a lot easier for them. You know, the stuff that you can go and hire at 15 and $20-an-hour work. I try to provide as much of that as we can so that you, as a sales person, can do the stuff that you have to do, which is going out, showing houses, writing offers, negotiating, calling people, looking for people that are thinking about buying or selling, doing the real things that will make you the money. So you take care of the low-income producing, but necessary, tasks to allow the salesperson to do the key high-income producing tasks like prospecting and negotiating deals.

Phil/Dan: *So you free them up. But I think what you're doing as well is you're giving them a roadmap to success.*

Francis: Absolutely.

Phil/Dan: *When you get your real estate license, they don't teach you how to sell. They don't give you a personality test to say that you'd be good at sales.*

Francis: That's right.

Phil/Dan: *They just thrust you into a world and then you're somehow expected to know how to do it. It's not like the insurance industry where you work for a big company and you're mandated to attend certain training.*

Francis: Well, it can be. It should be.

Phil/Dan: *It could be.*

Million Dollar Agent Key Idea #82

"In order to have a successful real estate business, the real estate agent needs to be freed-up to handle more and more high-income activities."

Francis: In our company, it is. Generally, it's not.

Phil/Dan: *And a lot of people have some preconceived notions about what sales is and what business is and how to be successful. But that doesn't necessarily apply to real estate because there are a lot of nuances about what you need to do in this business that I think are very different than other businesses by virtue of the nature of the business.*

Francis: Absolutely. And it's very unfortunate in the industry. So many brokers are just interested in getting the numbers, and that's their model. They need the numbers. They need to generate those monthly fees or whatever it is they do to make a profit. Our model is a little different. Our model is more of the old traditional model where we might pay a little lower commission but we provide a lot more service.

The other thing that I've done over the years, you don't have to reinvent the wheel. If you were to come to work with a company like ours, it's mandatory that you have a database. Well, I don't put any time, effort and energy into developing a database because there are experts out there like Morris Marketing, the one that we use. It's a phenomenal database.

And if you don't have a database in this business and you ask around, lots of people don't. If you don't have a database in this business, then what are you doing? You're not in the business. You can't be in business. You're doing one transaction after the other and you keep chasing the next transaction and the next transaction. And the other advice that

I would give people, new, old, experienced, it doesn't matter. Go to as much training as you can.

We all say that it's good to be physically fit. You need to go to the gym so many days a week. You've got to watch what you eat because we're looking after our bodies. And everybody's aware of that. Everyone is aware.

But when I bring in people, I tell them, "We have weight contests in our office. We have people that meet me at 5.30 in the morning to go walking or go running because I want them to be in good shape. That's the kind of fun things we do. But the other thing we do and that you can do as an individual yourself, as an agent, is to attend as much training as you can."

Anytime any training comes into town or you can go to Toronto, you can go anywhere to take training from some of the great trainers that are out there in real estate, do it. But don't just sit in on the training. There are a few things you should do when you take in training.

First thing you should do is try to meet 10 experienced agents and put them in your database so you can follow up with them for referrals coming in to your sales.

The second thing you should do is you should make a list of things that you're pulling out of that training that you want to do, recognizing you're not going to do them all. But make yourself a promise that you'll do one or two of the biggest ideas that you picked up.

Phil/Dan: That is so key. I notice that a lot of the agents would go to a two or three day training conference and they'll be buzzing with ideas, filled with ideas, and they'll come back and they want to do it all at once, simultaneously. And as a result, they'll do none of it. And then they'll go back to whatever behavior patterns they faced before and they'll become kind of jaded, "Ah, you know, that was all great in theory, but it doesn't work." It's better to do one thing and do it really well from the training. Take one learning or training from anything, from this book and implement it. It will make a world of difference.

> **Million Dollar Agent Key Idea #83**
> "The best realtors not only attend training seminars on a regular basis but they apply the learnings in their day-to-day real estate practice."

Then once you've got that habituated, add the second thing or the third thing, as you say, maybe pick 5 or 10 things. I think that's a very important point.

Francis: Absolutely.

Phil/Dan: But you know, what's interesting, if you look at the great brokerages out there, I consider you one of them, Francis, you really believe in training and education. What do you have to offer an agent? They need knowledge and they need application tools because it's not just about providing administrative support.

What agents need is to know what to do, how to do it, and the tools to do it most effectively. And I think that when you combine all those together, it becomes a very powerful force. And you do this so well with your agents, really, and it's quite amazing to me.

Francis: I'll go to a training program, and I'll assure you, this is where the growth is in the business. The growth in the business is the new people coming in the business, that's where the growth is.

Phil/Dan: The average age of realtors I know in North America is 57 years old.

Francis: That's right. And the average age of the buyers is the mid-30s, maybe low 30s. So, you've got quite a gap there.

Phil/Dan: The millennial versus the yuppie generation.

Million Dollar Agent Key Idea #84
"What agents need is to know what to do and how to do it effectively. I think when you combine these together it becomes a very powerful force."

Francis: Exactly. I'll go to a training session where there are 800 or 1,000 people, and very, very few brokers there. It's amazing. I never miss a training program with my agents because I want to work with them. Everybody is different. But that's the beauty of it. I mean, if they're not happy with where they are, they should find someplace where they're going to get coaching, where they're going to get support.

And there is professional coaching out there that they should look at seriously. But in the interim, as a new agent, as they're starting to grow, they want to find a place where they're going to get the support. Brand new people getting into the business don't be looking at the big commissions that you might pick up from a broker because if they're paying you big commissions they can do very little for you. In our organization, one of the things that we do is you go to training for both pre-listing packages, and pre-buying packages, those types of things.

We developed those for the agents – personalized, developed, and printed by professional printers. We have organizations set-up so that when you come in with us, you just need to give us a profile and we do everything else for you. Those are the kinds of things. So many people spend so much time trying to generate and create these things. We'll give you the tools and we want you to go and use those tools and put them to work so that you can find those leads and fill that funnel. And let people know, inform people as to what it is that you're doing and inform them how you can help them and those kinds of things.

One of the biggest problems in our industry is HST and income tax. We file the HST for the agents, we keep the HST. We prepare the income tax for the professional accountants to look at. We give spreadsheets to our agents. All they need to do every month give us all their receipts and we will compile it all for them.

Phil/Dan: *Isn't that amazing? I can't say how many agents I've spoken to that have had a lot of issues. Especially if they're coming from a non-entrepreneur environment, working a 9-to-5 job, and now they're an independent professional and they have to file all these tax returns. Now, that is a huge benefit.*

Francis: Most people don't like the detailed work. They don't like the administrative side of it. They don't like all of that stuff. So if you can get some place where they'll do a lot of that for you, then you're much better off. And you can do the stuff that you like to do which is interact with people, talk to people. That's what you need to do.

Phil/Dan: *You're so right on that, Francis. I think over all these years, I've noticed that the personality profile of the best agents is they've got great people skills, communication skills, negotiation skills, generally relationship skills. They love talking to people, they're extroverted. But they're not generally administrators. Nothing wrong with being great administrators, but they don't want to sit in front of their desk all day and push paper around. That's not who they are. As a matter of fact, if they did that all day and they weren't interfacing with people, it wouldn't make them great sales people.*

Francis: To me I think that is key, what you just said about making sure that they spend their time doing the work that they should be doing, that's going to generate income for them. We talked a little bit about looking after the body before. What we don't do enough of is feeding the mind – feeding the mind with the right information and with the right attitude. Like when I talk to new people, attitude is everything.

Million Dollar Agent Key Idea #85
"Real estate is a psychological game."

If you don't have the right attitude in the morning, if you don't feel like you're going to have a good day, then don't come to work because, first of all, you're not going to do yourself any good there but you're also going to drag everybody else down. So stay home. If you're going to waste time, I have a chair in the furnace room. If you're going to waste time, do it honestly. Go sit in the damn chair and look at the walls and waste time. Say, "Hey, I'm wasting time." That's good, you know.

Phil/Dan: I think the fact that you're bringing people to be conscious of that, this is why I love you, Francis. You take these concepts that we all know and you turn them into a practical reality. You do it in a very fun and humorous way.

I think what's really special as well is that you understand the power. This real estate is not just filling up forms, buying some houses. It's a psychological game.

I know you understand that sales in itself is about mindset, it's about attitude, it's about your consciousness – poverty versus prosperity consciousness. And it's about how you, on a practical level, implement that on a day-to-day basis. It's how you start your day. It's what you're telling yourself.

Francis: Exactly.

Phil/Dan: It's what you're visualizing in your mind. You could have all the skills in the world, all the talent in the world, but if you don't believe you can execute them, if you don't have the proper mindset or attitude towards this business, you won't be successful. There are plenty of talented people, naturally. When you're dealing with a profession where it's so ambiguous, you can live or die by your own thinking and your own behavior, it's useful having someone like yourself to make people aware of that. And having someone with your background and skills imparting that knowledge to your agents, I think it's so invaluable.

Francis: You're absolutely right. The biggest mistake that agents make is to hang around with agents that are down, had a bad open house, or agents that just lost a deal. That's the biggest mistake you could make.

Million Dollar Agent Key Idea #86

"If you're not happy with the results, it's got a lot to do with the way you think and the thoughts you're putting in your head. If you get negative results, you've got negative thoughts."

What I always say to people in very simple terms, if you're not happy with the results that you're getting, whether it be in real estate or within your life or whatever it is, your relationships, it doesn't matter, if you're not happy with the results, stop looking around you and stop blaming everybody around you. Stop blaming the company you work for, stop blaming the weather, stop blaming whatever, and start looking inward. Because usually, if you're not happy with the results, it's got a lot to do with the way you think and the thoughts that you're putting in your head.

If you get negative results, you've got negative thoughts. If you get a listing and you say, "Oh my God, I'm not going to be able to sell this listing. It's not selling. I haven't had any showings in two months. It's not going to sell. It's not going to sell." Well, guess what? You're not going to sell it.

I've had agents come to me and have that little saying, "My God, I can't get this listing. It's not selling. I'm not getting showings." And I would look at the agent, and I would say, "It's not selling because you don't see that house selling." And I tell them to go get me a listing picture on the home and they'd bring it in and I get a big red marker and I'd write sold right across the picture. And then I tell them go stick it right by the phone at the desk. And I'm telling you, without a word of lie, within a few weeks those listings would sell nine times out of ten. Because what happens is that agent starts thinking about the house selling. And once you open your mind to that thought, you'll attract things that are going to help you reach that. But if you close your mind, you're not going to attract anything.

Million Dollar Agent Key Idea #87

"People miss opportunities all the time because they're not looking for it. They're not waiting for them. They're asleep."

Phil/Dan: *That's so powerful, Francis. If you're looking for red cars, they're everywhere. But if you're not looking for red cars, they're nowhere, right?*

And so if you're looking for selling houses and your mind is looking for solutions, those solutions will pop in. But if you've limited your own thinking, all of a sudden you're blinded to all the opportunities. The brain distorts and deletes and generalizes information. I think that is so, so powerful.

Francis: People drive with me and I'll go to a parking lot, I'll go to a shopping center and I'll get a parking spot right up front. Yes, nine times out of ten. And they would say, "How do you do that? How come you're so lucky?" I say, "I expect to have a parking spot up front." And it appears. It's funny and sounds corny but that's how it works. Your thoughts control your feelings, the way you feel determines how you act, the way you act gives you results. So, simple logic - if you do not like the results, change the way you think.

Million Dollar Agent Key Idea #88
"Your thoughts control your feelings; the way you feel determines how you act; the way you act gives you results. If we created failure, we can also create success."

Phil/Dan: In the context of real estate, real estate being such a psychological game because you're not getting that paycheck, it's so important to master that inner game of sales, to master that inner game of mindset. I know that you do appreciate your intimate understanding of that and your ability to bring that to their consciousness because that's so important.

Francis: We all have to be reminded. I think the way I think and react, the way I behave most of the time, I'm normal like anyone else. Sometimes I'll get a little down, if I run into three or four different issues and I'll say, "Oh my God." Some days I'm sitting here saying, "What am I doing this for? Why don't I just go and sell real estate and forget this?" It's like I'm running an adult daycare center sometimes.

No, really. It's a matter of feeding that brain again. So I'll go back to reading. I've got a book, *You Were Born Rich*, by Bob Proctor. To this day, I still read that book. It's based on Napoleon Hill's book, *Think and Grow Rich*.

Phil/Dan: Those principles are ageless.

Francis: All the principles are there. They don't change.

Phil/Dan: They'll apply 2000 years from now.

Francis: Exactly. And what I say to people is, if there's somebody reading the book right now and they're thinking about getting in the real estate business here's what I would advise them to do. Sit down in a quiet place and think about how you felt when you were getting ready to write that exam, when you were studying for your course, the intensity that you put in. When a person is coming to me and we're coaching them and guiding them through the licensing course, they study day and night. They worry about that course. They come in and they take sample tests. They do all kinds of things, and then they wait a few weeks. And then when they pass that exam, they're just pumped. They're so excited. They want to tell the world they got their real estate license, they're ready to sell real estate. They let everybody know for about two weeks.

Phil/Dan: *Until they're out there.*

Francis: And then they stop. For some reason, they stop telling people what they do. It's scary. It's funny. It doesn't sound like it's that complicated, but I'm telling you that most people slip into a comfort zone and, for some reason, they slow down and stop talking to people. The very successful people, all they do every day is never stop prospecting. That could be cold calls, door knocking, going to events, it could be going to a shopping center. What is the best thing to do at 10 o'clock in the morning? Go to a shopping center. Guess what you find in the shopping center? You'll find all kinds of salespeople that are standing there. They're running a dress shop, a shoe shop, or whatever it is. They've got no customers, right? So go talk to them. Ask them how business is.

You know, when you talk to people, don't go in right away in their face and say, "I'm in real estate. Do you want to sell a house?" Don't do that at all. Get into the habit of asking people what they do, how is business for you, how do you find things. Let them talk, and eventually, they'll ask you what you do. And you'll be shocked at how many times you say to them, "Oh, I sell real estate." They'll start telling you, "Oh, I'm thinking about buying," "I've got a brother that wants to buy," "I've got a cousin." People love to talk about real estate. You just have to know how to approach them. You see, we don't sell real estate, what we're doing is we sell the relationship. And if they could understand that this is not a real estate business, this is a relationship business.

Million Dollar Agent Key Idea #89

"This is not a real estate business, this is a relationship business."

Phil/Dan: *Repeat that one more time.*

Francis: This is not a real estate business, this is a relationship business. Real estate sells itself. With the internet and with technology today, people don't need real estate agents any more to tell them how much a house is on the market for, how much it's sold for, where they are and what houses are going, they don't need that anymore. So you don't sell the house, the house sells. You need to sell the relationship.

Phil/Dan: *This is such a wonderful conversation. Francis, there's so much that you bring. I want to highlight the first thing, reconnecting to the desire. And I just want to go back to that and just start there. It's interesting because when someone has this passion, they have this desire, it carries them for two weeks. And then somehow it fizzles out. But I think what you said is brilliant because the successful people somehow reconnect to that original fire in the belly. And then what happens is they continually use that, you still reconnect to that fire in the belly.*

Francis: It is like the fire in the belly and the successful people have the ability like you just said to reconnect with that.

Phil/Dan: *Daily.*

Francis: Daily, that's right. And they have a passion. The fire in the belly is a passion for what they do and the passion is I love what I do. I've only been doing it for 36 years; I've got another 36 and all.

Phil/Dan: *And you're just getting started.*

Francis: I don't plan on retiring. And mark my words.

Phil/Dan: *I believe you.*

Francis: I hope you're still around, but I don't plan on retiring until I'm 100.

Phil/Dan: *Well, I'm glad to be with you all the way, Francis.*

Francis: I have a niece that'll be 65 when I'm a hundred. And I told that niece, when she turns 65 and retires, I'll retire with her at 100, that's it. But you know, my kids say to me, "When are you going to retire?" I say, "I have to get a job first." When you enjoy what you're doing, it's not work. And you talk about the fire in the belly, it's crazy but I get so excited. I get as excited about real estate today as I did 20 or 30 years ago. I love talking to people about real estate. And the reason being is that it's the business. It's the most rewarding business that you can get in the world. There are very few commodities that you could sell that will pay you the money and the size of real estate, and is the most value to people that is so easy.

I sold life insurance. I sold investments before. Years ago, and for little times in between different problems I was having. And to sell that stuff, that's tough. You're talking about rejection.

Phil/Dan: No one wants to talk about life insurance.

Francis: No. But when you talk about real estate...

Phil/Dan: Everyone is talking about real estate.

Million Dollar Agent Key Idea #90
"To be successful in business it is important to continually reconnect with your passion - your fire in the belly."

Francis: You can't necessarily sell somebody real estate. They don't have the fear that you're going to force them into buying a house. They love to talk about it because most of them want to buy a house, or they want to buy a bigger one or they want to scale down. But it's a matter of developing the technique to have that conversation. But let them start the conversation, not you. And the way you get them to start the conversation, just ask them questions. It's all about them, not you.

The problem with most sales people is we don't know when to shut up. But you need to ask the questions and let the people talk. And then you need to really listen to what they're saying. And you need to give them the information that they need so that they can make an informed decision, no matter what it is you're talking about, it doesn't matter. And they'll feel comfortable with you. That's it. People want to deal with people that they trust, and people that they feel that they can be comfortable with. So it's about relationships.

If you don't feel that you can develop relationships with people, if you don't think that you can meet a stranger and interact with them and start a conversation with them – I have a natural ability to do that because I'm from Glace Bay, Cape Breton. We have that ability just to talk to people.

Phil/Dan: Admirably so, yes.

Francis: But you know, it's the mistakes that are made. New people getting into business, if you happen to be an agent that's with a company and you're not happy with your environment, either do something or change it, but do something. Go speak to your broker and see if you can get the things you want. I'm not suggesting you leave because there's a certain amount of comfort there. You're there for a reason. Talk to one of the agents there and that fellow agent can buddy up and you can mentor each other, be accountable to each other.

We have sales contests all the time. It's accountability. If you're not able to do that, then get out of that environment. The most important thing that you can do as a salesperson is be in the right environment. That's why when I'm talking to brand new people, I tell them to interview several companies.

I say to them, "My job as a broker is to talk you into coming to me and coming to my company." That's my job, our company. But what I say to them, "I've got 20 something odd business cards out front at the desk with all the pictures. So if you were thinking about working for me, I would tell you to go pick out a card or two or three, anyone you want and call them. Call anyone and ask them about our company, and ask them about me as a broker, and ask them about our training and ask them about what we do. You'll find a broker that will do that for you then you know you're going to the right place."

Phil/Dan: *That's well said, Francis.*

Francis: That's true.

Phil/Dan: *Yeah, I know it's true and that's pretty amazing.*

Francis: I remember one time I was down in Vegas and I was with GMAC, they're out of business now, unfortunately. It was our second year with that company, I bought that franchise and we moved into this space back in 2004.

In the second year, we were the fastest growing brokerage in the whole network in North America at that time on a percentage basis. And we went from five or six agents to 20-something in that one year because that's what we decided to do. And I had a couple of elderly ladies that were there talking to me, and we were sharing some stuff. And these elderly ladies were really, really good on internet stuff, on websites and stuff like that. And back in those days, that's just when I started to become involved in that. I picked their brains about websites. I asked them, like, "How do you do this?" They seemed to have it all right. Well, they hired high school students to do it.

So I came back and I hired a high school student. It worked out really well. But they asked me, because I happened to be on the stage, my company got that award. They asked, "What would be the most single important thing you could say to us that would help us do what you just do as a broker?" And I said, "Very simple, treat your salespeople as if they're your customer, because they are."

Phil/Dan: *It's very simple but very profound.*

Francis: Yes, because we're in the real estate agent business as a broker and franchise orders are in the real estate brokerage business. I have to look at doing everything I can to make your job as a salesperson easier, right? I take away all the mundane tasks that agents love to do because it's their comfort zone and it keeps them busy, like writing ads or organizing an open house.

Phil/Dan: *I call it doing distraction.*

Francis: Yeah, exactly. Well, we do that for them. I take all the excuses away, right?

Phil/Dan: *A very wise person said that there are only two things in life – results and excuses. And once you take away the excuses, you have only results.*

Francis: That's right.

Million Dollar Agent Key Idea #91

"When it comes to success there are only two things: results and excuses. Take away the excuses and you are left with the results you want."

Phil/Dan: *So what's the greatest challenge a new agent faces when they start this business? Let's start with someone entering the business, and then I want to ask you, afterwards, about the challenges they face on an ongoing basis. And then we're going to look at what are the top agents that you reserve, the ones that really do well – and the key word here is consistently.*

Let's start with the new agents.

Francis: Okay. Well, there are a couple of things. The first challenge is to have a level of confidence that they can do the job. So when they first come in, they're green. And most of them are pretty good at learning a listing presentation, if they have that available. The biggest problem is pricing the homes and getting to understand the marketplace.

So the first thing they should do is look at every house they can possibly look at. They should always go out on agent viewings or these tours that other agents are having, they should go on that. They should talk to salespeople about value any time they get a chance because the more proficient they become at being able to decide what a home is worth or help people make a decision on the value of a home, the more confidence they have.

Then the more they can build a value proposition as a brand new agent. So what I do with our brand new people is that I usually pair them up with one of my agents that have their value proposition and help them with it. Or they use the company as the value proposition, right? And they have the tools to do that.

The other problem that they have is friends and family. They automatically think that friends and family that are going to help them with business. Well, I hate to tell them, they're going to get disappointed and let down because the friends and family are looking at them and they know that probably 60% of people don't make it in the business. They don't last. And they don't want to be a test case.

What I would recommend to those people is don't go to the friends and family and ask for business. It's about educating people on what it is you do so that they can become comfortable. If they become comfortable with what you do, then they'll help you with business. But if you go and start pushing and pushing, "Help me out here, I got to get leads, I got to get leads," I'm not going to refer somebody to you for what you do unless I'm really comfortable that I know that you can do it. Let's be honest.

Because I'm very, very proud about the people I refer. So what I would do as a new agent is I would get my listing presentation down pat and I would get my buyers presentation down pat. I would know how to answer the question -- why should I list my home with you? Why should I buy a home through you? You've got to answer that question really well. You've got to bring value to the table. You've got to feel good about what it is you're saying. You've got to believe that you truly can bring value to the table.

Phil/Dan: *I just want to touch upon the notion of value because this applies not only to new agents but all agents. There are over a million agents in North American continent, the U.S. and Canada. I've been asked by every audience I've been speaking with, "Why should anyone do business with you?" What's the why? There's a lot to choose from. Is it just because I like you? People in my opinion do business in real estate with people who they know, like, and trust based on their knowledge and expertise. I could like you, I could trust you, but if you're going to sell my biggest asset, my house,*

I want to know you're going to sell it for the right price and negotiate the best deal, and all of those things intrinsic in the value of selling homes.

And so many realtors think it's so important to articulate your value proposition. It's important for any agent, but for new agents even more so because the elephant in the room is what knowledge and experience do you have? You've only been licensed for six months or what have you.

Francis: Yes, you're right. As a new agent, you need to find a broker that's going to give you the value proposition that has it for you. You don't need to reinvent the wheel, right? We're continually looking at ways we can improve our value proposition. We are the leaders in the industry, as far as I'm concerned. And when people catch up to what we're doing, we're doing something else. So we're always racing to stay ahead.

But as a new agent, once you get that value proposition down pat, if you want to know how to be successful, this is what you do. You call up those friends and relatives, everyone you know,

Million Dollar Agent Key Idea #92
"People do business with whom they know, like, and trust and also based on their knowledge and expertise."

friends that you like and relatives you get along with. Don't call up relatives because you have to call them. These are people that you would think in your mind, "If they really knew that I did a good job, they would list with me, or they would refer somebody to me." Those are the people you want to think about, start there. Friends and relatives, it doesn't matter if it's 10, 20 or 30, it doesn't matter.

And make yourself a commitment. Every day, you book an appointment, five days a week, until you run out of those people. You book an appointment and you call them up, and say, for example, "Hey Phil, or hey Dan, this is Francis calling. How are you doing, buddy? I just want to let you know, I just got in the real estate business. Could you do me a favor?"

And here you are on the other end of the phone, thinking, "Oh my God, he's going to ask me to give him some business." I'm not going to say that. "I'm working on a program and a plan that I'd like to share it with you. I'd like to get your view on it. I'd like you to tell me what you think about the approach that I'm using. I'd love to get an hour of your time so that I could go over and show you what I do so you could critique it for me and give me some thoughts and some ideas. Could you do that for me buddy?" And of course they're going to do that.

Well, guess what happens? I go do that with you and I win and I give you the sleekest, best listing presentation that you've seen. I show you what we do for staging, I show you how we get professional pictures, I show you how we have a professional book that's second to none, I show you how I bring all the agents or I show you on and on and on and on. I'm not asking you for business. I'm not asking you for help.

Phil/Dan: *But they would be hard pressed not to do business.*

Francis: Right. So what happens is this, you as my friend because of that interview, what I did was I expedited the process. Instead of you waiting a year to see that I'd become successful I show you I'm successful right on day one and you start giving me business right away.

Phil/Dan: *And you dealt with the elephant in the room.*

Francis: Exactly, and if you do that with 10, 15 or 20 people, I'd guarantee you, if you can find 20 people that would commit to being loyal to you and to help you find business, that's all you really need. Think about it, that's how simple this is. If you have 20 people giving you a couple of leads a year, that's 40 deals. How many people are doing 40 deals a year? So you think about that. That's simple math. If you want to be successful in the business going in as a new agent, that's what you do.

Phil/Dan: *And also I think there's another added benefit that makes this so brilliant. I think when the agent who may need some confidence goes over their presentation, they will be installing a belief within themselves of their own capabilities in the process of convincing others what they're capable of. So it's like not only reasserting their belief in themselves and what they're capable of, but they're getting practice in their listing presentation.*

Francis: Absolutely.

Phil/Dan: *And here's the thing, if the agent doesn't believe in themselves, how the hell is anyone else going to believe in them? And it doesn't have to take five years.*

Francis: You have to do it with the fire in the belly. People know that, they can read that. They can pick up on that. You have to be

Million Dollar Agent Key Idea #94
"If an agent doesn't believe in themselves how is anyone else going to believe in them?"

infectious. You have to be excited. Like you and I are talking now, I'm excited about what we're talking about. I've been talking about it for 36 years; I'm still excited about it, right? These aren't all my ideas. This is stuff that I pick up from everybody everywhere I go. I'm the first one into the training session and the last one to leave. I pick your brain. I pick everybody's brain.

Phil/Dan: The key difference with you Francis is you take the idea, you distill them, you integrate them and you apply them consistently. And I think this is important also.

Francis: You're talking about applying ideas? I have a list as long as my arm of things that I want to do in the real estate company here. I have a list as long as my arm of new products I want to work on, new things I want to do. I never lose sight of that list and I'm always adding to that list. But I realized I can't get them all done but I pick the ones I want the most and I keep working on them every year. And as an agent, you've got to start adding to our portfolio every year; you've got to start adding to your value proposition. You've got to be assessing it all the time because times change, people change. What I did maybe 10 years ago is not going to work as much as today so I've got to come up with something else. And it's out there. You don't have to reinvent the wheel, just open your mind and implement these things.

Phil/Dan: There's so much there. Number one is being current. But the other thing is, there's this notion of big rocks, I call them big rocks where you literally list what are the highest 40 things, whatever skills are in that given year adding to your value proposition and work on those for the year and really perfect those. A lot of agents come into this business and they want to reinvent the wheel. There is a proven pathway to success. People ask me over the years, "What is the secret to successful realtors?" and I often

Million Dollar Agent Key Idea #95
"One of the secrets to be successful in real estate is practicing the fundamentals day in and day out."

say, "It's doing the fundamentals perpetually well over and over and over again." It's not rocket science.

Francis: People say to me a lot of the time, "Why are you involved in so many things?" I do a lot of volunteer things, right? We work with people, we don't disclose but we help them every way we can. I work at a community center any time there's a cause. I'll get involved to help, I do some stuff with political parties, whatever. And I just help people in general, people that need help. And people ask so what are you doing that for?

Well, what they don't realize is what goes around comes around. And I'm not helping people because I'm looking for something in return. I'm just helping people because they need help. And you know what? I've had situations not a word of lie where all of a sudden I'd be sitting here one day, and I'd be thinking things are a little quiet, I'd better see if I can pick up a commercial deal this year. And right out of the blue, one of my clients will call from the past, and just like that right out of the blue. That's because I was helping other people, that person maybe helped him in the past, or they're calling me to help me out. That's the way the world works.

Phil/Dan: The law of reciprocity. I often emphasize this, the ones that do well are givers. They provide, they ask questions, "What service can I provide, what value can I create?"

Million Dollar Agent Key Idea #96
"The best realtors ask the question what service can I provide; what value can I create?"

They approach it very, very differently. The irony is because they're giving of themselves, their time, their energy, and their expertise, it comes back to them many fold. And often in unanticipated ways. You're a great example of that, Francis. I've observed over the years that you give to your agents and you give to the community. No wonder you've been so successful and prosperous. And which is a nice way of talking about the traits of the top realtors. If you think about the agents that you've nurtured and helped grow to be top agents, what are the characteristics of the agents that are consistently the in top 10%?

Francis: They do the things that others don't want to do. Firstly, they all have databases. They get probably 75%, 80% of the business from repeat and referral business.

Phil/Dan: Okay, so they manage their book of business.

Francis: That's right. They developed the relationships with a systematic approach. They send mail out to their database, and they have it regulated and controlled when they call them. They have a minimum of maybe two events a year. One of them that we put on for example, but they do a couple of events a year where they bring these people out, they'll have lunch with them maybe once a year, they have a certain percentage of that database that's their centers of influence or their preferred clients that give them business.

Like our top producing agent here, who came to a Richard Robbins Training Program with me a number of years ago. And at that session, Richard talked about doing a special event with clients that give you referrals and then try to kind of create a competition. Well, this guy started that off 7, 8 years ago with a couple of couples, people that he had started with, because he was just new to the business. And last year he had, I think, 18 couples. All of which gave him a minimum of a deal to be there. And what he would do is give them a suite, bring them to an Italian club for a special dinner, pay for everything, open bar, pay for all the drinks, and he'd have a little hospitality room beforehand in one of the hotels. He would bring them in and he would have that little speech made where he would thank them all for their business. And in the course of the conversation, he would say, "Thank you very much for giving me three leads this year, I really appreciate it." And he would go around the table. And he would say to this group that "you guys are my team; you're my support. If it wasn't for you, I wouldn't be doing as well as I'm doing, and I truly appreciate it." He's very humble, he's very grateful for what they do. And he's just showing a little bit of thanks as an example. Phenomenal. And I don't need to tell you that he gets 90% of his business that way.

Phil/Dan: *Important points to really highlight. One of which is he gives back, he's client-focused in addition to having a database and creating value for his clients, he appreciates them and he's grateful for their business, he doesn't take it for granted. He realizes he's where he is because of the support, and he gives back to them.*

Million Dollar Agent Key Idea #97
"The best agents are willing to do the things that other agents are unwilling to do."

Francis: Yes. A lot of top producers do this; they really worry about what the clients think. Sometimes it gets in their way and I tell them the client is a lot happier than he realizes. They really overthink things in the sense that they want to make sure they're doing everything they can; they don't want to miss a step, they're perfectionist, it has to be right.

Phil/Dan: *They're client-centred, they're client-focused, as opposed to the transactional realtors.*

Francis: They're not expecting to get another one. But a good agent has a relationship with the client, not only do they sell to that client, maybe two or three times in a lifetime, but they sell to the client's kids, they sell to the client's brothers, sisters, they sell to the whole family.

Phil/Dan: *And if you take $5,000 in, that's a lot of money. That's a lot of money if you times it up by 100 people in the database. Each A-list contact is worth seven ends over a 10-year period of time, multiply that by 100 – by the amount of commission per end times critical mass of 100 people in the database – you don't need a lot of people.*

Francis: And these people don't work a full year, they might work 40 weeks out of the year, they take 10 or 12 weeks off.

Phil/Dan: *And they're the top 1% income earners.*

Francis: In this market here, I should have made a quarter million dollars plus. That's not bad for Halifax but it's not a matter of how much money they make. This is the other thing that I say to people when I'm hiring. This is not all about making 100,000 or 200,000. My way of gauging success and what I do with people is this, I say, "You tell me what your goal is. I have a good conversation with you about what is it that you want to achieve, what do you need in your life, right? I do budgeting with you and I find out what it is that you'd be really, really excited about. What would you like? And not everybody needs a $100,000 right? We might all like to make that but some people are happy pulling in $30,000 or $40,000 or $50,000 a year. As long as they're doing that with quality, what we do is we show you how to do that with a lot less work, and take a lot more time off if that's what you want, right? So it's not about your goal. I can tell you what you have to do to get there.

Million Dollar Agent Key Idea #98
"The ultimate goal of a successful real estate practice is not about the money; it's about creating a great lifestyle with the money you can make in this business."

Phil/Dan: *I don't think people are willing to trade wealth for health anymore. And if they're doing it, it's* *really fool-hardy and short-sighted. And it's not about the money. I think about the top realtors that I've interviewed thus far for this book, it really is all about the lifestyle. You get to a place where you can burn yourself out in real estate. I've spoken to realtors that have two or three marriages and are working weekends and nights, and don't want to deal with the business anymore.*

But then if I look at the really successful ones, they've got a lifestyle. They're making a damn good living, but they're also traveling, they're spending time with their families, they're working out. They have a good life as opposed to real estate being the mechanism or the process to get them there, the avenue; it's not the engine itself. And the money is certainly the fuel, but it is not the engine itself.

Francis: And another good thing to remember is budgeting is so important, budgeting for your business. If you're going to open up a retail business, you need to know how much inventory you have, you need to know what it's going to cost you to do your resource, you need to have a budget. Well, this business is no different. The successful people know exactly what they have closed, exactly what they have pending, they know how many listings they have, they know what percentage they're going to sell, they know how much money they got coming forward. They're not living from day-to-day. And they also know what to do with their money.

There are a lot of successful agents that make a lot of money and they have to keep making more money because they can't keep up. So many people have a tendency to kind of increase their living standard to their income and that's not good. I know people that make $60,000 - $70,000 a year that are a lot better off than people making $250,000 because they keep more of it. It's all on how you manage your life. If you're going to be advising and helping clients, you better have your own life together.

They can read that, they can tell. You've got to be comfortable with what you're doing, you've got to be really good top producing agents. They're very humble. It's not about them. If you ever watched the good ones, you'll see it. They're more interested in what you're doing, and they don't even bring real estate up, they don't have to bring up real estate. The people they're talking to will bring it up, right? They'll ask the question. And it's much better. If I can get into a conversation with you, and we can have a conversation, and I can get you to like me, and I can get you to ask me what I do, we're much better off. And here's how you do it.

Million Dollar Agent Key Idea #99

"Salespeople fail, for the most part, because they talk too much. Great agents listen more than they talk."

If I talk to you for 10 minutes, and a new agent should be thinking about this, and if there's an agent there that's not doing very well and is wondering why they're meeting all kinds of people, but they're not getting anywhere, they're not getting any leads, I'll tell them why they're not. They're talking too much, they're not listening, and they won't shut up because they know it all.

So you can get it to a point, and I always gauge this way, if I meet you on the street, total stranger, and I talk to you for 10 minutes, I talk for one minute, and you talk for nine, you think I'm the greatest guy. You know very little about me but you think I'm a nice guy because I let you talk. And at the end of the conversation, you're going to ask me what I do and I ask, can I get your information and carry on with you.

So you know, that's where salespeople fail for the most part because they talk too much. They talk about themselves and they talk about what it is they do and how great they are, and how many deals they made and how many listings they have. Who cares? I don't care, right? Don't worry about telling them what you're going to do for them and all that stuff; that will come later.

Phil/Dan: I think the last thing the world needs is another realtor saying how they're number one, and the greatest realtor that ever walked the face of the earth. I call that ego-based marketing. I think people really need to know that you understand what they want.

Francis: Yes. And I'll give you another tip - we're talking about marketing and realtors, and ego-based realtors, right? Anybody that might be reading this or looking at this, or thinking about this, think about it this way. I believe the industry has gone too far. The branding is gone; there is no branding anymore in the market place. There used to be excellent branding, there isn't anymore. It's all about the agent, and every agent has got a better way to do it. And it's all about how big their picture can be on the sign. Well, you can notice with our signs, there are no pictures on our signs, and there are actually no pictures on our business script because it's about our company, Press Realty, that's what it's about. And it's Press Realty that tells the public it's about them, not us.

I'll share a quick story with you. My top producing agent just changed their brand a few months ago. It's a top producing agent that has these events. He was getting a call from one of his clients that said, hey Marco, we really appreciate what you did for us, you did a phenomenal job when you served as a host two years ago, and we're thinking about selling our home now.

But they said, "We happened to see this sign that came up, it's all over the place, Press Realty. We want to try them, it's a new company." And of course, he had to tell them that's us, right? I share that with the people and he's got a brand of his own, he's dropped that brand. He is known as "The Friendly Agent; he's dropping that brand, and he's taking the team brand (which he came up with) and trying to keep it so that it's the public image. If you go to see a McDonalds, they all look the same. If you go see a Tim Hortons, they all look the same; whatever the case, but basically they're all the same style.

So brokers have got to get back to doing that. Agents should focus more on having a sign that doesn't sell them, having a sign that draws attention to the sign, not to them, draw attention to the house, right? That's what it's all about. So you know, you're absolutely right when you talked about ego-based marketing. I think you're going to see all that change. Especially with the internet today, with social media, and everything else.

That's where you want to have your face, that's where you want to be presented. The face is important; don't get me wrong, top-of-mind, top-of-mind awareness is important. There's no question about that. But it can go overboard, and especially today, like before internet, you had to have your picture in the paper because people would know your organization, those kinds of things, but with the internet today, with Facebook and all of those things that are out there today, that's your presence.

Phil/Dan: *So if you think about it, if you were to categorize it, the best agents that you've nurtured, so they're humble, they've got a database, what are the key things on a daily basis they've been doing? If you look at Marco's great example, he's your number one agent in this office, he's phenomenal, and he does it exceptionally well. How does he structure his day differently? What is he doing in the morning that's different from the average agent, the agent that's just getting by? What are the key activities that he's doing? What are the top three daily practices that he does consistently?*

Francis: The first thing would be, to have a things-to-do list, every single day. He writes a things-to-do list whether it be the night before he's finished, or in the morning. And then he takes a look at the things-to-do list first thing in the morning, and he prioritizes the things-to-do, and he makes sure that he has the ones that he has to get done that day, and he gets that done right away.

He does his prospecting early in the morning so that he doesn't waste his time thinking about it all day, he gets great at it. Believe it or not.

Phil/Dan: When he has the most energy?

Million Dollar Agent Key Idea #100
"Great agents have specific written goals; they prioritize and focus on their most important tasks that lead to the accomplishment of these goals."

Francis: That's right. And believe it or not, they don't enjoy making phone calls any better than anybody else does. I mean you know, but it's something that has to be done. Top producing agents know how to ask for referrals.

For example, the best time to ask for a referral or the best time to go after for sale or buyer listing is right after you made a deal, right after you found a listing, or right after you got a sale. You're pumped, you're excited, you're confident, you're feeling good, that's the time to do it because that's what these people need, they need help. The top realtors have systems, they follow the systems, and they don't drop off, that's the difference.

Phil/Dan: They work them consistently.

Francis: Exactly, they time block. They consistently do what they have to do, and that doesn't mean they don't get off track every now and then. They do. But they also control the business, the business doesn't control them.

Million Dollar Agent Key Idea #101
"The best agents control their business; business doesn't control them."

Phil/Dan: So they take the elements of the business that they can control and do them very well and consistently. And it's not always that glamorous. I was speaking to another agent and he's making multiple hundreds of thousands of dollars a year, his goal is to make $1 million. And I asked, what stops you? And he says, well, discipline. He said, even though he's doing *really well, he said, I don't want to do more, all I have to do is just focus a little more. That may not be everyone's goal, but I think the one thing that's worthy of emphasis is that the best agents are disciplined in what they do. Cold calling in the morning is so important because rather than it being dreaded all day, and doing it when you're most tired, it'll be a real accomplishment if you get this out in the morning.*

And then you can go out and execute. In Japan, company men go out for dinner and drinks, and they make all the decisions about what they're going to do, and day time is not for meetings, it's for execution. I think it's called Nemawashi, but I think it's an admirable thing. I think that the best agents execute consistently day in, day out.

Francis: The successful agents are more than willing to help anybody and everybody they can. That's one of the things that are ironic in the top producing agents.

They're more than happy to help other agents. They really are. And if you're a newer agent, or if you were an experienced agent, and you're not happy with the results you're getting, find the biggest producing agent that's around your area, not necessarily even working with you, call one from another company that you know is a big producer and ask them out for lunch and they'll tell you what they do.

Phil/Dan: That's a very good point because whenever I hear that two newly licensed agents are getting together to form a team, I

Million Dollar Agent Key Idea #102
"The best agents are disciplined and get the key, most impactful things done early in the day."

say a silent prayer to myself because it's a little bit like the blind leading the blind because they think that they're going to sit around a coffee shop and share ideas, well, they might get a few. When I was learning karate, I remember I always thought this was a very funny thing, they had the black belts at the front of the room, and in a linear line, they had the black with brown stripe, and then the green, and blue and red, all lined up, and I was lined up on the white belt. And I was watching each one. The black one was demonstrating the movements, but you couldn't see the black belt, all you see was the next belt in front of you. So I was modeling the guy who has the least amount of skill and experience and I was learning very little because he was doing it no better than the yellow belt and so forth. I kept thinking to myself, I should be standing behind the black belt and seeing how to do this correctly because that's the fastest way of being successful.

Francis: You're right. If you associate with successful people, surround yourself with successful people, you'll learn how to be successful. I've seen an interview where you can talk to all kinds of top executives in that field, and ask them questions. I knew one guy that never seemed to do anything. But yet he was a senior vice president of the company that I worked with at the time. And I asked him, you never do anything? How did you get to that?

Million Dollar Agent Key Idea #103

"If you associate with successful people - surround yourself with successful people - you'll learn how to be successful. And if you want to be the best you need to model the best."

And he was my boss at the time because I reported to him as a VP. He was a senior vice president of strategic planning. He said, Francis, the secret is not what I do, but the people I surround myself with. As an experienced agent or new agent, don't go ask the top producer for help, make a little switch to your thinking. Go ask the top producer if you can help them. They're busy, maybe you could do an inspection for them, maybe you can arrange to meet somebody that's taking a picture at the next listing for them, and maybe you can work on a CMA for them. Do anything you can to help them. Maybe you can do a pre-closing inspection. Just ask them if you can help them because what that will do, is that'll get you interacting in real estate, that'll get you doing productive things even though you're doing it for them. And I guarantee you that you'll get that returned to you handfuls.

Phil/Dan: *Whether you're dealing with your clients, other agents, you don't want to come from a place of being needy. You come from a place of providing value and service. It's so damn simple, but it's worthy of reemphasizing.*

Francis: Other agents are actually your customer too if you think about it. You need them whether they're with your company because you need to be known as the agent that is great to work with, that can get along with everybody, that works to make a deal happen, that when there's an issue, you're going to do everything you can to resolve the issue. You're not judgmental of other people. You want to be known as an agent that when I have a listing, people are going to come to my listing because they're going to be taken care of; those kinds of things.

So it is important that you develop a good reputation and a good relationship with agents in the industry no matter who they work for. That's a big part of your business. You think about it. You're going to come and list your home with me, and I can sit there and I can say to you, "by the way, there are 7 agents that work this market, I know them all personally. I have lunch with them every now and then; I'm going to do a little special open house just to introduce them to your property." Powerful.

Phil/Dan: *Very powerful. And it's a small world too.*

Francis: And those 7 agents have the buyers. I sell their listings, they sell mine. They sell mine when I'm down in Florida or wherever I might be on holiday, not that I do a lot of that, but you know, other people do. So yes, you've got to be thinking about your career as a lifestyle, as an extension of you. It's how you treat people; it's all about the relationships.

Phil/Dan: *So very important. When you look at all the marketing strategies, you have everything from what I call commodity-based strategies which are geographic farming, some people call you, you have bus ads, you have newspaper, radio, TV, you have internet marketing. And then on the other hand, you have relationship, which is what we've been talking a lot about, referral and repeat. If you look at the agents that do very well, what ones really are the most effective?*

Francis: This is what I've observed. The problem with some of the marketing that's out there, like Facebook and social media, you're not controlled when you do it, and you can get lost in it very easily. It's a comfort zone; you could spend a lot of time on social media.

Phil/Dan: *It could be a time vortex. There's one realtor I know who spends hours in discussion forums and blogs. It's very good what he does in that realm, but he never seems to have a listing.*

Francis: It's funny you say that because I was coaching somebody this morning, we were having the exact conversation and they're going to meet me next week, they've got some homework to do. But you know, we need to take all of those contacts. This person has a huge following on his Facebook and Twitter account, but he just doesn't resonate with any kind of business. The difficulty that you'll discover is that until you start to figure out a way to connect with them and offer them some value, it's going to be hard to do what it is that you want to do. There's so much out there. What I always recommend people to do is pick one type whether it is Facebook, LinkedIn or Twitter, and focus on it, do it properly, and get it done right, and schedule the time you put on it.

We have a new website now, we're already generating some pretty good action to that site with optimization and all those things, the same with our Facebook. But it's not a matter of how much time you spend on it because what happens is, as people get panicked and they say, oh my god, I've got to work on my Facebook. So they spend the whole day down. You've got to book your time, you don't need to spend a lot, but you book half an hour a day or 20 minutes a day, and you schedule it. You do certain things. There's ways to do that. If you get overwhelmed, you get nowhere, you don't make any headway. And people use it as an excuse, unfortunately, not to talk to human beings.

Million Dollar Agent Key Idea #104
"You can't use social media as an excuse not to talk to human beings."

Phil/Dan: *What I do for my clients is provide them the email marketing, social media marketing, direct mail, contact management websites, the whole bit, and the purpose of having a fully integrated system which we provide, is to free the agents so they're doing a high income producing activity. But anyone who tries to do all those things themselves, it's a time vortex. They're taken away from working with clients, negotiating deals, talking to people.*

I remember speaking to one of the top agents, who owned his own brokerage in North Vancouver, and I asked him, you're very successful, he picks up his clients in a limo, and takes them on tours, American investors and they buy multiple million dollars at a time when houses were in the million dollars apiece. I asked, "How do you pick up a lot of clients? How do you prospect?" He said, "What I do is I go out to those upscale stores and I buy one item and I stand in line, and I talk to people. And by the time I get to the cash register, I've got their name, I've got their number, I add them to my database, and then I get a million dollar deal just by doing that sort of thing and not sitting around trying to write blogs for my internet, or whatever, for my website." So it's knowing what to do, but not getting lost in the details of things.

Francis: Times have really changed over time. I started selling back in 1970, selling life insurance, going door to door.

Phil/Dan: *That's real sales.*

Francis: If I could give you a formula for success, if I could tell you to do a few simple things, and guarantee you that you can make whatever amount of money you wanted to make, would you do it? That's the key. So if you're reading this, and you're looking at this right now, you want to go home and you want to think, what are you doing with your life right now in sales? It could be real estate or whatever it is. And the key is that you need to communicate and talk to 10 people a day, 5 days a week. That's it. If you talk to 10 people a day, do whatever you've got to do to do that.

Now when I say talk to 10 people day, I don't mean 10 cold calls, I don't mean 10 door knocks, I'm talking about face-to-face conversations, whether it be private cold call, part of a door knock, prior to calling in to your database. Talk to 10 human beings a day about real estate and you'll be shocked, you'll be so busy that you'll need an assistant. The problem is , various people do that. You talk to those top producers you're talking to, that's what they'll tell you. You've got to talk to people because you're the best kept secret in town. And you know what, the funny thing is, it's the agent that is concerned about talking to people because, "Oh, I don't want to bother people," but what you don't realize and what you find out is that those people love to talk to you because if they have a need for real estate, they want to talk to you. They need help, they know they need help. They love to talk about it.

Phil/Dan: You know, it's one of these topics that everyone thinks of almost daily. They're bombarded with media and the internet and when they drive down the street and they see houses for sale, it's the biggest life investment and their whole life is wrapped up in where they live. I often say that all the great truths in life are simple. If they were complex, everyone would understand them.

Francis: That's right.

Phil/Dan: Francis, this has been so fabulous and we could go on for hours and

Million Dollar Agent Key Idea #105
"It is so important to focus on the high-income producing activities."

hours and I've got to be very cognizant of the time, and I'm very appreciative because someone of your stature sharing your wisdom, you exemplify what the top agents do. They're very gracious with respect to their knowledge and wisdom. And there's no surprise you're where you are.

Francis: I appreciate that.

Phil/Dan: I say it from the heart. So, if you think about all the communication channels we have: email, direct mail, social media, face-to-face, telephone calls, etc. What in your view have been the most effective?

Francis: I consider social media aspects, the Facebook, the Twitter and the LinkedIn to be passive communication. The audience, on the other hand, doesn't really have to communicate. They just read and do what they want.

Phil/Dan: They did a study of what's called semantic response, people's misinterpretation of language in a text or on an email because you're dealing in a written form. If you take all the human communication, 55% is body language and 38% is voice tone, only 7% of it is words and you have to be pretty damn precise in an email to convey meaning. And so they figured there are billions of dollars, millions of dollars in misinterpretation.

Francis: You're right. The social media in my mind is just another form of newspaper, another form of media, and another way to reach out to people. And it's one that's a lot better and can get the quantity and you can measure it, but when it all boils down it's for you to be able to reach more people and inform more people of what you can do for them or inform more people to give them more information.

You try to figure out ways, you don't try to sell a house on social media, it doesn't work that way but you want to give them some valuable information that may help them, that you can engage them in conversation. But the most effective means of doing business is going right back to what we said in the very beginning, this business is about developing relationships. It's hard to develop relationships until you meet people, until you talk to them face-to-face and phone calls, you've got to do that.

Million Dollar Agent Key Idea #106
"No matter where you meet someone, online or anywhere, it is important to move the relationship ultimately to a face-to-face meeting."

Phil/Dan: It's funny how the more personable, the more in touch you are and especially in real estate which is such a people business, the more powerful it is.

Francis: And you've got to understand now depending on the client, let's say one of the millenniums, they'll stay on emails, they'll stay on social media, they'll ask you some questions, they'll do their research, they'll do everything but if they see you as a presence, and they see you as a trusted place to go and to get information, as a real estate presence, when it's time for them to buy, you'll get a phone call from them that'll go something like, "Hey, Phil, we saw this house - we want to go see it."

Phil/Dan: They've done all their due diligence, they're ready to buy.

Francis: They'll say, "We need you to make sure we do all the right things, get an inspection, so we're not missing anything," that's what they want you for.

Phil/Dan: They were already pre-sold. But you have to provide your credibility and knowledge for them to be pre-sold. When you go to an open house, and you give someone your business card or you meet someone at a mall, kiosk, they're googling you, they're googling you and they're checking you. So it's not that social media is important – it's part of what I call the credibility enhancement process. They're using it but it's part of the process, it's not an engine of itself. So they check you out, someone gives you a referral, we've got to call Francis MacDonald he's really great. I'll Google who is Francis MacDonald, and I see on his website, I see on his blog, he's got useful information. Okay, he looks like he knows what he's doing. I've done my research now I'm going to pick up the phone and Francis, I want to list my property. So it's part of a process, it's not an engine of itself. You've seen this business evolve. A lot of times the fundamentals haven't changed in 37 years since you started. What do you see as the future of real estate, Francis? How do you see things evolving in this business with all the technological advances with all the regulatory changes everything else, what do you see as the future?

Francis: I see that younger people are going to enter the business which is a good thing, that's needed anyway.

Phil/Dan: Well, it is. The average has been 57 so there's going to be a whole bunch of people retiring.

Francis: I still see that those people that are proficient at developing relationships with individuals are going to be where it's at more so today than ever. They no longer need access to the information, they have the information. So what they need is somebody that they can feel that they can trust, they can like to work with, and that can help them.

Phil/Dan: Help them interpret what the information means.

Francis: Exactly, help them and give them other information that's not readily available, like today to show you a house and say this house is beautiful because it's got this, this, this, and this. We're not selling a house, we're selling the neighborhood, we've got to know about the neighborhood, we've got to know about the schools, we've got to know about the transit, we've got to know about special needs, if there's a need. We've got to know what employment is in the area, somebody's moving in, you really have to know communities. And you have to know and understand what lifestyle these people are looking for, and so that's all about relationships.

Phil/Dan: *They say that wealth is packaged experience. And I will say if that is the case, your words are gold, sir, you've got a hell of a lot of experience and wisdom which are rare commodities these days. You've shared some valuable insights. For those reading this book, I think they should go back and take a look at some of these points over again because all you need to do is just absorb them and integrate them in your day to day experience and like so many of Francis' agents, and the agents he's worked with and helped become successful, you will as well.*

Francis: And what I'd say, in closing, to anybody that might be reading this book, there's a wealth of experiences and knowledge right around them, around everybody. And if they would just develop the habits that they need to develop, of communicating with people and asking questions, don't be afraid to ask questions. And then be quiet and listen to what people have to say because you'd be absolutely shocked sometimes where the good ideas come from. Some of the best ideas that I've implemented are from people that are just on the first week on the job, just by asking the right questions.

Phil/Dan: *Because you were willing to listen and learn and look at the world through their eyes.*

Francis: And don't lose the fire in the belly. If you're not pleased with the environment that you're in, if you're not happy with the circumstances that you're involved in, then look at it very seriously, see if there's anything you can do to change those things within the environment you're in, and the circumstances you're involved in, or get the hell out and do something else.

Phil/Dan: *That is great advice. And I think when you're connected to that desire you have all the mechanisms in the world, but if you don't have the right intention, if you're not coming from the right place you won't be able to use the tools, but if you have the right desire, you'll invent the tools* *to become successful. And I think that's a great place to end it where we started.*

Francis: The excitement and enthusiasm and the fire you've got in your belly when you make that sale, right after that sale is made, is time to wait for nothing.

Million Dollar Agent Key Idea #107

"It all begins, ends and continues with desire."

Phil/Dan: *On that note, I want to thank you Mr. MacDonald. It's been a pleasure.*

Francis: It's been a pleasure. Thank you.

Million Dollar Agent Key Ideas Summary

$ You have to want to feel comfortable getting out of your comfort zone.

$ Successful people will do all of those things that the ordinary, everyday person or the not-so-successful agent doesn't want to do. We're tough.

$ In order to have a successful real estate business, the real estate agent needs to be freed-up to handle more and more high-income activities.

$ The best realtors not only attend training seminars on a regular basis but they apply the learnings in their day-to-day real estate practice.

$ What agents need is to know what to do and how to do it effectively. When you combine these together it becomes a very powerful force.

$ If you're not happy with the results, it's got a lot to do with the way you think and the thoughts you're putting in your head. If you get negative results, you've got negative thoughts.

$ Your thoughts control your feelings; the way you feel determines how you act; the way you act gives you results. If we created failure, we can also create success.

$ This is not a real estate business, this is a relationship business.

$ To be successful in business it is important to continually reconnect with your passion - your fire in the belly.

$ When it comes to success there are only two things: results and excuses. Take away the excuses and you are left with the results you want.

$ People do business with whom they know, like, and trust and also based on their knowledge and expertise.

$ When people catch up to what we're doing, we're doing something else.

$ If an agent doesn't believe in themselves how is anyone else going to believe in them?

$ One of the secrets to be successful in real estate is practicing the fundamentals day in and day out.

$ The best realtors ask the question what service can I provide; what value can I create?

$ The best agents are willing to do the things that other agents are unwilling to do.

$ The ultimate goal of a successful real estate practice is not about the money; it's about creating a great lifestyle with the money you can make in this business.

$ Salespeople fail, for the most part, because they talk too much. Great agents listen more than they talk.

$ Great agents have specific written goals; they prioritize and focus on their most important tasks that lead to the accomplishment of these goals.

$ The best agents control their business; business doesn't control them.

$ The best agents are disciplined and get the key, most impactful things done early in the day.

$ If you associate with successful people - surround yourself with successful people - you'll learn how to be successful. And if you want to be the best you need to model the best.

$ You can't use social media as an excuse not to talk to human beings.

$ It is so important to focus on the high-income producing activities.

$ No matter where you meet someone, online or anywhere, it is important to move the relationship ultimately to a face-to-face meeting.

$ It all begins, ends and continues with desire.

BILL PARNABY:
Always Do the Right Thing

RAISED IN CALEDON, Ontario, Bill Parnaby attended Wilfrid Laurier University for a degree in Biology & Physics, and then returned to continue as an actively involved resident of the town.

Bill is an active supporter of many local sports programs for youth, an ongoing supporter of Caledon Community Services and has spent time as a Director of the Caledon Chamber of Commerce.

Bill's ability to help families match their needs in this extraordinary part of Southern Ontario is what he does best! And since becoming a father of two, it has given him an even better appreciation for the needs of families faced with the daunting task of buying or selling a home.

Bill has been ranked in the Top 1% of Canada of all Royal LePage agents. He specializes in selling Town and Estate properties throughout Caledon and its many villages, and couldn't imagine doing anything else. He has been awarded the Lifetime Award of Excellence for his efforts.

Bill's knowledge, honesty and common sense approach work successfully, hand-in-hand with the team's core values and beliefs. This combination of traits and values is appreciated and respected by his clients, colleagues, and his community.

Bill and his beautiful wife and business partner, Tina have two kids, Joseph and Mia.

Bill has been helping people buy and sell homes in Caledon and the surrounding area for over 25 years.

BILL PARNABY IS great example of an agent who came into real estate at a very young age with very little experience yet understood that if you want to be successful you need to learn and model what successful people do. After surviving his first year real estate barely making a living, he partnered with another agent whom he could learn from and grow with. Committed to lifelong learning, growth and development he is one of the top agents in Canada in every respect. The way he conducts himself and his real estate practice is a model of excellence that any agent can learn from.

Phil/Dan: Well, good afternoon Bill. We really appreciate you taking the time to do this. We are doing some research for this book and the premise is to really capture the journey of some of the best realtors in Canada. And you're certainly amongst them. Wherever we turned, multiple people said that you've got to interview Bill, and as well, at the Richard Robbins events you're a key panelist. He uses you as an example of the Secrets of the Masters seminars and so forth. So, thank you for taking the time to do this. We can't tell you how much we appreciate it.

Bill: My pleasure.

Phil/Dan: And so, we've got a couple of questions for you.

Bill: Okay.

Phil/Dan: Bill, what did you do before real estate? How did you end up in this crazy, wild business?

Bill: Well, I graduated from the university in 1990 and I had been doing landscape construction for seven or eight years. I do backhoes and excavators and big machinery but it had taken a toll on my body so I wanted to find something else, something that's more business-related. And I toyed with insurance. I toyed with thoughts of doing other things. But then a girlfriend of mine, her family owned a brokerage in Bolton, they were real estate brokers, and she said to me, "You should give real estate a try." And I kind of laughed and said, "It's never been something on my radar," but at that point I was willing and open to just about anything. So, I said, "Sure, I'll give it a try." So I went and did my courses by correspondence, then I finished up the formal courses in class. And next thing you know, I was hired.

Phil/Dan: So here you are. You're in a brand new field, somewhat related as you were in construction in real estate. But they don't teach you how to be successful when you get your license. And so, what was your greatest challenge?

Bill: I would say my greatest challenge was pretty much everything.

Phil/Dan: Okay, so what the hell do I do now?

Bill: In all honesty, I was 23 years old. So I looked rather young. I had a borrowed suit, I had a bad car. I had really no idea what I was doing other than being textbook-taught on paperwork, but no idea how to actually do the business or run a business. And it was also the beginnings of the deepest recession that we've experienced, especially in the country, to this day.

Phil/Dan: Wow!

Bill: So, it was after my first year, I had sold a house. A full 365 days and I thought like what the hell am I doing here?

Phil/Dan: You tell that to a realtor today, you'll never live through if they don't sell 10 houses, or at least enough to pay their expenses. They quit.

Bill: I'd like to say I'm a slow-learner. I like to say I'm a bit stubborn. So, I wasn't going to let it sort of beat me, if you will. And first year was based in my idea to see whether or not, getting my feet wet. I was actually going to just see how it goes down. So, I did like how it went down the one time. And I was proud to make my $6,000 and go home and say well, I've given it a good shot. And then I got approached by Royal LePage and they said, "If you want to be serious about your career, you need to leave that small broker." You can come to Royal Lepage and it was then that I made the jump. And then I met up with a partner and then my career just went from there to one step bigger and bigger and grew basically ever since.

Phil/Dan: Almost exponentially. So did you get mentored? Was it the training that made the difference?

Bill: Yeah. It was actually no formal training, but I partnered up with a guy who had been in business six months longer than me, and he was maybe around 50. But, he was a former business owner.

Phil/Dan: Okay. So, that's a key point. He had business experience. As people go into this business, they have dollars signs in their eyes that it looks easy and it's clearly not. And they don't realize it is a business that operates based on fundamental business principles. So your guy may not have a lot of realty experience. But, he could parlay a lot of his business experience.

Bill: Totally. And that's what he brought to the table. He had very strict discipline.

Phil/Dan: Okay.

Bill: Not that it has much to do with it, but it has something to do with his German background. And my experience with Germans is that there's a very strict platform of performance. In other words, it's very strategic. It's very deliberate. It's very significant. And that fit him to a T. Everything we did was strategic and plotted and planned and it was fantastic to learn from, because it was the foundation of systems.

Phil/Dan: Interesting point. So there was a road map and there was a purpose. It wasn't just totally chaotic and just reactive. But you were saying that he had a reason and a process and a system for everything that he did?

Bill: Yes. He was the one who basically brought the business background to the table. And it was simply real estate that was the new product. Now, it wasn't that we weren't totally reactive still because both of us were still learning how this business worked.

So we had our times where it was very, very demanding. And we did exceptionally well as a partnership that was very much a good cop, bad cop.

Phil/Dan: Your personalities complementing one another.

Bill: Absolutely and we dominated the market here during a 90s period where nobody dominated anything. So it was a huge learning curve. But then after a five-year window, I decided that was enough. And I needed to spread the wings and do my thing.

Phil/Dan: Which is I think a natural progression because I look at teams and they have a lifespan of their own. And you grow and you don't stay still. You evolve as a person in where you are professionally. You're not the same person when you start.

Bill: That's right. And that was it. We hit that spot and we just wanted to do things a little bit differently. And so, we just went our separate ways and still remain good friends to this day and I still speak with him even though he's retired. But it was probably the most valuable relationship I had in my business life.

Phil/Dan: So you made sort of this pivotal shift. You've been in real estate how long now?

Bill: It will be 25 years this coming February.

Phil/Dan: Amazing. Looking back over your career, obviously there's been a number of different course corrections along the way, learning experiences. What would you say has been the greatest challenge? And obviously, when you're starting, that's one thing. When you're established, if you look back and you think 25 years, what has been the biggest challenge as you would define it?

Bill: I think it's still managing the reactivity of the business, the demands of the business. And the struggle to manage those demands and still have any sort of quality of life.

I've got two kids. And there have been very pivotal changes in my career where I built a team as many as five and then we had shrunk to three, and then it went to four, it's always morphing. And that was the one thing that I picked up from my coaching was the idea of leveraging. Because it wasn't so much anymore about selling one more house or one last house. It was more about, how do I get my weekends and how do I get my Friday nights and how do I try to work 40 hours a week instead of 80?

Phil/Dan: I learned about the reverse engineering process. But instead of a reactive nature where your things pile up, you look back for, what are my major goals and how do I create my business to fit those big, big rock goals, whatever you want to call them. Those big chunks? Major important life goals. I see so many realtors completely at the whim of whatever is going on in the moment.

Million Dollar Agent Key Idea #108

"In creating a successful real estate career, it is important to define your major life goals first and then figure out how your real estate practice can serve to accomplish those. It's a reverse engineering process."

Bill: Yeah. And I honestly think too that one of the biggest shifts that ever occurred was the implementation of the internet technology to our world. I think about our smart phones and it's going to be the death of most of us because we've now all become so conditioned like Pavlov's dogs that every time it makes a whistle, a tweet, a sound, a horn, or honk, we are in a constant state of distraction.

Phil/Dan: I recently heard about a hotel in New York City where you can lock up your phone for the weekend as a service. So that you could actually enjoy going to a play, dinner with your spouse, what have you. If they ever built a monument for the 21st century, it would be a guy looking at his cellphone.

Bill: A hundred percent.

Phil/Dan: You know, frozen in time, right?

Bill: Yeah. With really a big thumbs.

Phil/Dan: Interesting. So why did you get into real estate business? What was your underlying motivation? I know you were in a somewhat related industry, but what was the 'why' for you?

Bill: Well, I was probably very immature at that time. At 23 you just want to try and make a living and try to make some money and get yourself going. So, I would be lying if I didn't say it was about some of the money. But more importantly, it was about establishing a business because I'd come from such a physical labor intensive job, that this was now about using my head more than my hands. And so, it was a low barrier of entry to get into this business. It looked from my perception that you could do well financially if you were good at it. And the freedom of what appeared to be time.

Phil/Dan: Which you feel, which is a real issue?

Bill: Fallacy. I don't know where that false pretense actually comes from. I don't know why anybody would think that you have more time. And the reality is, if you grow a successful business whereby, let's suppose your target is you want to sell 50 homes a year. Well then, if you think about the number of people you have to go through to get to 50, all those people are your bosses. So, the idea that you are your own boss is for the time that you actually can hang on for your life, because the rest of the time, it's them. And if you don't do the job when they need it to be done, then you're not hired.

So it's a very quick learning curve that you say "Oh my god, this is like survival." If they've thrown you in the lake, you've got to swim now, and swim very hard. Because the next boat is not coming by.

Million Dollar Agent Key Idea #109
"The real estate business is a business - if you want to be successful it's going to take time, energy and money."

Phil/Dan: *And there are sharks swimming.*

Bill: And there are sharks everywhere.

Phil/Dan: *Exactly. Bill, so you're very successful now. Here we are 25 years later and you're forty seven. How would you describe your lifestyle now versus your lifestyle back then?*

Bill: It is kind of comical because I would like to think that it's a bit more in control. My lifestyle per se is that yes, I have a house and yes, I have cars and yes I have the freedom to do a few more things. But it's interesting that I still face the same struggles today that I did 20 years ago.

Phil/Dan: *Is that on a different scale?*

Bill: Just on a different scale. You build a machine and then you have to feed and I maintain this machine. There's overhead now and I've got staff. So it becomes just a different animal altogether and it's the blessing and the curse.

Phil/Dan: *It's the blessing and the curse. So it's something you've created, but it's insatiable in a lot of ways?*

Bill: That's right. I would think that in the time I've been doing the business, that the biggest change would be the availability of information via technology. And the reason I say that is because information used to be rather sacred before.

With our MLS books, catalogs and sheets that you couldn't share in board, we'd fine you if you did. To now, the public – Joe Public believes that they are every bit an expert as you are.

Phil/Dan: *Now you need to create value. You need to contextualize information in such a way to define your own value in the eyes of the people who hire you. Because unfortunately, in the low entry threshold of real estate you get people from every walk of life, and the ones that really rise above are those that really get that. And I'm sure you would agree to that value proposition. Not only within information, but everything that they do for these multiple bosses.*

Bill: Yes the reality is that the perception of the public is that your job is to sell their house. Well that's an expected outcome. That's why you get hired. So, if that's expected across the board, then how do you differentiate yourself if you're all expected to do the same thing? Because then it becomes about compensation, then it becomes commodity. And then it becomes a race to the bottom for values. So you're right, just keep adding value to the equation so that you begin to stand out.

It's a good thing in a sense that it will raise the bar. We like to do things in our mind. It's our measure of just doing things right. And we try to explain to people the fact that we're going to sell your home is an automatically given expectation of our arrangement.

If the other things that we're looking after, limiting the risk and liabilities, the fact that we're there at the end making sure that you get your check before we get our check. That everything goes till the end of the day when you can sign off and be done.

Phil/Dan: It's optimizing the amount they get for their house. And it's articulating that in the eyes of your clients.

Bill: Correct, and navigating the world, that it's not as easy as what they see on the outside. I can go on to the internet with a sore throat and diagnose myself as having tonsillitis. But it doesn't make me a doctor. I still have to go somewhere to get it confirmed. We're navigating through what information they're being inundated with now.

Phil/Dan: You're successful, you're prosperous, you're doing really well, and you've got a team. What drives you to take your business to the next level?

Bill: We've had this conversation about what is the next level, what does that look like? Because you can always be on that treadmill to try and chase more money or bigger fish. For me, it seems to be more about optimizing a better lifestyle. I'm not talking about things, bobbles or cars or trinkets. I'm talking about lifestyle where you have more time to do the things that you want to do. To me, that's the next level. I want to make sure that I can take an afternoon off and hang out with my kids or go ride my ATV.

Phil/Dan: At a certain point in life, you want to trade things for experiences because those are priceless and certainly, time with your kids and things like

Million Dollar Agent Key Idea #110
"When you really boil it down, the purpose of the real estate business is about creating a great lifestyle; however you define that."

that, you can't put a price tag on. So I get it. Whereas in the earlier years, it's all about what?

Bill: Building.

Phil/Dan: Building and creating something. But now, you want it to serve you. What do you like the most about being in real estate? I think it's a fascinating business from many standpoints, but what do you like the most about it?

Bill: I like the people puzzle. I see every situation where we'd call them to help or to move somebody or to buy for somebody, wherever, as a people puzzle.

Phil/Dan: You have to be a psychologist. You're dealing with people, if you're looking at the dynamic; you've got family issues, legal issues, and financial issues. The big one for people is change. Nothing stresses people out more than change. They seek change and then they resist it. You're dealing with every aspect of human condition.

Bill: Well if you think about it, I mean, the people puzzle is really what drives everything. You're either coming together or going apart. You're either going up or you're going down. You're getting a job. You're losing a job. It's always how the people puzzle interacts with itself.

Phil/Dan: Getting divorced, people getting married, having a family, growing a family, downsizing from a family.

Bill: So to me, the object is just the house. That's not the real driving force. It's the people puzzle that's at work. Once you can step in and understand the people puzzle, you can help them put the pieces together or take the pieces apart in the best way that's right for their puzzle. And it's not always easy.

Phil/Dan: You don't often see that because you're so much a part of that. I think that in and of itself is part of the value you provide. Is the objectivity of having circumnavigated all these different situations, that you can see the bigger picture?

Million Dollar Agent Key Idea #111
"Being a great realtor is understanding and putting together the people puzzle."

Bill: It's very ironic too, because I can see the bigger picture for them, but sometimes, you don't see it for yourself.

Phil/Dan: *Ah, okay. Elaborate a little bit more on that, because I think that's really powerful. We don't see the water where we're swimming.*

Bill: We're in our own waters. We're not looking at it. So sometimes, dealing with other people's people puzzle allows you to be reflective of your own. And maybe that helps to keep you grounded. Maybe that helps to keep things in check or gives you that wisdom to build, to give people advice on things that maybe you've experienced because of other circumstances that you've been through.

Phil/Dan: *I think that's very powerful. Whenever I hear one of my clients or realtors are moving, I smile to myself and think, well that will make them a better realtor because they understand the intrinsic stresses going through that process. And they get advice from the outside, but when they're in a place full of boxes and there's always ambiguity in their lives and everything is moving apart. It's absolute chaos. They can kind of appreciate that. There's a light at the end of the tunnel mixed with all of that.*

What makes you the best at what you do?

Bill: I've been asking myself that question.

Phil/Dan: *I know probably someone else could tell me what makes Bill good and I would have a few perceptions on that. But what in your mind, what have people told you, what makes you the best?*

Bill: We get people who give us feedback on lots of different things; we'll get told that we're really good communicators or we're down to earth, or that we're good listeners and that sort of thing. Maybe for me, what works is that I don't really believe that I'm the best.

Phil/Dan: *So is it the humbleness?*

Bill: I guess it's humbleness, but I have a problem with people who are the boast and bragger type. I have an aversion to that. I think you just need to do

Million Dollar Agent Key Idea #112

"As a realtor you do not always do things right but it is important that you always do the right thing."

your stuff and the rest will take care of itself. The moment you have to tell people that you're the best, it's probably not true.

Phil/Dan: *Right. A lot people believe their own press where that's concerned and there's certainly an incongruence. One of the greatest business principles is don't judge people on what they say; judge them by what they do. And I think that's very powerful. In the best people, their actions speak for themselves.*

Bill: And I make mistakes, I am far from perfect. I may come across sometimes like I really am in control or I really know what's going on. And you hope to God that's the truth most of the time. But there are times that I'm a complete fish out of water. And I'm in the tank with you. I think, we've got to try and figure this puzzle out because this is a new one for me. Rich and I always talk about it as you don't always do things right, but you always do the right thing.

Million Dollar Agent Key Idea #113
"I think one of life's greatest skill is mastering ambiguity. No matter how we think we're experts at things, especially in business, there are so many moving parts. It's very important to have that ability to navigate ambiguous circumstances."

Phil/Dan: Right. So you have a moral compass that you use. I think one of the greatest skills is mastering ambiguity. No matter how we think we're experts at things, especially in business, there are so many moving parts. It's very important to be certain to also have that ability to navigate ambiguous circumstances. If you want a total certainty, you would work nine to five in a cubicle downtown, pushing paper, even that's not completely certain, but my point being is that you're dealing with so many scenarios. How could you know everything?

Bill: You're learning and I think that's the key thing that most people would respect about you is that as long as you're open to continue to learn, and admit when you don't know something. One of my old clients, he's a builder and he used to say to me, Bill, money talks, bullshit walks. And I say, don't bullshit a bullshitter. I think about just coming clean with whatever you got. Be completely transparent if you have to. If you don't know anything about that, just say, "You know what? I haven't got a clue."

Million Dollar Agent Key Idea #114
"If you don't know something, admit it; people will respect that."

Phil/Dan: And people respect that.

Bill: They're going to totally respect you, because if you try to blow smoke...

Phil/Dan: *People have built-in bullshit detectors. They know.*

Bill: They know. Just let it go the way it's supposed to go.

Phil/Dan: *So, if you want to define it, what separates you from the competition? Why would someone choose you?*

Bill: Two things. One is, that I'm incredibly loyal, so I'll stick with you, I'll back you up, we'll do everything we can to make sure that it's the way it's supposed to be. And I have a high meter of integrity, in the sense that I'm not going to do anything wrong that I'm going to be conscious of. I'm not going to bend the rules. I'm not going to do something that's going to be in your best interest because we work in an industry every day, where we are faced with a decision to be made between doing what's best for our clients or putting bread on our own table.

Phil/Dan: *What an interesting position to be in.*

Bill: And not everybody can make that decision.

Phil/Dan: *Because they're thinking in the short term. And what I've noticed is that people who make the*

Million Dollar Agent Key Idea #115
"Transactions are not about the deal, they're about people; always do what's in the best interests of your clients and this will serve you well."

right decisions for your clients or the situation or knowing this business a long time, it comes back to them in multiples.

Bill: I think it's a given. I think that's where I think a lot of realtors miss the boat. The transactions are not about the deal. They're about the people.

Phil/Dan: *And the relationship.*

Bill: The relationship and the puzzle. My first broker said to me, first opening remarks, "you always do what's right for them." You do well by your people and the rest will follow. I tried to live by that my whole career. One of my better skill sets is that I don't bend when it's not the right thing.

Phil/Dan: *This is very admirable. That's one of the key things that I think separates the best from the others. And as Richard has said, for 10% of realtors in this business, it's a great business; for 90% it's pure hell. Because I don't think they're making those wise decisions along the way and I think that's one of the reasons that you were able to point it out. How do the best realtors view the world differently than everyone else? What's their mindset?*

Bill: I would guess that what they think is that everything that we do, we do through the lenses of being professional, number one. But then our complete focus is about the client and not about ourselves. And I think the more you can do for your client, the better. And ultimately, the fact that you just created such a solid relationship and a respected professional relationship, performance, is already given. I think that's how the top 10% continue to make it because as the world expands with demands and needs and things from professional people, I think the numbers of people that are in that top 10% of whatever the trade is, whatever the businesses, it's becoming slimmer and slimmer.

Million Dollar Agent Key Idea #116
"I would lose a complete commission if it was to make somebody happy."

So just because you're in a business a long time doesn't mean you're good. It means that you've made it that long. But when you confine those people that are great, you tend to stick with them. You get a great mechanic, you have a great doctor, you have a great dentist, you have a great realtor, and you had a great teacher.

Phil/Dan: It's valuable and people don't want to waste time. One of the lessons my father taught me, when I was young, I used to buy cheap shoes and go through them every three months. And he said, let me give some advice. Spend $200 on a pair of shoes as opposed to $50, because they'll last you a long time. And you know, there are certain things you don't compromise on. Well, the same is true for professionals. Once you find a good professional, you really know they're worth it.

Bill: And that goes back to the loyalty issue. When I called the guys at Morris, they've been doing my newsletter forever and we had a glitch at some point where we had made a mistake. It was our mistake, but those guys took upon themselves to swallow it for me. Those are the guys that I will never leave because I would do the exact same thing.

Phil/Dan: I think it's taking full responsibility for everything, that's part of the shift and focus. So just to recap, the top realtors in the interviews, their focus is on creating value. Their focus is on the client as opposed to their own interest. They'd take responsibility for the process.

Bill: Yeah, and it's the client, not the deal.

Phil/Dan: It's the client, not the deal. And that's very, very important. How would you complete this sentence?

Million Dollar Agent Key Idea #117

"It's the client, not the deal that is important."

The real estate business is what in your life? I love asking this question because I get so many varied responses.

Bill: I was going to say, it depends on the day. Or the minute.

Phil/Dan: Yeah, that's right.

Bill: I'd say that it's rewarding. It's a very rewarding career from a monetary standpoint because you get paid very well for being a very good realtor. It's rewarding in the sense that it's centered around helping other people and the value that you get in the face of somebody that you're helping who is at their worst, is something that doesn't even translate into money.

Phil/Dan: Very few professions get to that feeling that you've made a difference.

Bill: Satisfaction, like significance.

Phil/Dan: You made a contribution.

Bill: I think it's one of those things where I used to say to one of my clients, it's like the real estate business client is like the idea of intense dating. You are with them in such an intense environment for a very short period of time relative to their life.

Phil/Dan: It's got all those elements. It's got drama, time wise.

Bill: It's swirling. You have intimate details.

Phil/Dan: There are issues, there are problems.

Bill: And they can be two

Million Dollar Agent Key Idea #118

"The best realtors have ways of keeping that relationship feeling alive with their book of business - they have systems to do this."

weeks, two days, two months long until they need you the next time and you're basically gone to the wind. But you're not forgotten. They know that you're there and that the moment you reconnect with them, you're back in that same environment, that instant speed of trust is established in a second.

Phil/Dan: That's a critical thing you've said. I think a lot of what I call transactional realtors, they date their clients and that there's this romantic relationship transactionally, but then there's no contact. They go out to the next deal, the next deal, the next deal and they suffer from what I often refer to as realtor guilt. They're really good people-people, really good relationship people, but they go from deal to deal to deal and then they wonder why overtime they're without a system of maintaining that relationship. I think the best realtors have ways of keeping that relationship feeling alive with their book of business; they have systems to do this. Because how many deals have you done over that time?

Bill: 2,200.

Phil/Dan: *Okay, so how do you stay in touch with that many people without a system? It's physically impossible. When you grow your business beyond a certain modicum of clients, you couldn't do it.*

Bill: I was one of those realtors at the beginning because I was ignorant. I didn't know any better.

Phil/Dan: *When did you make the shift from transactional to relational? I mean you've always been good with relationships. In order to go beyond the feast and famine cycle, the roller coaster of real estate to creating a business that grows exponentially, how did it happen?*

Bill: I would have to say that the light went on when I started with Rich.

Phil/Dan: *Okay, coaching?*

Bill: I wasn't even in coaching yet, but I was on an event. I didn't join after that event, but I knew that I had to. He talked about, why is it that we spend 80% of our revenues, chasing people we don't know, when 80% of your business actually comes from 20% of the people that you do know? So it was an inverse relationship. We were doing the wrong things in the wrong directions for the wrong reasons.

Phil/Dan: *We're spending time, energy and money on people we don't really care about and ignoring the people that have the greatest economic return.*

Bill: That you've already served.

Phil/Dan: *And I call it the elusive obvious because people wonder where the next deal is coming from, right in front of them.*

Bill: It's right there.

Phil/Dan: *In relationship, but it's not automatic. So you made that cognitive shift. Often it's amazing because if you look at realtors who get that,* *their enjoyment goes up because they're no longer dealing in a commodity-based world, but a relational world and there's so much more reward and you've alluded to that in our conversation.*

Bill: Absolutely, absolutely. I don't know any other business where you can measure all the units in terms of the value of each client. If you are a client of mine and we bought or sold one house, I can say yes, you're worth $10,000 or $14,000 to me. But what people don't realize is that, you're only going to move maybe two or three times in my career.

Phil/Dan: On average, every four to seven years.

Bill: So there are 40 or $50,000 there, not to mention the fact that you're going to know three to five people every year over the next 10 or 15 or 20 years, which is another 50 or 60 people.

Phil/Dan: I do the math when I do my seminars, Bill. It's interesting that if you have a book of business of a hundred rock-solid people, a critical mass point, and what's the average commission?

Bill: Here, it's going to be close to $14,000.

Phil/Dan: Okay. So let's say it was 10.

Bill: 10, easy math.

Phil/Dan: I deal with everything from Saltspring Island to Newfoundland. I was recently in Moncton, New Brunswick where the average house price is $175,000. I said I would take five thank you very much. And then I have clients at Vancouver where it's going to be $2,000,000 they project by 2020. But in any event, let's use 10 grand and people move every four to seven years, literally $70,000, seven transactions over a ten-year period times a hundred, that's $7,000,000 worth of business in your commissions, and we know it's higher than that. Over a ten-year period from a book of business of a hundred people. You multiply that in your case by two, three, four, 500 people. Talk about an annuity-based business. But here's the thing, it's not automatic.

This is what transactional realtors don't get. They go to the one-offs, because they're always chasing the leads or new business, they never nurture those relationships to create the residual business.

Million Dollar Agent Key Idea #119

"Transactional realtors are always chasing new business; they often don't realize the sheer wealth of business to be had in the clients they have worked with in the past in terms of referral and repeat business."

Bill: Yeah. And I think it's very easy to fall back. I have been guilty of falling back into a transactional mindset, especially if and when things get a little tight. Because you go into panic mode.

Phil/Dan: *Right, you've got the machine to feed, you've got staff.*

Bill: That's the thing. So we need to be able to snap the band and maintain your position on the other side.

Phil/Dan: *Make that mindset shift. So let me sort of focus a little bit. Drill that a little bit. On a daily basis, what are the key things that you do? What are the key daily practices or behaviors that you do that lead most to your success? There's a mindset in the philosophy and the approach here on a daily basis, what are the things that you do that you think consistently lead most to your success?*

Bill: Well, I would say that there are probably different levels of things that get done every day. There are those things which are systemized that happen because I put them in place to happen.

Phil/Dan: *Okay, so they're automated, self-perpetuating.*

Bill: Exactly. So, if you're looking at things like anniversary letters and different ways to touch your database and all those things are systemized, that's one of the key things.

Phil/Dan: *Whenever I hear of a realtor that's stuffing their own envelopes, 25 years into the business, I get the fact that it's nice to read handwritten little notes and all that stuff, fine. But if you're doing everything yourself with your family in an assembly line in front of the TV set, it can be an issue because you don't put value on their time*

Bill: That's it. So I would say that from a day-to-day perspective, I think you've really got to be good at doing your follow up. I refer to it like pushing the train cars, not pulling them, but pushing the train cars. The train car is bringing your leads and your prospective people you're going to be doing business with and you're gently pushing them down the track every day.

Phil/Dan: *It's incremental.*

Bill: It's incremental. It's just like, here's a little nudge.

Phil/Dan: *It's not a discourse, but ultimately it's a nudge. You're managing the process?*

Bill: Yes. So you push a little, push a little, push a little, push a little. And I'm not trying to push them into doing anything. I'm pushing them with information. I'm pushing them with opportunities. I'm pushing them with communication. I'm pushing them with follow up and feedback. So that I'm constantly in touch with them, but we're moving our process forward. And it may take a week, it may take a month. In some cases, it may take a year before we actually connect and put something together.

Phil/Dan: Now, you have to be pretty organized to do that. So you must structure your time in such a way to time block.

Bill: I try. I just know there are a few simple tasks that have to get done. It doesn't matter when they get done in the day, but I've got to get them done.

Phil/Dan: But by the end of the day, you've accomplished them?

Bill: X amount of phone calls, so many e-mails to my clients. Different forms of communication for different clients.

Phil/Dan: What are the top three things that you consistently do?

Bill: Follow up.

Phil/Dan: Behavior that leads to most of your success.

Bill: Following up, is key.

Phil/Dan: Okay. With both leads and...

Bill: Current.

Phil/Dan: People of current business.

Million Dollar Agent Key Idea #120

"There is no magic bullet in being a great realtor; it is a matter of doing the fundamentals well each and every day."

Bill: Whatever's on the plate that needs to be followed up on. The second thing is, I would say that I have a personal ritual where I go to the gym three days a week and that happens in the middle of the day - 11:30 to 12:30, Monday, Wednesday, Friday. That's for my own psyche. I think the last thing and probably the most important part is that I get home at a reasonable hour.

Phil/Dan: Because this business can be all-consuming.

Bill: Yeah. So I think you need to have a balance between doing your work really well. I look after myself physically in a well-balanced way and then I try to be with my family in a well-balanced way. And it's even interesting as I say it out loud as sometimes still the family balancing part is still the last one on the line. I think that's probably my biggest failure is that I constantly struggle with prioritizing them to the front.

Phil/Dan: This is meant as a compliment, the fact that you think it's a failure, it means that you consider your work and family very important.

Bill: I know it.

Phil/Dan: Now, you're telling me your guy travels two months a year and you're trying to circumnavigate that. I've probably lived over the last 13 years in a hotel room almost two years of my life, missed. I suffer from the guilty father syndrome, but I could appreciate that more than you know.

Bill: Yes, yes.

Phil/Dan: So, I often use this as a metaphor. When you think about what's the magic bullet in real estate? What's the one thing I could do that will turn on the tap and lead to my total economic prosperity? If you look at the great athletes, if you look at the best in any field, they're doing the fundamentals really, really, well consistently. Would you agree with that statement?

Because they may not be exciting and it may not be the most glamorous thing, but they've mastered the discipline. I mentioned Peter Gain out of Port Moody and he was saying he has to do X amount of these key activities everyday if he wants to push the process forward. And he may not feel like it, but he'll go through and he'll do it consistently. And the results are very consistent.

Bill: Repetition is boredom but it creates results. And it's 100 percent the truth because you'd be sitting there and thinking, "I really don't feel like picking up the phone. I'm not in the mood to pick up the phone." But you go through the motions and you do it anyway.

Phil/Dan: And you learn to love it and the irony is because you'd see the bigger picture, the end result's been agreed.

Bill: Yeah. It's also important to understand that, whatever I don't do today is going to affect me 90 days from now.

Phil/Dan: So you see the causality relationship? A lot of people don't think this way.

Bill: Failure to do what you do today shows up. Now if I do that for a week, I'm going to have a horrible looking 90-day month down the way.

And I don't want to face that.

Million Dollar Agent Key Idea #121

"The actions you take today will affect your business results tomorrow."

Phil/Dan: *I think that's a very critical point because when you see the bigger things and how they all link together and you see it's the small little behaviors done consistently that lead to the bigger, you chunk them down, you see how one interacts with the other. I think your metaphor of the train, of pushing the train along is a very good way of thinking about this.*

Bill: That's how it came to me. It came to me in a visual. And then get her going, right?

Phil/Dan: *That's right, get her going. It gives it all the lift. And it's the cumulative effect of all these micro tasks.*

Bill: I think that's right, it's cumulative effect.

Phil/Dan: *So, just shifting a little bit of focus to when you started out. You're a systems guy. You're a relationship guy; you're the plane in flight. You can course correct, go up or down depending your choice because you've made it. Not that you think you have, but you're at that critical mass point. When you started, what was your expertise? Was it farming, FSBOs? Expired listings?*

Bill: To be honest with you, I think where we mastered the marketplace was in marketing.

Phil/Dan: *More specifically, was it advertising?*

Bill: Yes.

Phil/Dan: *The world was different. We didn't really have much of an internet back then. This is pretty hard for people to understand.*

Bill: My partner was from the media background. And so we would be at the office until one and two in the morning designing ads. With cut and paste paper tape putting these concepts together. And we would inundate the town with our propaganda. Clever creative. This was ahead of its time for real estate in the 90s here because it was a very old farm town. We would take pictures of ourselves and say this is what team work looks like. We would lie down on the train tracks and take a picture of the train track and say, don't let your deal go off the tracks, very cliche now, but at that time it was rather cutting edge. But we did it again with lots of consistency to the point that we used to get people calling, saying, "Could you stop sending us all this advertising material?" But what was happening was, we were building up our own critical mass to the point that we were doing our 50 transactions a year in a market that would see the normal agent do about eight or nine.

We were just on top of it and everybody knew who to call. In those days, the 90s, if you are earning 400 to $500,000 that was a couple of million today. So we basically marketed our way into the business here because neither one of us did well with cold calling. Neither one of us likes to get out and knock on doors. I had a huge aversion to what we now would call rejection-based marketing or rejection-based prospecting. Why do I want to go to somebody's door, knock on it and get it slammed in my face?

Phil/Dan: I've met a few crazed door knockers in my time and there's one guy in particular in Vancouver, he has to knock on somebody's door, he's addicted to the process. Most realtors would rather die than door-knock. Yet, you'll look at new realtors in their first year, I've known a lot of realtors who made the shift from an ego-based to a relational approach, but you've got to do what you've got to do when you first start. So, of all these areas, farming, FSBOs, expired listings, especially referrals, referral and repeat website, lead generation with all the technology, what is the area that has generated the most business for you, when you think about those areas?

Bill: I think what has happened over my career is that my marketing ability has led to the opportunity to create relationships. And I think those two things put together got me the opportunity.

Phil/Dan: But then you took the ball...

Bill: And developed it. Yes.

Phil/Dan: You made the shift once you got to a certain amount of clients, and then they became referral and repeat. You've got what I would refer to as an annuity-based business.

Bill: Yes. At least 80 percent referral at this point.

Phil/Dan: We saw it to the point where you can have a team to handle all the business.

Bill: Yes.

Phil/Dan: You can't do it all yourself. How would you define your expertise in generating new clients?

Bill: I think what we deal with most often is going to be again marketing and this market place allows me to be recognized, if not referred. Because people will check with their friends and say, oh yeah, I've already used Bill, and I see this stuff everywhere and he's everywhere. And then we meet face-to-face and they actually realize that I'm a real guy that they can actually connect with me and then our relationship will build from there. And it's not that I build up with everybody. I don't typically like to turn people down, such as at times when it just doesn't work. For whatever reason.

Phil/Dan: So things have changed in the last 25 years. What is your primary methodology for communicating with your book of business? Is it internet, e-mail, social media, direct mail, in person, face-to-face, telephone or is it all of it?

Bill: Well, I don't do any e-mailing on a mass broad sense at all. I am not a believer in mass marketing through e-mail or even through social media. And the reason I say that is because I get enough emails in the day that I don't even want to read one. And that's why we have always maintained the relationship through snail mail. Because there's a better open-rate. It's multi-sensory. They can conjure up images and memories and whatever.

Phil/Dan: In the UK they did a survey, a study where they hired a neurologist to look at the effect on the brain of someone who opened a piece of snail mail versus reading on a screen an e-mail. When you see an email it's fleeting. You don't remember any e-mail you got two weeks ago. But if you had to feel something to open it, it's multi-encoded in the brain.

Bill: Yup. So I still maintain the old snail mail and then phone call and then the random e-mail. I'll say, I will state like a personal note of interest to the person not, "Hey, are you thinking of moving?" I'll say, "Hey, I went past your house last week, great job on the landscaping, it looks great" or "I saw your mom last week." Strategic.

Phil/Dan: So how do you convert prospects into clients?

Bill: Well, if it's a listing prospect, then I still maintain a two-step approach when I go to do my listings. And that's a bit old school still and that's because I want to get two chances to have the relationship built. So I go the first time, I bring them a brochure on how and what we do and then I go to the house and make my notes and then I come back and do homework. I arrange that second visit to have a coffee and talk about it in person to interview other people. Please make sure you're going to have two or three people that you're interviewing. Because I want them to see that I'm not attached to being the only one or that I'm afraid of something.

Phil/Dan: And I think there's a subtle point here that by encouraging them to speak to other people, knowing you, you're saying you believe in your abilities to do it. You say, you're going to do it, but I also think there's integrity there. You come across as somebody who would like the business, but you don't need it to put food on the table.

Bill: It's a very different approach and one of the things we talk about at the table is just that. I tell people that, we're very fortunate that we're going to sell 60 families this year in properties. And so whether it's one more or one less, it's not going to make a difference to my world. But it has to be a good fit for your world that I'm your guy.

Phil/Dan: Which I think is very powerful itself.

Bill: It's okay, right? If you're not feeling comfortable with this, I'm good with that. And it's the same with the buy side. It's very interesting, that the government gurus have said to us, you need to sign our agency agreements and sign up your clients. I still don't do that until I have reason to put them into an offer situation because I want to earn their business.

Phil/Dan: If it's only the reason we're doing this is by virtue of a contract...

"I need to earn the right to work together."

Bill: Not doing it.

Phil/Dan: I still do business on a handshake with people because I'm old school, but if the trust and the feeling aren't there, then what's the glue that's holding them?

Bill: A hundred percent. Piece of paper is not worth anything. I've had people sign multiple representation agreements. So what good is it? Is it my job to convince you to sign this thing to work with me? No. I think I need to earn the right that we work together.

Phil/Dan: And based on that, based on relationship, that's going to mean so much more business down the road anyway.

Bill: It's a natural flow and I believe in the natural flow more than forced procedural tactics and sales tactics. I don't look at myself as a sales person, right? This business is really not about sales at all. It goes back to the puzzle. You want a blue house, okay, let's go look at all the blue houses we can find and find the best one. I'm not selling you a blue house; I'll show the blue house. What do you think of that blue house? I don't like it. Okay, let's find a different one. It's not rocket science, right?

Phil/Dan: But to make it happen, there's a lot of nuance along the way.

So Bill, what marketing strategies do you currently use for your business, like the main ones?

Bill: All of them. So, we use an internet presence. We use print media. Both newspaper and magazine. Newsletter communications with our current data base. Direct mail. Our touch system which is the existing data base and we provide them with opportunities and experiences as well. So we'll send 400 people home show tickets.

My database is 400 people large at this point that I manage regularly. We'll invite them to a movie screening. We'll have an ice cream that's coming this month. We're having all 400 and we got invites, come on down. It's free ice cream on me from six to seven o'clock on Friday at the Happy Days Ice Cream parlor. So we try to make these contributions to them because I look at it and say, you guys are the ones responsible for giving me the first 10,000, not to mention every other 10,000 that you've given through your referrals and repeats. So the least I can do is include you in my world and then give you something just to say, hey I appreciate you or thank you. Let's just go do something that's kind of fun.

Phil/Dan: So there are a couple points here. You give back through experiences because people remember experiences much more than things.

Bill: Right.

Phil/Dan: The other thing is physically. There are some trainers who will say, you have to visit all your clients individually. Well, that's not going to happen where you're concerned. You've been in this business 25 years. You've done 20, 200 or whatever deals. You've got 400 core people that you may define as your A list, your advocates.

Bill: I can't see them all.

Phil/Dan: You don't have enough hours in a day. So, the fact that you get to see them collectively in a couple hours, you can see a certain number of them.

Bill: Correct.

Phil/Dan: *And I'm sure that pays for itself multiple times.*

Bill: It absolutely does.

Phil/Dan: *What's the value of your time visiting each one of your clients individually?*

Bill: And what's the value of a lost client or a lost deal?

Phil/Dan: *People never look at that side of the equation. People know how much business they have, but they don't know how much business they have lost because of the things they haven't done.*

Bill: Right and to me, that's one of the key differences.

Phil/Dan: *That's very powerful. Let's look at the future of real estate. If I was coming to you as a brand new real estate agent, having just got my license, what are the things you would tell me today?*

Bill: Well, I think you can relate back to the basics. I would say that you have to be trustworthy. You have to be a clear communicator. You have to be a servant to those that you are working with. You have to know your craft, so know your product inside and out. And do right by people. So when you are given those opportunities, make the best of those opportunities for not only yourself, but for the people that you're with.

Phil/Dan: *Have you ever talked someone out of this business? I don't think a lot of brokers do enough of that. This business is not for everybody.*

Bill: No. I think what's interesting about this business is that there is a place for everybody. So if you want to get in as a part-time person, do one or two transactions to help your family, that's great. If you want to be a 50, 150, 300-a-year-unit person, there's a place for you. You want to work in Port Moody? You want to work in Burlington? You want to work in Alliston? There's a place for you. And all those things will shake out to wherever that level will be.

Phil/Dan: *There is too much expertise required.*

Bill: The world is smarter than that. They don't need a talker.

Phil/Dan: *They say wealth is packaged experience. But there's a lot of knowledge and expertise required in doing this right.*

Bill: Yeah. They don't realize it until there's a mistake.

Phil/Dan: *That's right.*

Bill: Until there's a huge error because the lawsuit that follows is going to be way bigger than the commission you think you saved, is going to eat up three years of your life before you get into a court, is going to cost you tens of twenties of thousands of dollars by the time you're done. And your life will be off the rails until it's finished.

Phil/Dan: What has changed Bill, in your view, for those getting into the real estate business today?

Bill: I would think that the biggest change is a compounding effect with the availability of information to the public. And their belief that they are now as prepared as well as we could be. That new realtor has a bigger challenge with the cynics and the skeptics, to try and prove value.

Phil/Dan: To demonstrate their value, given the proliferation of information available.

Bill: Yes.

Phil/Dan: And what do you think is the biggest challenge faced in the industry as a whole?

Bill: I don't think there's anything else that has greater risk.

Phil/Dan: Do you think that those people entering today have the same prospects as you to be as successful in this business?

Bill: I'm sure some of them have the right idea. But for many of them it's getting into business that's built on a false premise. It's the car, the time, the money, the whole thing.

Phil/Dan: It's like someone looking at you, saying here's why Bill is so successful, I can do that. Or I'm looking at a professional athlete at the top of their game. They don't realize all the incremental tasks, the hard work.

Bill: I think the better you become in your industry, the easier it looks to the world.

Phil/Dan: Interesting. Because you are more skilled, you are more adept at what you do. You're at the mastery level.

Million Dollar Agent Key Idea #122

"I think the better you become in your industry, the easier it looks to the world. To be great at real estate is a result of a lot of accumulated expertise."

Bill: So they look at that and say, wow, that looks pretty easy. Or they would say your real estate equation is, you sold my house one day, and made $14,000.

But they are making a time and money equation out of it, which it's not. So I could say, well, that's easy. Would you like me to take six months to sell your house, and that way we could rationalize the $14,000 better. No, it's outcome-driven. It's liability containment-driven. It's efficiencies.

Phil/Dan: *I think new realtors don't appreciate it.*

Bill: There are so many opportunities to go and join a team. And I think as a team leader, you'll understand that you're going to get lifers, which in this world I think is about five years for realtors. Or you get those guys in for a year. But at least you've helped them to realize that okay, now you can take your tools and go on your way.

Phil/Dan: *One last question. This has been incredibly valuable. In your view, what is the future of real estate generally? This is a big-chunk question, but if you look and project into the future, how do you see the profession evolving? What do you think is going to help in the future?*

Bill: Well, I certainly don't think that the internet and information is going away. I think it's going to become an industry of more specialization. I think it's going to become more about the 10 percent running the 90 percent of the business. And I think my projection would be that you would see less people actually getting into it or remain in it because of the specialization of the upper crust. The way it currently stands, I think there are a lot of people who are – with no disrespect, feeding off the bottom.

Phil/Dan: *But they're not making a really good living.*

Bill: They're not making a living at it. So for those people, it's desperation and it's drastic measures and it's a race to devalue themselves as quickly as possible to try and get the next deal. And they will always exist and they will always be the shortest term possible that's in this business. But, the people who are at the top of the chain who are doing the best they are doing for their people, I think will always survive and flourish. And I think the industry will focus more and more on that type of profession.

Phil/Dan: *For the business and for the consumer.*

Bill: We're all going to do much better by dealing with the professional people at a higher grade. That's for sure.

Phil/Dan: *And on that note, you certainly exemplify that Bill, and I want to thank you for this.*

Bill: Thank you. My pleasure and it's been my honour.

Million Dollar Agent Key Ideas Summary

$ In creating a successful real estate career, it is important to define your major life goals first and then figure out how your real estate practice can serve to accomplish those. It's a reverse engineering process.

$ The real estate business is a business - if you want to be successful it's going to take time, energy and money.

$ When you really boil it down, the purpose of the real estate business is about creating a great lifestyle; however you define that.

$ Being a great realtor is understanding and putting together the people puzzle.

$ As a realtor you do not always do things right but it is important that you always do the right thing.

$ I think one of life's greatest skill is mastering ambiguity. No matter how we think we're experts at things, especially in business, there are so many moving parts. It's very important to have that ability to navigate ambiguous circumstances.

$ If you don't know something, admit it; people will respect that.

$ Transactions are not about the deal, they're about people; always do what's in the best interests of your clients and this will serve you well.

$ It's the client, not the deal that is important. I would lose a complete commission if it was to make somebody happy.

$ The best realtors have ways of keeping that relationship feeling alive with their book of business - they have systems to do this.

$ Transactional realtors are always chasing new business; they often don't realize the sheer wealth of business to be had in the clients they have worked with in the past in terms of referral and repeat business.

$ There is no magic bullet in being a great realtor; it is a matter of doing the fundamentals well each and every day.

$ The actions you take today will affect your business results tomorrow.

$ I think the better you become in your industry, the easier it looks to the world. To be great at real estate is a result of a lot of accumulated expertise.

NOAH DOBSON:
Well-Taken-Care-of Clients

NOAH WAS BORN and raised in Southwestern Ontario, but moved with his wife to Victoria, B.C. in 1990. He is educated in Business Administration as well as Human Resources. Prior to becoming a licensed realtor in British Columbia, he was a personnel director with a world-renowned private health-care clinic. Noah has worked with many people from around the world and continues to enjoy working with people from both British Columbia and abroad. According to Noah, real estate is truly a "people-business" and he continues to enjoy meeting the wants and needs of his clients.

NOAH DOBSON IS in class all by himself. Like so many agents he came into real estate after achieving success in a totally unrelated industry. After receiving considerable media attention for his landmark work at a world renowned health-care clinic, Noah sought to reinvent himself in the real estate industry. That he has. Noah understands that real estate, above all else, is a people business and this permeates everything he does. His clients absolute love him and send him a steady stream of referral and repeat business. He is greatly admired and respected by his peers, so much so that when he goes on vacation his colleagues do not want to take care of his clients for him because they are hard pressed to provide the same level of service clients are accustomed to working with Noah. In this interview Noah provides valuable insights into how to be a great realtor.

Phil/Dan: Good afternoon, Noah, we're delighted to be able to interview you. Noah Dobson is one of our favorite realtors in all of Canada let alone Western Canada. We've known Noah for many, many years and he is a fabulous person in addition to a fabulous realtor. Thank you for taking the time to do this because we know you are an extremely busy guy and that's an understatement. What did you do before you went into real estate? Your background is very, very unique.

Noah: Sure, prior to being in real estate, I'm actually a human resource generalist and I spent 10 years with a company. Then, I was a program director and personnel director with a world famous eating disorder clinic for another 10 years.

Phil/Dan: And that led you to some interesting experiences. While you were the director at the eating disorder clinic, you had some interesting experiences related to that, you were invited on a number of talk shows. Do elaborate.

Noah: We did a *20/20* program with ABC which was a launching point for our little clinic that had been running for four or five years. Somebody came through our program that had family at ABC, the *20/20* program, and they came and dedicated only for the second time in the history, a full hour to one idea and that idea was our clinic. And from there we were inundated from around the world, with people arriving on our doorstep to media from around the world wanting a piece of what we were doing. And that led to some really rewarding programs, we did two Oprah Winfrey shows, the first one being dedicated to men suffering from eating disorders, which had never been done on a daily talk show and we moved on from there doing numerous pieces throughout the world, in Germany, Britain, Australia and went on to do Dateline pieces. So just numerous, numerous pieces, too many to remember.

Phil/Dan: *Well, so you caught fire through the 20/20 exposure?*

Just to clarify Noah, this was dealing with the other side of the equation because all the rage was thin models at the time and women's eating disorders, but your clinic specialized with men?

Noah: We specialized in both, we didn't discriminate. We had such an alternative program to what was being traditionally done in the model.

Phil/Dan: *That's amazing, so here you are. Once that career ran its course, you found yourself as a realtor. Why real estate and how did you get into that from where you were?*

Noah: I have always had a passion for people and my first profession was working with people. I love the differences in people and when I decided to make a transition from the human resource field, I thought to myself, what have I been thinking about what I wanted to do but had never really vocalized it, and my wife said to me, "What do you think you would really like to do?" And I said, I think I would really like to get my real estate license. And I had never said it out loud before and thinking my wife would say, "Oh, dear God, no."

Valerie's life was like, please go into an office and be Noah again. I thought to myself as my wife said, "Then, why don't you do it?" And I really took some time to talk to myself and I thought, "Why am I not doing this?" And for numerous reasons or maybe a couple of reasons, I thought I've always had stability in my life, I've always been able to rely upon myself and make a good living and have a nice lifestyle but I want to do something that I'm going to enjoy. And not be in an office anymore. I thought to myself, well, fear is the only thing that ever holds anybody back. And that's obviously what was holding me back. So I took the next step and I called the UBC office of real estate here on the West Coast and I ordered the real estate package and waited for it to come. So it was really as simple as that.

Phil/Dan: *Now, so here you are, brand new profession, you are doing something that you think you are going to love, you don't know exactly how it's going to be until you are actually into it. What was your greatest challenge when you started?*

Noah: Way back then? I had some wonderful connections here in Victoria because of my previous profession. And so I wasn't too worried about that part of it. I think the biggest challenge for me was going from Noah sitting in an office with 150 employees to the isolation of sitting in my car and thinking, "Okay, what is today going to hold?"

Phil/Dan: *So lay it out for us. And this is a common question for people going into real estate, it's not nine-to-five anymore but you go to a physical place and here you are in real estate, your car is your office most of the time, you are dealing with so many different physical locations. And really you are it; you are the commander of your own ship. A lot of people don't actually make that transition very well, and they end up wasting a lot of time or spending a lot of time on what I would refer to as feel good distraction work as opposed to money making activity.*

Noah: I would agree.

Phil/Dan: *Go to any coffee shop in North America and just scream as out loud as you can, are there any realtors here and at least one or two will stand up, depending on where you are looking.*

Noah: True absolutely.

Phil/Dan: *And that's not an indictment of realtors, it's just an indictment of the need for such a difficult challenge for many people to structure their time. So the challenge was how do you go from a structured environment to unstructured environment where you are? What would you say has been your greatest challenge over the years? And I am sure there have been a number of them but if you look back at those challenges, what would be the biggest one you faced?*

Noah: Maybe the greatest challenge really has been myself. When I think about when I started out, getting over the fear, getting over some of the failures that I initially had within the industry and trying to keep self-motivated and learning to do that. And I think that I have now, in my 16th year. But that was certainly a great challenge. When I look back now and I think about the things that used to cause me angst and certainly all of those have gone because I have structured my career the way that I would like it to be, and that's worked well for me.

Phil/Dan: *I'm going to get to that in a moment because as I interview across the country, great realtors like you, the ones that I would say "have made it" or make it on a continuous basis, they've really defined real estate on their terms. It wasn't always the case, many at times they had that what I call a walk-in–the-park moment where they say, I don't want to do this anymore. In other words they realized they had to make some changes in their career to really define the profession on their terms. Did you ever have a moment like that throughout the years where you said, you know what, the way I'm doing it isn't the way I want to do it and I need to re-invent myself?*

Noah: I think I had two moments; one was in year number two of my real estate career. And now you know for me, I sold my first home on day number two which I didn't set out to do but I certainly did which was a great oomph for me. I had a fantastic, great first year, in all aspects. And I had a really great mentor who just kept saying, "My goodness, I've never seen anyone come in and do so well in this kind of market." And so all of that was such a wonderful boost for me and I soared along with that. The next year, about half way through, it felt like everything had dried up. And I of course had never been through any kind of cycle in real estate. So, I actually hung up my license for two weeks.

Phil/Dan: Oh, that's interesting.

Noah: Yes, I probably never told you that.

Phil/Dan: Yeah, I have known you for years Noah, I have never known this.

Noah: I thought to myself, oh my goodness, I don't know if I can do this for a lifetime. I mean the ups and downs, I had such a great first year and everyone kept looking at me like I was the golden boy or something like wow, look at you and so I thought to myself, okay, so I don't know if I really know how to turn this around. I was certainly still making a living; it just wasn't compared to my first year. And I thought, okay, maybe this isn't the profession for me. So I hung up my license and accepted a position in human resources. I hung up my license on a Friday, on the following Monday I was sitting in an office with a company here in Victoria and by Thursday afternoon when I picked up my wife after work, we were both done at four o'clock. I picked her up and she looked at me, and she said, "You look miserable." And I said, "What have I done?" And she said "You can change it," and I said, "You know what, I can change it." And so with that, I gave my notice at that current position, they were kind enough to let me walk away within a couple of days. And by the following Thursday, I was relicensed as a real estate agent and doing an open house on a Saturday. And that got all of that angst out of my system.

Phil/Dan: It's almost like you needed to be shown what the alternative was.

Noah: Exactly. I never really had a moment like that in my professional career. Everything had always sailed along nicely and then I was making these decisions and I thought to myself, oh my goodness, I think I need to be in an office. Where do I find the business from now and on and on and on and on. And so I had all of this self-doubt, so I felt, well, just fall back on what I know I can do.

Phil/Dan: You know it reminds me of an ancient Chinese saying, "You can never step in the same river twice." Because it's changed and you've changed and you remember how it was, it is never the same because you are a different person and that's the experience you had.

Noah: It was.

Phil/Dan: And it was a vindication that you had made the right decision but did that eradicate all the self-doubts that you had?

Noah: Yeah, it was gone, it was done. I can remember exactly where I was standing there doing the open house, most people had no idea that I had stepped out of real estate for two weeks, except my agent and the people I worked with, some of which I still work with here at Newport by the way. Because they were at Bowman's at the time and what I did, that they were all saying, "Why would you do that? You've been so successful" and it was all about me and my self-doubt and I learned a really valuable lesson in my life. And so when I stepped back in, I never looked back. I never looked back and I know I'm not the only person who's ever done that obviously but you know it was something that I think I had to do. Definitely, it was part of the process.

It was part of the process. And when I look back on it, I mean that's how I see that and I never have any regrets that I did that. It allowed me to just take a deep breath and say okay, I chose this profession, I have worked very hard, you know my first year and a half plus you know the few months of getting my license and what have you. And I know that I can make a success of this and that's how I moved forward.

Phil/Dan: And in retrospect, what a wise decision that was. I often suggest to people who are considering going into real estate, that one of the biggest challenges, if you live in a structured environment, is embracing ambiguity when you are dealing with uncertainty; it's not like working in an office. It requires a faith, it requires a confidence in yourself, in your ability and to believe in your own ability, to create abundance in your life and that's something that you have to reassert on a continuous basis. So it's totally understandable that you would do that but by doing that, it really cemented yourself in ways that you can't even define, I think that's wonderful.

Noah: Absolutely, it was like a paradigm shift; it happened for me. And I needed that to happen and that's my personality anyway, I don't want to be thinking I should, could, what have you. You know it was something I felt that I needed to do and honestly I've had no idea that I would within two weeks, be back doing what has turned out to be one of the best things I've ever done in my life.

Phil/Dan: And I'm sure that your clients that you've worked with over the years, your colleagues, myself personally, we are glad you made that decision, Noah.

Noah: Thank you. Yeah, my deep dark secret is revealed.

Phil/Dan: It is revealed for all to know.

Noah: You are as good as Oprah, Phil.

Million Dollar Agent Key Idea #123

"Being successful in a business where you are your own boss without the structure of working for someone else involves having faith and confidence in yourself."

Phil/Dan: My hair isn't as good though. Maybe someday I will have my own network, you never know.

Noah: You might.

Phil/Dan: Noah what is your greatest challenge today? So we are looking 16 years later, you have been a tremendous success and I could say that you are too humble to ever say that but I could say that. I've observed you evolving over all these years; your challenges are obviously very different because you are established now. You have a modicum of past clients and people seeking you out and you are defining the profession on your terms. What is your greatest challenge as you would define it today, Noah?

Noah: I think my greatest challenge today is continually servicing my clients to the standards that I have expected of myself and I think that they expect of me as well. I do find that a challenge on some days. When I have someone in my car at eight o'clock in the morning, I'm doing a transaction mid-day and then I have a fresh group of people I pick up after work at six o'clock and they need me to be something else as well. And I have days where I have to do a little self-talking and say, okay, Noah you know, just re-energize and you will be fine as soon as you get into the car. But you know 16 years into it and with a busy practice, I find that a challenge some days, not all days. But the days that you find it a challenge, you really have to pull something from inside of you that you maybe don't think you have that day.

Phil/Dan: And I think that separates the people who really are excellent with what they do, are really at the top of the game, is their ability to access those inner resources when they need them and I know that as a speaker, there are some days when the last thing that I want is to get up in front of an audience and speak and you have to. You know to do that, you have to be that much more animated than everyone, have that much more energy than everyone else. And the same is true for when you are dealing with clients who have these great expectations and that you may have been putting out fires all day and all you want to do is just go home and be mindless in front of the TV watching a movie or something, having a glass of wine, as opposed to negotiating a deal into the wee hours of the night or morning.

Noah: Very true, very true.

Phil/Dan: And boy, that's a mark of a true professional to be able to do that and I know you do that so well. So obviously we are a similar age but your lifestyle has evolved a lot in the last 16 years. How would you describe your lifestyle now from when you first started in the business? What's the biggest difference in your lifestyle now?

Million Dollar Agent Key Idea #124

"Being the best is doing what you need to do even though you may not always feel like doing it."

Noah: You know I really love my life.

Phil/Dan: I love your life too, Noah, I'm just aspiring to get to where you are.

Noah: I love it. I feel incredibly grateful for my life and if I say that to my wife, she will say that it has been hard work, you have worked hard and I guess it's all how you put it in perspective. I feel very congruent, I have for the last certainly three or four years in my career and I think that's just having the balance of knowing that I really built a strong practice that continually rewards me in what I do. I feel very fortunate and very grateful at this point in time.

Phil/Dan: To draw on that a little bit, when you started out, I'm sure you weren't taking the vacations you are taking now; your lifestyle was different because you were building a business. If I am not mistaken your business was more controlling of you because you were trying to get established. You've taken back control of the business, you decide when you want to work, often times who you want to work with and how you want to work, generally speaking. Would that be a true statement, would that be an accurate statement?

Noah: Yeah, very much. Part of being congruent for me is feeling that I have a sense of control over my professional life and I feel that it helps me move forward year-to-year now knowing clearly the advantages of what I do, that I can take a nice holiday that I can take a weekend away. That I can do these things knowing that I still have the same practice.

Phil/Dan: Your income won't suffer; in some cases you will make more money by taking vacations and being more refreshed and energized.

Noah: Absolutely, if I don't take care of myself, no one else is going to. I have said that my whole life and I am very good at preaching that but I absolutely believe that. So I do the right things for myself to make sure that I can be the best that I can be which is what my expectation is for my clientele. As you know I'm in the gym three days a week, I take vacations, my wife and I will fly over to Vancouver for a weekend, sometimes maybe a night, catch a play, what have you. I come back to Victoria and feel refreshed, even just doing that, it doesn't take much for me actually.

Phil/Dan: Well, I think that's so important, I need to remind myself that on a regular basis. So, Noah at this stage of the game I'm sure the money doesn't

Million Dollar Agent Key Idea #125
"It is essential that if you want to be the best and do a great job for your clients you need to take care of yourself mentally and physically."

drive you, what drives you to take your business to the next level? Because you do very well financially, I am sure. I know you do based on the amount of work that you do, but what drives you to the next level? What motivates you to do things, to go to that next level, how would you define it?

Noah: You know, part of feeling congruent is feeling successful and for myself the number of people that I can take care of successfully that continue to refer me, really continues to drive me. And I strive for excellence, I don't always get there, certainly my clients may think that I have gotten there but I don't always feel that I've gotten there. But it's really the people that I work with; I still have a passion for people. I love the diversity of people and I welcome that and certainly working in such an international market as I do here in Victoria, I have the ability to meet the most interesting people from all over the world, and that continues to drive me today in my practice.

Phil/Dan: You've got a very interesting profession, you are dealing with people that have various education levels, various income levels, some very famous A-list actors, I'm sure you are able to relate to that strata of humanity and that requires a lot of skill. I deal with realtors across North America and one of the things that fascinates me about realtors is they come from every walk of life. Because they come into the profession as a secondary or a third profession as I said. And that's amazing to me but in your case, given where you were located in a very high end market place, you are dealing with such a wide strata of humanity and I think that is not something just anyone can do.

Noah: It's all about your people skills and we hone them as we age in our profession. I think I was telling you the story last week about David Foster's mother and how I sold his home and David had said to me, "You know my mother would go to the opening of an envelope because of all these pictures of openings, walls and walls and walls of that." And he obviously adored his mother and so what a small world it is that who is our district manager for Christie's, (we've just become affiliated with Christie's International in the past year which is very exciting for us), Zack, lives next door to David Foster in Beverly Hills. And so Zach and I were having a conversation and he was saying, "Oh, David was saying so nice you're going to Victoria, I love Victoria." So I was able to tell him that story and he said "Oh, I love it," he said "the next time we are sitting around the pool, I'm going to share that with David," and I thought "What a small world," is that not a small world?

Phil/Dan: It's a very small world.

Noah: It is a very small world but somehow that conversation I had with David Foster quite a few years ago now which I shared with other people over time and I was going to go back via Zach sitting around a pool in

Beverly Hills. So it is a very small world and it's always good to put your best foot forward.

Phil/Dan: *It certainly is. Noah what makes you the best at what you do? There are a hell of a lot of realtors out there and if you go to the Toronto Real Estate Board there are literally people lined up out the door and a big queuing station to get their license but not all of them make it. It's the same in Vancouver and you are in Victoria which is not exactly Vancouver, but there are a lot of realtors in Victoria. What makes you the best at what you do?*

Million Dollar Agent Key Idea #126

"Great realtors give a damn about their clients and understand and anticipate the stresses and challenges they face."

Noah: Oh dear. I'm just better at doing some things, obviously. I think one of my abilities that set me aside from a lot of the other great people that I work with in this profession is my ability to really empathize with my clientele; go the extra mile. I really believe that in what I do, that it's all about the details and so I think I try and set myself apart as Noah Dobson the real estate agent to be what my clients need or want me to be. So you know that's one of the things that I would say that sets me apart from other people in my profession that have had great success.

Phil/Dan: *Well, I think to sum it up, Noah, you give a damn. You are able, as successful as you've been over the years, to still look at the challenges and stresses and issues faced by your clients and to be able to navigate that for them in such a compassionate way. It's not about a number for you, it's about a relationship.*

I get that sense that how you relate to people, you really put them at ease in a time of great transition in their lives and you take each situation on its own.

Noah: Yes, I certainly try to do that. I deal with people who may have lost a spouse or are going through a divorce or lost a parent that has been a component in their lives for 10 or more years, I know the family. I have a very good client in her late 80s now. I have worked with the whole family; I just worked with her daughter in the last couple of months for the very first time helping her make a transition. And for me it's always making sure that, I always get right back to the source and let them know how much I appreciate their confidence in allowing me to help a family member make a transition. With that particular client, her adult son had a lot of health challenges which I was privy to because I had done a lot of work for them. When he passed away it was making sure that I had flowers delivered to the home and then I left her a personal message. I just do what I feel is the right thing to do for me always, but I think that by planting all of those seeds, you reap the benefits of that over a long relationship. People actually know my clients; I want them to know that I actually really do care.

Phil/Dan: This book I'm working on is about the best realtors and the best realtors are the ones that have compassion. You certainly can learn how to do it but it's the ability to translate their own life experience into the service of others.

Noah: I do agree with you.

Million Dollar Agent Key Idea #127
"Truly great realtors are authentic and the same person whether you are dealing with them personally or professionally."

Phil/Dan: How do the best realtors look at the world differently from everyone else? I speak with a lot of realtors out there and it's all about the money or it's all about the deal but in your view, how do the best realtors look at the world differently? What do they do differently from everyone else?

Noah: Some of the top agents that I work with here in Victoria have really brought the profession into their life and the two have worked together very well. I know some of the people that I greatly respect in the industry here in Victoria, they're going to be the same whether they're doing a transaction or if you meet them at the gym. They have the stability to incorporate and create a really structured business and continue to be successful by bringing it all together. That's how I feel.

Phil/Dan: That's a very powerful point. I do a lot of speaking and no matter what their profession is I think the best are not afraid of being themselves and bringing themselves with the authenticity and a humanness of who they are rather than being plastic fantastic. Some of the TV anchors are trying to be someone else's speaker and you can tell that they're being their persona and if you see them in a different context, they're someone else. I think the best in real estate, there's real sincerity in there. They're the same people whether in a coffee shop or dealing with a client. There's a kind of alignment to who they are.

Noah: And people are attracted to that. I'm attracted to that. I'm attracted to authentic people, and I think a lot of people are because it's like the law of attraction. It's real estate and you could choose from 1400 real estate agents give or take here in Victoria, so why are people going to be attracted to me again and again and again? It's all part of that experience and that attraction. It's my challenge to keep up to the standards that I have set; as I was saying some days it's more difficult than others but I'm a human being. It's realizing that I have the ability, I can get through this next hour, and I can do that. I will be okay at the end of the day. You know it's clearly knowing that and always being forward thinking.

Phil/Dan: *I think that if you look at it, it's kind of a scary question for a lot of people but your clients are often a reflection of who you are. As a person, it may not start out that way but this dawns on me from time to time when I realize that I'm the common denominator in all my client inter-relationships and over time I tend to attract a lot of clients that are just like me, in one form or another. Be it a good day or a bad day but it varies from time to time. How would you finish this sentence Noah? The real estate business is what?*

Noah: I was going to say stressful but that's because of my day.

Phil/Dan: *Oh yeah. Let's look at it from a wider context.*

Noah: I'm going to say rewarding. That can encompass a lot of things for myself.

Phil/Dan: *Overall, you would say it's rewarding.*

Noah: Yeah. Personally it's rewarding.

Phil/Dan: *Okay that's wonderful. Let's look at things at a much more a chunked down level. On a practical level, what do you think are the essential habits to be successful in real estate? If you think about all the things you do in a day, the phone rings and you're running in one direction and then you're putting out a fire somewhere else. And all best laid plans are laid to rest but what are the key things, the key daily practices that most lead to your success as a realtor?*

Noah: Being proactive. Before I end one day, I always have a plan for the next day. So I don't wake up in the morning, and think, "Okay, what do I need to do today," I go to my planner and say, "Okay, so this is what I set out yesterday to accomplish today. I will attempt to accomplish that."

Who knows, as you say, how many fires I might have to put out or what have you but you know being proactive has worked very well for me.

Phil/Dan: How can you be flexible enough to adapt to changing circumstances. What are the things that really sharpen the saw for you or really contribute to your success? Would you say exercise or what other things you do consistently, it may not be everyday but certainly on a frequency?

Noah: Monday, Wednesday, Friday I am in the gym. That is part of what keeps me successful so that I have a healthy body, a healthy clearer mind and so that's something that I have structured every Monday, Wednesday, Friday. I have done that for probably the last eight years of my professional career. You have to create structure in your life when you are a real estate agent. That's how I see it obviously, is that you have to create structure, so that's certainly part of what I need to do for myself.

Phil/Dan: So, do you block off the time to do that? It's so easy to say I'm going to exercise three times a week but those three times a week never come. So do you book an appointment with yourself, how do you do that?

Noah: Absolutely. It's probably the standing joke that my clients absolutely will know from me if they are working with me directly that on a Monday, Wednesday or Friday, if they call me between eight and nine thirty in the morning, they will get my voicemail and I will happily call them back as soon as I am available after my gym appointment. That's just a part of who I am, but if something comes up that I have to deal with, obviously, I certainly will.

Million Dollar Agent Key Idea #128

"As unpredictable as real estate is, it is important that you take back control of your time and your life by blocking off time for yourself."

Noah: I really take that time for myself and if you look at some of the top agents like the million dollar guys in New York, what do you see these guys doing? And they are very much younger, you see them reacting if you watch one of those shows and I think to myself, I know what it's like to be there. You know, to say okay all right, I'm very successful but what am I doing for myself? Having the ability to do that, has allowed me to continue to have a successful career.

Phil/Dan: So looking at the top realtors generally, what do you think the top three things that they can do consistently that lead to their success in real estate? If you had to crystallize it to top three things, what would you say they are?

Noah: The first thing would be, being organized, that's what I think the top agents are.

Phil/Dan: *Which by the way, I've never met a realtor that's completely organized. Some do it better than others.*

Noah: Very true, very true.

Phil/Dan: *But that is an admirable thing when they are, believe me.*

Noah: Exactly and I admire that in some of my co-workers who are organized. They have a set plan when they are listing a property, they have a list to check off, so that they know that they are doing, everything appropriately and consistently. I think top agents as well have to be consistent. You have to live up to the image that you've created and that's not always easy for people to do, but I know when I work with other agents or I might work with someone new who says, "Noah, I've never worked with you before but I just spoke to so and so who said that it will just be a wonderful transaction and you are very professional." And I take that as a compliment. I have got a standard that I want to try and meet. So those are certainly two things. A third one is a really good suit.

Phil/Dan: *Right, at least one good suit.*

Noah: At least one good tiger suit, exactly.

Phil/Dan: *I remember the first time I went to speak on Vancouver Island. I think it was in Nanaimo, and I remember two or three people in the audience had on Hawaiian shirts. I was the only guy with a tie on and I looked like the town undertaker that day.*

Noah: I bet you did.

Phil/Dan: *But Victoria is a different animal, you need a suit there given the nature of the market.*

Noah: Everybody has a separate image. So for me, people have an expectation that I will certainly kind of meet that standard. When I bought my first BMW, my very first BMW, I drove into my office and one of my colleagues said to me, "Oh, aren't you afraid of what your clients are going to say, you driving such a nice car?" And I thought no, I want my clients to know that I am going to be successful for them, I am going to put my best foot forward, that's what they expect from me and that's what

I'm going to portray to them. And I haven't wavered from that because I know that people have that expectation of me. I know that they have that and so I want to make sure that they know that I feel successful and that I am going to be successful on their behalf.

Phil/Dan: *And there is also a kind of a subliminal message there that if you don't value who you are, how is someone else supposed to?*

Noah: Agreed. I don't even know when that comment came to me from my colleague, I don't even think I know how to think that way. It was very interesting, it really took me back.

Phil/Dan: *I remember once I went in to buy a suit and the guy that was trying to sell me a suit was wearing a ripped suit and I kept looking at his suit. He wasn't reflective of someone who understood how to wear a suit.*

Noah: It's all about the details and for me that's important, for some other people it might not be. I have met agents at showings and the client says, "Oh, is that the client?" I say "No, I think that's the real estate agent." Oh, they go, "They don't dress like you, Noah" and I go, "Not everybody does." This is how I prefer to dress but everybody is different, thank goodness.

Phil/Dan: *And just for the record, for those people who have never met Noah, he is an immaculate dresser. If anyone should be a television person-ality or anchor, it should be Noah. And I can say that because every time I meet you whether we are having dinner or what have you, I always feel like I have to go back and change.*

You are a well-dressed, well put together gentleman. But Noah, when you first started out in real estate, there were a lot of ways to generate busi-ness, you have farming, for-sale-by-owners and expired listings, specialty referrals or referral and repeat. What did you do to get established, where did you make your money the first year, that wonderful first year you had?

Noah: The wonderful first year, I went out to every person I possibly could know here in Victoria through my previous profession and per-sonally gave some of them business cards, had a conversation with them, took them out for coffee. I went to all of the places that I had received such wonderful service from. So I went to the place where we had the cake baked for our clinic, I went to the restaurants that we used to dine in with all of the celebrities and had all these wonderful wait staff and managers and what have you. And I really spent the first two months of my career making sure that everyone knew I had made this transition in my life to become a real estate agent.

I also went ahead and did some branding which, at the time, a lot of people I worked with said, "How

Million Dollar Agent Key Idea #129

"If you do not value yourself, how is anyone else supposed to?"

much did that cost? Oh my goodness." I felt that I really needed to let people know that I had become a real estate agent and then I followed up with those people, not everybody by any means. But really what happened was that, as I said the first couple of days, somebody had been looking at a home they saw at an open house, didn't have a real estate agent and it was a former server from a high end restaurant that we dealt with here in Victoria and I helped them purchase their first home.

Phil/Dan: *So really it was all about the relationships?*

Noah: All about the relationships - all about the relationships and I felt that I am very personable that I had built some really strong relationships over time and how are any of those people going to know that I have made this transition in my life? Were they going to wait around to hear that I had become a real estate agent or was I going to let them know? And I just started the process of letting people know.

Phil/Dan: *That's brilliant because I often advise new realtors that their business is going to come from the people that they knew before they went into the business and the biggest challenge there, is establishing credibility because they are so new. And they need a strategy for that. And the other one is face-to-face; you combine both of them with what you did. This is really admirable. When you think about all the areas that have generated business throughout your career, what has been the one area that has generated the most business?*

Noah: Two things: open houses, referral and repeat business. Without a doubt and still to this day - I'm just listing a new property this afternoon and I will be in there on Saturday to attempt to get it sold for my client.

Phil/Dan: *So what is your main strategy for communicating with clients? Is it email, social media direct mail, impress and face-to-face telephone? How do you communicate with people generally? I know it probably varies depending on the nature of your relationship but what medium do you use now?*

Noah: Yes, it varies. Real estate has changed a lot; social media is a very big part of what I do now. I have embraced it and love it. Certainly direct mailing has really just continued to form those strong bonds that I had prior to starting with you, Phil. When I look back now on my connections and how I stay connected and communicate, that's certainly part of what I do.

Phil/Dan: Someone asked me the other day what is the difference between email and direct mail when it comes to your clients. I put the question on them, "When you open up an email, where are you when you read that email?" They said, "Well, it's on my smartphone, it could be anywhere." I asked, "Where are you when you open up the piece of direct mail?" They said "I am in my home." And I said, "What are you in the business of buying and selling?" and they said, "Homes." I said, "That is known as associative marketing." You want to deal with people where they are going to use your services. When someone calls me, emails with 12 questions I often call them and address them all in a two minute conversation as opposed to writing a 'gone with the wind' email. Notwithstanding that, you need an email strategy and you need a social media strategy these days. But I think the buzz word is diversification, you can't have all your eggs in one basket; you need to do it all.

Million Dollar Agent Key Idea #130
"If you effectively manage your relationships, the longer you are in real estate, your cost-per-client acquisition goes down as you get more and more business from your previous clients."

Noah: You absolutely can't. If you've been in the industry long enough like I have and I've used different venues for branding and advertising. I often have magazines really trying to get me to come back, and if you are going to put a certain dollar amount into something, you would like to know what the results are. And at this point in my career, I don't feel like I need to do any further branding but I still need to be visible. So I say okay, I have done that for a year and that's great and I have had a wonderful response to it. So what will I do next year, you know to take myself to another level, to create some buzz around who I am. And you have to constantly be thinking about these things.

Phil/Dan: Have you ever analyzed cost-per-client acquisition? It's probably a lot less than it was in the early days, only because you get a lot of referrals because you've reached a certain modicum of past clients, not-withstanding all of the advertising you are doing and which I have seen. Some of the ads you have placed look phenomenal. A lot of your business comes to you by virtue of the relationships you have already established.

Having said that, when you get a lead, someone who doesn't know who you are, maybe they found you via your website, what's your main way of communicating and converting them? I mean how do you convert them from a B list contact to an A list client?

Noah: Generally, with a conversation and a skinny caramel macchiato.

Whenever I am contacted, my first response is always thanking them and if they've contacted me via email or text, I will respond that way because that's their comfort level to start. First of all, I thank them and ask them who referred me. And then ask them how I could communicate with them, do they have a cell number, could I meet them for coffee, etcetera. I take it from the initial contact, and always respect them by contacting back the same way. And then moving it to a way that I can have a face-to-face.

Phil/Dan: *That's such a powerful point, Noah. The best in the field understand it's an escalation process. If it's email they want to escalate the relationship through a voice communication until ultimately you are meeting in person, as opposed to just leaving it online because that's a road that often leads to nowhere.*

Noah: I had a young woman recently who called me about a property I had downtown and just by chance the conditions were coming off that day. But I had a nice conversation with her on the phone. I knew it was a cold call calling from a site, so I wanted to have a bit of a conversation to find out where I am going to go with it or if I could help somewhere. And so that young lady, within one week, I sold her very first condo and her boyfriend, I sold him his very first condo - we close on it this Thursday. And what she said to me while we were sitting in one of the condominiums having a conversation, she said, "You know, I had looked at properties with two other agents; just called and asked if we could see the property. Neither one of those agents asked me what I was looking for. You called me back, told me, I'm sorry, but I have an accepted offer, I will let you know if it doesn't come to fruition, but what are you looking for?" And she said, "And now, you sold the home to myself and my boyfriend."

Phil/Dan: And in addition to that, each one of those relationships have their sphere of influence, people that they know in their age group that will be buying and selling.

Million Dollar Agent Key Idea #131
"Every person you treat well and take care of is an opportunity to be referred business from their friends and family."

Noah: I met both parents, of course, because the parents were helping with the transactions and the father is now considering selling his home, and moving to Vancouver. He would like me to come and value it next week. I am open to all of that because that is what I do for a living, so yes I have this great pool of clientele that has been so good to me and continue to be. But I still need to keep moving forward every day and build new relationships.

Phil/Dan: There is this notion of what I call critical mass point, when you have 50, 100 rock solid relationships and you add to that, even if it's on an incremental basis each and every year. You are there Noah, where you are creating business as you go through life and it is coming to you and it evolves. It's like one relationship leads to a Venn diagram to 10 others but all you have to do is focus on one relationship and provide excellent service to one person at time. And a lot of realtors don't see that, they see it as if they are not going to do something the next 24 hours, they don't look at the long term nature.

Over the 16 years of being in this business, what has been the most successful strategy for you? Of all the strategies, what would you say has been the most successful in generating business?

Noah: I guess the most successful has been taking care of the clients who have taken care of me.

Phil/Dan: So referral and repeat, basically?

Million Dollar Agent Key Idea #132
"One well-taken-care-of client leads to many more down the road."

Noah: Referral and repeat, absolutely. I walk across the street and run into someone I sold a home to 10 years ago, they still know that I am Noah Dobson, their real estate agent and have a lovely conversation. Prior to working with your company, Phil, I would be still making sure that I took care of the people who took care of me. Whether it is a phone conversation, sending them a birthday card, remembering the day that they moved into the home and dropping off a platter, having flowers delivered…

Phil/Dan: *What's interesting, Noah, if you look at the best realtors, how are they supposed to remember? I mean you go to the detail of remembering what type of coffee they have. I mean you can't do that unless you have a photographic memory or something.*

Noah: And I don't, but I have ways of documenting all of that information.

Phil/Dan: *Right, you have a database; you have a system of keeping in touch. A lot of realtors in your position would suffer from what I call realtor guilt because they want to do it but they feel guilty that they can't.*

Noah: I have just managed to give away all of my realtor guilt now. It's gone; I have never had it since I watch people's faces when they speak to me.

Phil/Dan: *Which is such a difficult thing to do?*

Noah: Well it is for a lot of people and I have this ability. Somebody recently was saying to me "Noah, I really want to sit down and talk to you about this; I want to see how it's working for you because I don't have anything, I'm just running around taking care of clients but I don't have anything." And I said, "My philosophy has always been you have to take care of the people who have taken care of you."

Phil/Dan: *I call this the elusive obvious because people look for where their next deal is going to come from. Very often it's in front of you, it's not in the next magazine ad you put out there, and it's in taking care of that person you met at the condo, the person in front of you.*

Noah: Absolutely, absolutely. I dropped off a platter the other day. I double ended a property in my building where I'm currently living, a loft. I sold it to my client 12 years ago and I was helping her move on in her life with pleasure. To help her do that was to sell it to my own client at an open house. And so I made sure that I went down to my favorite place here in Victoria and had something custom made for this client. And those are the details that people remember. I would remember that.

Phil/Dan: *I think Noah you create experiences as well as relationships and you get that.*

Noah: I think that's key. I like a good experience and I guess that's probably what I try and do and often I am very successful, my friend.

Million Dollar Agent Key Idea #133
"Creating great experiences for your clients not only enhances your relationships, it also ensures they will want to work with you again and send you referrals."

Phil/Dan: A new realtor getting in the business will seek your advice and they come to you and say Noah you are successful, you are prosperous. What do I need to do to get to where you are? What do you tell them? What would be the key things that you need to do to get established?

Noah: I recently had this with Dirk in the office who just started into the real estate world coming from a different world and the first thing I said to him was, "You have to get out there, Dirk." Get out there, make sure that you are putting a call out every Monday, page everyone in this office and tell people that you are available. Get out there, meet people, that is the key; people need to know that you are a real estate agent that you are a great guy to deal with. So get yourself out there. And secondly, make a plan, make sure that on Sunday you sit down and say, Okay, this is my week. Make a plan for the week so that you have a focus to know where you want to be on Monday. Do you want to come in and spend three hours in the office? Do you want to come with me and shadow me, working with clients? Really getting yourself out there and having a plan is a really great place to start. You can't sit down and think, "Oh, maybe someone is going to walk in the front door and they are looking for a real estate agent. You have to be proactive.

Phil/Dan: That is very valuable advice. What has changed for those new realtors getting in the industry today? Technology has changed but what do you think the key difference is for those getting in the business today versus 16 years ago?

Noah: The biggest change is the technology. Generally, our practice is pretty much the same; we are still doing the same things. We've changed how we do them now of course, it is computerized. But it's embracing the technology and finding a way for that to fit into your business model. I think for some people if they are second or third career, they may be coming into the industry, they may be well into their 50s and they haven't had the ability to learn about social media, how that works. I think it can be a really big learning curve for people coming into the industry. There is an expectation now.

Phil/Dan: Just on that note one of the intrinsic challenges is because of that technology and the proliferation of information people think they know about as much of the real estate as the realtors themselves. So realtors need to be a step ahead of the curve. You've embraced things like social media, you've embraced technology, and I think that is one of the reasons you are so successful. Let me ask you one final question Noah and I could speak to you for hours. I just want to be very respectful of your time.

Noah: And vice versa.

Phil/Dan: Well, the pleasure is all mine. In your view, when you look to the future of real estate as a profession, what do you see, how do you see it evolving, how do you see it as a bright future? There have been so many changes up until this point in time. What do you see in the future?

Noah: I see great strides in real estate, there will always be ebbs and flows certainly, and that's what comes with the housing market. I think there will be, and I see it already happening, there will again be a paradigm shift sometime in the next 5 to 10 years where we see people really searching out to have more of an experience, be it old school, where there is more personal contact. There is the ability to utilize social media but be able to transition that and have a real conversation, have the ability to sit down and to speak to someone. I don't know how far the technology will go for us in the future and I have had this conversation with other agents, in the last couple of years where people are really searching for that experience, that personal touch. And I think we are going to see a lot more of that.

Phil/Dan: Your insights are bang on here. I look at this one sort of philosophy, the commoditization of real estate where it's 'what do you need a realtor for?' It's a transactional process, and yet there is a yearning. There is a real need, I think it will never stop, the need for true professionals in this business. People that understand as you do Noah, that it's the human element and to be able to help people navigate that process because of the dynamic involved in real estate and the issues that are involved. I think that there will always be a need for true professionals like yourself.

Million Dollar Agent Key Idea #134
"You have to take care of the people who have taken care of you."

And that will never go out of style and I say hallelujah because were it to be an antiseptic transactional process, it would be a great loss to the people, it would be a great loss to the profession and certainly the industry as a whole.

Noah: I absolutely whole heartedly agree with you, and I am certainly working towards that in my personal practice, to really set that standard that doesn't make me invaluable but people feel that I am an invaluable resource to them and that's what I am here to do, and that's what I want to do. And again that has repeated back in my repeat business and I have reaped the benefits of that. So on a personal and professional level and I will continue to strive for that in my career and I respect that and anyone that I am dealing with and I remember that.

Phil/Dan: *In conclusion, although you could retire Noah, I hope that you never do. Because the profession needs you and people like you.*

Noah: I have many, many years, many, many transactions ahead, my friend, before I decide to hang my hat up for sure; I hope, anyway - that's my hope.

Phil/Dan: *I don't think you have anything to worry about where that's concerned. On that note Noah, thank you so much. The pleasure has been all mine and you provided some very valuable insights, more than you realize.*

Million Dollar Agent Key Ideas Summary

$ Being successful in a business where you are your own boss without the structure of working for someone else involves having faith and confidence in yourself.

$ Being the best is doing what you need to do even though you may not always feel like doing it.

$ It is essential that if you want to be the best and do a great job for your clients you need to take care of yourself mentally and physically.

$ Great realtors give a damn about their clients and understand and anticipate the stresses and challenges they face.

$ Truly great realtors are authentic and the same person whether you are dealing with them personally or professionally.

$ As unpredictable as real estate is, it is important that you take back control of your time and your life by blocking off time for yourself.

$ If you do not value yourself, how is anyone else supposed to?

$ If you effectively manage your relationships, the longer you are in real estate, your cost-per-client acquisition goes down as you get more and more business from your previous clients.

$ Every person you treat well and take care of is an opportunity to be referred business from their friends and family.

$ One well-taken-care-of client leads to many more down the road.

$ Creating great experiences for your clients not only enhances your relationships, it also ensures they will want to work with you again and send you referrals.

$ You have to take care of the people who have taken care of you.

GRETA TORLEN:
Offices like Ours, Working with Companies like Yours

GRETA TORLEN IS the Sales & Recruitment Manager for Coldwell Banker Preferred Real Estate in Winnipeg, Manitoba.

Since joining Coldwell Banker in 2012, Greta has brought her more than 30 years sales and professional sales management experience to her position working with real estate sales associates at all stages of their careers. Working to assist them in building rewarding careers, while maintaining personal life balance, is her goal.

Greta's experience has included working in real estate, luxury product sales with individuals and corporate clients, territory sales, national key account management and business development on a global level through the expansion of companies outside of Canada. This has led to the development of a varied skill set and flexibility in understanding the needs of those she works with, as well as the importance of business planning and accountability.

Coldwell Banker Preferred Real Estate has been providing excellence in service to the Winnipeg and area market since 1986 and is a proud member of the one of the largest and most established real estate networks in the world.

Here is what two long-term realtors in her office had to say:

"Greta Torlen is a tremendous support to those new to the market, as well as seasoned agents with years of experience. She has an innate ability to determine the individual's needs, motivations and sensitivities, and presents a clear and concise plan of action that anyone can understand and follow."

> — Marianne Krieger, Realtor,
> Coldwell Banker Preferred Real Estate.

"Greta is detail orientated. She has so many people to keep on track on a daily basis and she does so with amazing accuracy. When asked a question she will have the answer ready from her vast professional experience or if not she will have it for you within the day. She never seems overwhelmed at any prospect given to her, she goes to work and gets it done and moves on. She has the ability to minimize mammoth problems and put them in perspective while keeping you focused on the task at hand. Her motto - "put it in the rear-view mirror" - has become a favorite quote for many of us, and it works! We are all very lucky to have this professional working with us."

> — Diane Graumann, Realtor,
> Coldwell Banker Preferred Real Estate.

GRETA TORLEN IS a wonderful example of a sales manager who not only understands what it takes to be successful in the real estate business, she also has the knowledge, practical experience and ability to coach and mentor her agents to achieve their own success. In addition to having successfully bought and sold real estate, she has vast multi-industry managerial and sales expertise. She knows exactly what it takes to be successful and prosperous in real estate and personally works with all her agents to ensure that they have a clear vision and strategic plan for their business. She holds her agents accountable, thereby ensuring that they achieve their desired outcomes. Greta is a true model of excellence in what she does and with whom many valuable lessons can be learned.

Phil/Dan: Good morning, Greta. How are you?

Greta: I'm very well, thank you. How are you?

Phil/Dan: Excellent. First of all, we want to thank you very much for doing this. Initially, we spoke when I was last in Winnipeg and this is a follow-up interview. So, we appreciate you taking the time to do this. And out of respect for your time, we'll be as succinct as possible. But we really value your expertise because for those of you who have never met Greta, Greta is a tour de force. She's a wonderful mentor, coach, trainer, who works for Coldwell Banker in Winnipeg, Manitoba and she does some fabulous things for their agents and really helps them optimize their success. So we're glad you're taking the time to do this because we want to capture some of your insights, Greta, in terms of what the best realtors do, what you've observed the best realtors do. But let's start off with a little about you. Greta, what did you do before you went into real estate?

Greta: I worked as a sales manager, trainer, and recruiter for an international optical company. I also maintained a territory in the Caribbean and South Central America that actually provided me with access to 23 countries on a regular basis for several months of the year. I did all of our trade shows in Europe, as well as North America, and designed all of the programs and marketing strategies.

Phil/Dan: Wow. You know, if you ever want to learn about how to handle jet lag, Greta is the person to speak to because you're amazing. When you described what you did when you worked for the optical company between time zones and meeting with doctors in various countries often with little sleep, it's just amazing. You're talking with somebody who travels a couple months a year within North America, but when you look at your experience from an international context, it's absolutely amazing. You've got vast sales experience. You've also bought and sold real estate as well back some time ago now.

Greta: I did, many years ago I worked as a realtor in the city and worked on condo projects as well as new-builds and resell properties during a time that interest rates were very high. Market was difficult. Let's say people always have to remember that people need a place to live and real estate will always buy and sell. No matter what the market conditions are, there is a living to be made and a career to be built within whatever is going on in the economy.

Phil/Dan: *You certainly have a unique role now within Coldwell Banker, not only in Winnipeg but you're often called upon across the country and internationally for your expertise on helping to train agents. How would you describe your role now in Winnipeg? What do you do in terms of your day-to-day functions within the Coldwell Banker office there?*

Greta: Well, it's an interesting thing. It changes all the time. I think that's because I take myself wherever I go. And one of the big things that I've always believed in is accountability. I've helped develop accountability programs for every company that I've worked for and making people accountable when they're on the road and away from their homes.

It's a lot more difficult than I believed, having realtors become accountable for their actions. I spend my days, every day, meeting with as many of our people in-house as I possibly can. I structure training days within our office. I run our sales meetings, which is very important. It's not about selling, pitching a product or just covering housekeeping from the board, but there actually has to be something that helps these people to elevate their actual sales and skills and professionalism. So for me, that's critical and very important especially when you're working with agents that are starting out or trying to boost their career to another level.

Phil/Dan: *And a lot of people go into real estate and it's a business and they often know what they should be doing but they don't often do it. And when you're faced with a situation where you*

Million Dollar Agent Key Idea #135
"Being accountable for yourself and your actions is so important to creating a successful and consistent real estate business."

live and die by your own success by what you do or don't do on a consistent basis. I think the notion of having someone not only provide you with the skills and knowledge, what you so effectively do with your agents, but to hold them accountable is so important. This is the whole value of coaching, oftentimes, the agents know what to do but they don't do it, and to have someone hold them accountable for those necessary things that will lead to their success. Having spoken to thousands, worked with thousands of agents throughout my career, it's absolutely invaluable. That is critically important.

Greta: I think that this is a business, unfortunately, where there's no actual vetting process. Nobody interviewed you in a constructive way. And one of the things that we do is, if we're lucky enough to get a hold of them before they even start with registering for the course, I ask them a lot of questions. I want to know about their background. It shouldn't be just filling a body into an office and then saying what your success rate is and covering of your failures with volume.

If your people are not succeeding, you're actually failing as well, not just them. So I think it's important that when you're talking about accountability that you make yourself accountable, whether it's getting them through the course, whether it's getting them started out in the right direction, whether it's helping them to reach the numbers that you had helped them to set for themselves because one of the key ingredients when you're coaching people is to actually have goal setting and business planning. When you're that person that is helping them to reach, assess their goals. You have to have a plan in place for what you're going to do to help them achieve it.

Phil/Dan: *That involves seeing their potential or what they're capable of even when they don't yet see it them themselves, because you have the larger picture in mind. You see agents come in all excited about real estate. They don't necessarily have the skills which you impart but you help shape them and mold them and help them believe in themselves and see what's possible when they may not see it yet. It's a very daunting thing when a realtor gets their license and they have all these expenses and they don't have any business, a lot of them don't make it through that initial phase, they don't last. Especially if it was not a good market when they started.*

Greta: They absolutely have to know what to do from day one. I try very, very hard to have them so organized that by the day that they're done writing their exam, before they've even done the orientation or have their license in place, we have a set of tasks that have been completed so that on the day that they start here, they know exactly what they're doing, they know what direction they're going, instead of standing like a deer in the headlights saying what direction do I go now. There is just not enough of that in the industry.

Our offices that have a training program, they wait till they have a number of people to fill a class, and they might have one of their top producers do it when it works for them. There's a variety of ways that they do it, but I don't think that they sit down and make sure that they have the structured system that works for each and every person.

Phil/Dan: *Let me ask you, Greta. What would you say are the biggest challenges faced by brand new agents?*

Greta: I think that the group challenges are they don't have business yet so they lack confidence. They have a difficult time often engaging in the conversations that lead to people having the confidence in them to try to buy or sell their homes through them. They need to have a strong set of scripts to allow them the dialogue to put them forward in the industry to allow people to have confidence in their abilities and they don't have it in themselves yet.

So you actually have to give them enough information and enable them with the right tools, the right materials that give them the confidence to go forward. And I think that is overcoming the biggest challenge that every one of them has. They show up, they have their new phone. They may or may not have a new computer. They often don't know how to use it depending on what career they came from and they don't really know what they're doing. They have absolutely no idea what to do.

So I think if you set them down and you have them systematically do everything, from let's sit down and find out who do you know, what do you belong to, start building a database and giving them an actual task sheet that they have to complete every day. And then sitting down and going through that task sheet at the end of the week and figuring out what worked for them, what didn't work for them, what they did complete, what they avoided? Because that is one of the biggest challenges, is when you don't have confidence you will avoid tasks that you find unpleasant or uncomfortable. And you have to teach people not to be frozen by fear.

Phil/Dan: *That's interesting. I think there's a couple of things you touched upon, Greta, that I just want to elaborate on, because there are just golden nuggets there. One of them is, it's one thing having the skills to do something but it's also the self-belief. It's the self-confidence. It's believing in themselves. It begs the question, how are their clients or potential clients going to have confidence in them in their ability if they don't truly believe in their own capabilities? And I think having someone like you help install that or instill that in them is invaluable. They're not mutually exclusive, you need both.*

You need knowledge of what to do and how to do it in a direction. But there's also that notion of they need to believe in themselves. You get that through experience, obviously, after succeeding and failing over time. But it's nice to have someone coach you and guide you to expedite that. I think that's so very, very important. But also, you touched upon the need to confront your fear. That goes hand-in-hand with self-belief and confidence. It's very scary. It's very scary to do things that you haven't done before, especially for the first time in a sales context. There's often fear of rejection and all those things. And I guess you must deal with that on a regular basis.

> ### Million Dollar Agent Key Idea # 136
> *"One of the absolute keys to a realtor's success is not only to acquire the knowledge and skills to be successful but also the self-confidence and self-belief in order to apply the knowledge and skills that they have obtained."*

Greta: Well, I had an interesting thing occur last week, for the very first time. I've been in this office now for over three years. And for the very first time last week, one of the shareholders for the company brought forward a candidate and asked if he could sit in on my interview and presentation. And I've never had that. I've never actually had anyone audit what I do. And it was interesting because I thought about it in advance and I thought to myself, "Well, how am I going to feel about that? Will it affect my presentation to this person? Will it affect my ability to draw the right information to ensure that they're right candidate for us and that we're the right fit for them?" Because I do not believe that everybody should be grabbing at agents and just filling up a roster. I really do believe that you should be looking for fit, and I think that it affects your office culture. So I thought, "Will this affect my decision-making?"

And it was very interesting for me because that was my big concern with how it would affect me. We all have that little moment of hesitation where we feel somewhat thrown off our game. And I've always had control in these things. Now, I have an agent that's been in the business for 30 years and that shareholder and the company that I work for sitting in and watching and observing this? It didn't bother me at all. I used a really strong visual aid. I have really good materials. I'm consistent and know exactly what I'm going to say to people, what I'm going to ask of them and I know what I'm going to discuss about our company.

And I think that having people prepared and ready to set out, whether it's on a listing call or working with the buyer, having them have a set of questions, having them understand what they're going to do to present their value, I think does the exact same thing as what this did for me, is that it removes the fear. And you don't know until you try it, how much that will benefit you, by being prepared for everything that you do and knowing your materials so well that you're not going to falter. This is critical to the success of a new agent, someone that's at the middle of their career or someone that's been in the business for decades.

Phil/Dan: *So, there are some universals here that transcend whether someone is new or experienced. And just to reiterate, continually refining your skills, being prepared, leads to more self-belief even though we have fears, but helps manage them. Think about the more experienced agent, an agent that you've observed that's been in the business for, say, 10, 20 years, sometimes longer, what are their greatest challenges?*

Greta: I find that depending on when they got into the business, it's adapting to change because they get very set in their ways. They've come into an industry in the last say decade or 15 years, it's been so solid. We haven't had any major downs but we've certainly had some ups. And it's interesting to see how they react to fluctuations in the market with panic and fear, which has been a surprise to me.

These people were here before I came on board or if I'm getting

Million Dollar Agent Key Idea # 137

"Whether you are new to real estate or have been in the business for years, it is very important that you continually learn and grow and challenge yourself. It is very easy to slip into a comfort zone and ultimately the amount of business you have will reflect this."

them from other offices, I again, have to work on their mindset as well. But for the ones that are in our office, just probably having them adapt to change, also to taking on new ideas, I find they do get very comfortable and very settled in things and they've been doing it over and over again. And the times are changing, and I find that depending on what age group they're in, will depend also on what their challenges are, but I would have to say change.

Phil/Dan: *People will often say people seek change and then resist it because they don't want things to be too the same. But being in a comfort zone, it's very easy to get in a rut. That's what I term in real estate where you reach a certain modicum of success and then we look at the dynamics of the industry in the last 10, 15 years that have been incredible. And then when you factor in technological change on top of that, it's pretty amazing.*

There's been some huge 'ifs'. Manitoba, where you're from, is the most stable real estate market in the country. It has its ups and downs but relative to Toronto and Vancouver which tend to oscillate more frequently. It still can be quite traumatic being open to change, so how do you deal with that? When you're dealing with an agent that's in their comfort zone, they know they have to change because the ground is shifting under them, how do you deal with them? How do you get them to deal with the fears surrounding that?

Greta: If they're an existing agent that was in our office and you have to say, when I came onboard here we did our business very differently as well. I had to not only find ways to change how they think about their business but also to accept some of the ideas that I have. And for those agents that are the ones that you're really speaking of – and I do agree, they get complacent and they get comfortable. They make more money than they did in their previous life and then they come and sit there. So they have not been through a terrible, terrible market yet, like where some of the older agents that are really the top producers started in a really difficult market.

And if you can succeed in that, you're going to ride to the top and stay there. So that's almost like a gift that happened to them. But for these agents that started off when things were very stable or on the upswing in our economy, they get very comfortable because now they're making more money than they did at their previous jobs but they're also not planning for any change. So they get very stuck. So it's one at a time again, I do these things that I do as an accountability sales manager that believes in accountability coaching. I try as much as I can to have conversations with them and I try with them to make very small steps.

I introduce ideas often through our sales meetings where I have our top producers speak or I will ask someone who's just had an innovative idea that's doing something well for them at that time, something where they can hear about an experience from another agent. If it's something that I feel that should be brought in or implemented that isn't really being done by realtors at this time, I will ask somebody to participate. It's sort of like a test run for my idea, and I will try it out and then have them speak at the sales meeting. And then I'll target those people that are sitting in the middle.

We also are very blessed within our Coldwell Banker network to have a program called Boost which is really all about taking people from one level to the next. And again, it gets them very accountable for their actions. These people that sit in the middle, they don't like accountability. So they don't want people to know how much TV they watch or how many days off they take or how early they knock off or how late they start, they're still making decent money. They're still paying their bills. Their families aren't starving. They're doing okay. But they would not weather a storm well, if they don't do something different going down the road. So what you're basically trying to do is get them to change their mindset, take it up a notch and maybe have a look at every part of their businesses.

Some of them may have systems in place but they're not really watching them very carefully. So it's, again, evaluating what they're doing, evaluating what systems they're using, having to make a change from that. I've created a great system for people to use within our office to do everything from tracking their numbers, tracking their expenses, comparing what their return on investment is, and looking really strongly at evaluating what they do.

And a lot of the mid-line agents again, they're the ones that will throw the bus bench advertisements up that they think are getting them business. They don't really realize that you have to be totally multimodal in order to have the successful marketing campaign work for you. So, it's basically the biggest thing that I have to do with them is change their mindset and have them look at things bit by bit by bit, and bring them along. But it takes time and patience, and most sales managers won't have it and if they've got a sales manager that's a top producing agent, they're not doing that for them, either.

Phil/Dan: *Or they're too focused on their own business.*

Greta: Absolutely.

Phil/Dan: *There are a couple of things I want to highlight, and one is change – not only is it is essential but it needs to be incremental. To do cataclysmic change all at once is often too daunting for most agents caught in a comfort zone. So I think what you're doing is very important, starting with the right mindset. Again, if they don't have the right mindset, they'll revert back to their old behavioral patterns.*

Million Dollar Agent Key Idea #138
"Successful behaviours that lead to positive results begin with a success mindset."

Greta: And you have to find a change that you know is going to bring a result for them. That's how you have to start them off. You have to feed it to them. So when you start off making a change on how they do their business, you have to figure out something that they're doing that you think that if they'd changed slightly, would give them a positive result. Because people are results-driven, they're not driven by a pat on the back. They're results-driven. Especially people who work on commission, they want to make more money. So if they do something small or one change that results in something, where they're seeing a difference fairly quickly, then you've got them on a hook, and it's basically baiting fish.

Phil/Dan: *Interesting. So small successes, in succession, lead to larger successes rather than try to go for everything all at once. And that's very, very important. And seeing the results of that which in and of itself becomes a motivator to do things different. Greta, if you look at the top agents that you've observed over the years, at their conferences, being in your office, the agents that do well consistently year after year after year, what I call the top 10%.*

What would you say drives them to take their business to the next level? What is their motivation? I spoke to a realtor in Edmonton and he said, "Well, I'm doing a half a million dollars, this year I want to make a million dollars in sales." What do you think drives the top agents to take their business higher when they're already doing well?

Greta: I think they have a natural mindset that they need to see their business going up, because oftentimes the guy that's making 500 thousand and goes to 700 and up to a million, doesn't change his home, doesn't change his car, he saves a lot. He maintains the same number of weeks off every year. And that's the one of the things that we've really noticed with some of the top producers in our market is that not much changed within their lifestyle.

They are making a lot more money but it seems to me—and perhaps they're giving it to their church or whatever they're doing, I have no clue what they do with it in terms of that,—but I think for them that they are so results-driven and so success-oriented. And they never allow themselves to become complacent and they never allow that little tiny bit of fear that things might end if you don't continue on an upward swing. I think that they allow just enough fear into their lives and then just enough insecurity to keep them chasing that rabbit.

Phil/Dan: There's a great metaphor for this, that in ancient Roman times, they use to give the victors, glad-iators in battle, a crown of thorns to wear on their head. And one of the reasons they did that with thorns was so that they would never let their victories go to their head and they'd always feel that edge to want to take things to the next level.

Million Dollar Agent Key Idea # 139
"Successful realtors never rest on their laurels no matter how well they are doing."

And I think that if you look at the best of the best, they're not compla-cent. They realize there's something within them, this fire that burns within that drives them to the next level even though from outside appearances, you'd say, "Well, if I was making a half a million, I would be pretty satisfied." You're either growing or expanding or you're deteriorating. No one stays the same. In other words, you can't stay the same in what you do, you have to both grow and expand in your horizons or you're deteriorating over time.

Greta: I totally agree. These are the same people that never lose their rou-tines. They get up in the

Million Dollar Agent Key Idea # 140
"You're either growing or expanding or deteriorating."

morning, if they workout it helps to get their day going. And I do find that they're very, very structured whether with their fitness routines, with their diet, with getting enough sleep, they're very, very focused people, and it's a part of how they live their life. They schedule very well their personal time. They're just very, very focused people and it's something that I greatly admire. And interestingly, you often see them with large teams. One of the top producers in our office and who this past year was given an award for being in the top 10, I think he was seventh in Canada for units sold for Coldwell Banker Canada.

He does every single transaction, does every detail himself. He has no assistance. He takes care of everything. He's extremely detail-oriented. He has an unbelievably high level of customer service and satisfaction. And something that he feels that he has, that's the only way that he can accomplish it. The way it needs to be done is to do it all himself.

He stills manages to maintain a personal life, he has a family. I find that people that are successful at that level are successful at everything that they do.

Phil/Dan: It's cross-contextual. Let's break that down a little bit. If you look at the top 10% of realtors, the best realtors, one of the things you'd mentioned is that they do things in a specific way, they have routines. In other words, they have certain, perpetual behavioral patterns or perpetual habits. What would you say they are?

Greta: They're incredibly good at time management. I did a talk recently to a group of women regarding time management incorporating the talk that I was doing in our office, because time management is something that we all struggle with. Top producers struggle with it a little bit less because they never, ever go off of the schedule. And I think that they manage their time extremely well. They schedule things in such a way, they don't treat their phones like a fire alarm. They make sure that everything that needs to be done for their business is done so that they stay away from becoming transactional. In their personal life and their professional life, everything they do is in accordance to a schedule that works for them. I do believe time management is the key. That would probably be the greatest crossover with each and every one of them.

Million Dollar Agent Key Idea #141
"Success has a structure and one of the best ways to learn this structure is to model those realtors that are already successful."

Phil/Dan: You know, it's interesting you should say that. They interviewed Bill Clinton once and asked him, what was one of the books that inspired him as he was developing himself. There was a book written and I think it was in the '70s, called, "Take Back Control of your Life". It's about time management. The exact title escapes me, but once he got it, he needed to control his time and value time and control his life. Everything else fit into place and a lot of things are intrinsic in that. I think that if you look at the best, what I've observed is they're not reactive, they're proactive.

They pre-plan the structure, how they want things to go. One agent I interviewed said, he blocks off so much time to do prospecting, and then he blocks off a certain amount that he's going golfing later on that day and he doesn't deviate. There are certain things that come up from time to time but he is not at the whim of whatever happens. And I think if you look at a lot of agents, they're very reactive. The phone rings and it's like a fire alarm going one direction and they're often in the other direction. And before they know it, they've lost a day, they've lost a week, they've lost a month, and they haven't really accomplished a lot.

Greta: It's interesting because I have one of our new agents that started with me in the last couple of months. And he started off, immediately had three listings. So he's very good at the first few weeks when he wasn't so busy, coming to training and following all the rules, and doing everything and all of a sudden he's busy and he's running around. He's not really getting a lot done. And of course, they take listings, they don't necessarily sell or they're harder than they thought. And then at end of it, once they sold those three listings, they might have picked up a buyer or two and did that also. So you have four or five transactions out of the way and then it all stops, because they've done absolutely nothing to build a business.

Phil/Dan: *Right. And that is so important. And I think if you look at the top agents, they're always seeding the future with their current behaviors. So they're not just involved to what I call client maintenance activities which can feel good and distraction where they think that they're busy, they make this linear projection that the world is going to be like that forever, and they go from a period of intense activity to no business. So, by managing their time and realizing they have to dedicate so much of that time to prospecting, so much of that time to future business as well as dealing with current business goes a long way. That's very, very, very important. What else on the behavioral level? What are other characteristics of top agents?*

Greta: I think what they do is involve themselves in their community. They join things. They definitely don't see themselves as an island of real estates. In order to be somebody that is going to build a business that has that level of success, they don't ever forget where they came from. We have set a prime example of one of the best networkers I've ever seen in my life as a realtor in our office. He's amazing to me. And you wouldn't expect that necessarily when he's around the office, but he goes to every conference, love that.

Million Dollar Agent Key Idea #142

"The top realtors understand that even though they are very busy now, they must still do the key activities they need to ensure they have a steady stream of business in the future."

And when you see him at a conference, it's amazing to watch the way he works. He never sits around with the same group of people. He's constantly meeting new people. And if you're out somewhere and you run into him in the public setting, he's doing the same thing. He's constantly meeting, seeding, basically.

It isn't all about advertising. He shows up at hockey games for teams that his kids no longer play because he knows parents of children who were a little younger starting in. He maintains contact with people. He maintains that, but on the personal level, as opposed to just sending something out he's constantly maintaining personal contact. And he'll sponsor things. He belongs to business clubs. That's how he basically builds a business, not just being known as the realtor but as their friend and someone that they can connect with. And I think that's really important. He's truly a good neighbor. I don't know how else to say it.

Phil/Dan: *You've said it so eloquently, Greta, I think there's a couple of things here. I think one of the first things a lot of the good agents realize is that it's not all about the money. It's about giving back to community. It's about being other-focused as opposed to always self-focused. The money in and of itself, once you get to be at a certain modicum of financial success, that's not motivating at all.*

I once interviewed a billionaire, or pretty close to it. He said something interesting — very profound. He said you can only eat so many nice meals, you can only wear so many nice clothes, and you can only live in so many nice houses and drive so many nice cars and after that it is all about giving back. That has the most meaning. If you look at the top realtors they involve themselves in giving to others whether it is through their community, sports teams. And that involvement actually comes back. So having that sense of 'other' focus is really, really critical.

Greta: I think it is. Just understanding that this is all about relationships and finding ways to seek those relationships out build upon them and develop more. So I think that that is what good realtors do. I think strong realtors are out in the community.

Phil/Dan: *And let me ask you, Greta. How do the best realtors from your perspective, how do they think differently than those that are struggling?*

Greta: I'm very proud to say that in three years I've only had one that's left the industry.

Phil/Dan: *That's as much to your credit.*

Greta: It's something I'm proud of and I lose sleep over that one because I think that she has so, so much potential. She just wouldn't do what had to be done. And I think to myself maybe there was something else that could have been done to help her.

Phil/Dan: *Obviously, there were mitigating circumstances that probably led to that decision. When you think of the best agents, how do they think differently?*

Greta: I think that they know that they have to be working hard constantly for success. I think there're still some out there that are very much about vanity in the marketplace. But I think the really, really, truly successful ones that manage their life as well as they manage their business, have really put their ego aside and they know it's about hard work and they work very, very hard.

I think they're also very generous and they are also helpful with the new people that are starting out. I rely upon them to do as much mentorship and to assist me in training as possible. And I reach out to them and they seem to be very kind and good about sharing their insight. Some of what they do is different than what I would do. But again, if you ask for help, you take what you get. And it's interesting what evolved from that.

I think that they are very, very much focused on their business, and they put aside some of their ego. I think that they have to because what happens with a lot of them when they start to reach success, and you see it a lot with young agents, if they come in and things go really, really well for them right away, they get very, very excited but they also get that little bit of cockiness and arrogance that comes with that and then you just have to wait. You have to wait till they hit a wall.

And then just call them when you know things are starting to freak them out and it does really fast, these things usually happen within the space of a month. You make that call and say, "Okay, are you ready to talk?" And I think that for them, these are good lessons that they learned along the way because that will help them to be better when they have really failed at business and if they have worked hard to get to the level that your top producers are at.

Phil/Dan: I've met a lot of ego-based realtors in my time but I think the best ones that truly are really successful have evolved beyond that. Oftentimes, they're very humble and oftentimes they are not as ego-based as they were in their early years. Maybe it's part of a maturation process, but I've noticed the top realtors are really more relationship-focused as opposed to ego-focused.

I think that comes with time but often comes through surviving failures and realizing and being humbled by them because, when you're used to a lifestyle very quickly and then everything is dependent on a certain modicum of success and then you have periods of difficulty, it can really moderate one's thinking. I know I've lived through that many times.

Million Dollar Agent Key Idea # 143
"The best and most successful agents are the ones that do the most transactions and actually keep the money in their pockets to create referral business for themselves and build relationships with people."

Greta: I actually do, every once in a while, a sales meeting on the satisfaction of failure.

Phil/Dan: Yes, because we learn more from that than we do from our successes because we make this linear projection but it's not going to be that way all the time. Greta, when you think about the top agents again and there are so many ways to create revenue or revenue streams in real estate. There's farming, there's FSBOs, there's expired listings, there's specialty referrals, there's referral and repeat, and there is website lead generation - you would refer to this as one needs to be multimodal. Do they do it all?

Obviously some realtors have preferences for one or the other. What are the strategies that you have seen top agents use most consistently?

Greta: The best agents and most successful agents are the ones that do the most transactions and actually keep the money in their pockets to create referral business for themselves and build relationships with people. Multimodal campaigns are very important. And we have to think in terms of there have to be face-to-face components in there. There has to be typically something that you're doing with the mail components, where they're getting something from you, handwritten notes are amazing or a card.

If you are to send a Christmas card and actually sign it instead of stamp it or something, it's personal. It's amazing how that makes people feel, just a little note inside of a card during the holidays, whatever the holiday is, acknowledging someone that you're thinking about them. Keeping in touch with them when you have a spare moment, sitting down with your list of people and actually making phone calls and just checking in with them, you won't tell who's got a good reception, you won't tell who's got a hold with people but at least you're reaching out.

I think if you look at the people that you've done business with the most over the years especially if you've been in business a long time, some things get harder and harder to do with time. But, you know, if periodically, you say, "Okay, well, these people have been in this house for three, four years," the average person moves every five years, I should send them a little quick CMA and what the value of their home is, using different contact that you could have that actually gives something back to them as opposed for you asking for something from them.

And I think that if you're able to maintain that contact with people over the years, check and see how they're doing once in a while, I think it's very important. I think having a setup with the referral marketing system that sends out a valuable piece to them but they can read. And again it's addressed to them. It's very, very important. All of these things are important components of a multimodal campaign.

I'm a big believer in social media and I think social media does a lot for both the agent and for the client. You're allowed to share information as well as successes so people know what's happening in your life, and you should still keep the social in it and let them know a little bit about yourself. And that's one of the big things that social media does. It allows people to connect with you without you having to be constantly keeping in touch with them by phone calls, at every other outlet. But it also allows you an opportunity to see what they are doing. It allows you to keep track of their children when their children are growing up, when they're being born, if they're getting married, if there's something new that's happening, because people post their lifetime events.

Lifetime events mean change. Change means home-selling is on. So I think that by building relationships, we actually care about what's happening in their life. You're actually able to serve them in a way that helps and assist them into the next step that they have for their own life-planning.

Million Dollar Agent Key Idea #144
"If you don't have enough business, you need to go out and make more friends."

Phil/Dan: *What I've observed when an agent starts having the business, they've got to do it all in a way. They don't have any past clients and they get to business oftentimes through their generalized sphere of influence, people that have never done business with them, and also through face-to-face and other mediums. And they often have to engage in more what I would refer to as commodity-based strategies because they just don't have a lot of people that they can call upon for business.*

And then as time evolves and they get a certain number of clients over time, they evolve to become more relationship-based as you're describing. They get to this place which I call a critical mass where they have enough relationships, whereby if they focused on enhancing them and working with this sphere of influence, the business more and more comes to them. Then their cost-per-client acquisition goes down because commodity-based strategies tend to be a whole lot more expensive than relationship-based. Have you noticed that sort of a trajectory that naturally occurs with the top agents?

Greta: I see top agents in our marketplace that are absolutely blowing their brains out without protesting. They can't get enough of their selves out in the marketplace. And I think to myself, certainly, they're probably getting some business with that but what is that costing them?

Phil/Dan: *The cost-per-client acquisition.*

Greta: I don't encourage that actually with new agents, even. If they want to do something in a small farm area, that's up to them. And of course we've got agents that go against this with me and they'll ask me to help them with the piece and I do. But it's really not what I've approved of at all. I think they should be getting out and meeting more people.

Million Dollar Agent Key Idea #145
"People do business with a realtor based on trust and likeability but most importantly based on their knowledge and expertise. Both are essential for a realtor to be successful."

There's a great trainer that I've seen speak many times. And I really like what he says. He says, "If you don't have enough business, you need to go out and make more friends." And I think that at the end of the day, what did it cost you to get one client with your advertising and how much energy were you using chasing bad leads that came from pieces that you mailed out to people that are not qualified in any way that you have no knowledge of? Or if you could be spending your time and your efforts being involved in activities that are going to bring you people that are already getting a sense of who you are. And I'm so glad, no matter where they are in their career, whether they're beginning, middle, or end, I'm really not all that in favor of a lot of advertising.

Phil/Dan: *Commodity-based marketing is very expensive and then you're also competing with every other realtor in town. You're also competing based on price as opposed to when someone calls you from a referral of your pre-existing relationship, you're having a different conversation. And I often say, Greta, people do business with the realtor based on two funda-mental reasons. One, they know, like and trust them. But based on their knowledge and expertise, not liking and trusting someone isn't enough, they also have the perception that person will be able to assist them in buying and selling a property and selling your house at an optimum price.*

Greta: And you've got to do both, you're dealing with people in real estate at a time of great change when you're the facilitator, so having the relationship skills, having to trust people is so critically important. And you can't convey that in a generalized ad in a magazine somewhere.

If you have any kind of difficulty making new friends or finding ways to converse, there's Toastmasters, there are things they can do to hone that skill. I would rather see them focused on building a database with people they're meeting face-to-face out there.

I don't care if you meet them at the grocery store, but at least you're going to have a conversation with somebody that can get a sense of who you are and vice versa. And maybe you go to your neighborhood. I'd rather see them knock on every single door, up and down by a listing that they have in an area that they've worked in regularly and get to know the neighbors. And you know what, it doesn't always work but you're going to eventually meet somebody and have a conversation with them.

If you put a for-sale sign on a lawn and sell it really quickly, it's like a virus in the area. Once that sell sign goes up, everyone starts listing, why wouldn't someone list with you. Build a relationship with those people, invite them to a pre-open house because you really don't want the neighbors in your open house talking about what was going on in that house, what kind of stories they're going to tell. So, I'll say invite them, give them a special invitation. Get to know people in the area that you've got your listings and find that to be a way that you can build your database, as well.

People will want to talk to you if you treat them as though they're special and you're interested in them. And you can build a database from a variety of sources. Join an organization or do something else, but I will never, ever, ever be an advocate for advertising.

Phil/Dan: I once heard a great sales-trainer say the mark of a good salesperson is when they are flying from one city to another, sitting in an airplane, and they have a genuine interest in the life of the person sitting beside them. They're curious and they want to know about that person and have the inclination to spark up a conversation. That's not something that most people will do, but I think the best realtors do. I think the ones that are curious, they like people. I know it's simplistic but it's very, very important.

Million Dollar Agent Key Idea #146
"To be successful in sales you need to be curious and really like people."

It's so important for an agent if they're going to build their business based on relationships to maintain a database. If you're going to do door-knocking, you're going to meet people, you need to take that information and put it somewhere because you can't keep it in your head. The transactional realtors try and remember all these things and even the best memory experts can't do that.

Greta: And I think your system has to include everything from contacts to sheets and letters in your database, on your phone that you're using, and syncing it to your computer or if you're using paper, there has to be a component of getting as much information as possible. If you go to their home and you don't know their last name, it shows that you really aren't paying attention.

Do you have their e-mail address? Their phone number? If you're going to operate a business, you need to have phone and complete address, you need their email address, you need their full names, you need to find a bill that Mr. and Mrs. have the same last name. There are a variety of things that you must ask and just ask the questions when you're speaking to them.

It has to be multimodal. You have to be able to provide information. They're going to be opening an email from you when they requested information from you. They can't request it if they don't know what you do. So they need to receive it at their home. You need to have everything about these people.

So when I sit down with our new people and I ask them to bring me their database, I'm always surprised. "Okay, but that's not a real address. That's from your Facebook." What you can do is compose on Facebook that you're going to be sending out a newsletter whether it's monthly, bimonthly, quarterly, and that you would like to have their complete contact information including their email address in case you want to send anything that way. And I said it's surprising when we have our agents do that. We had one agent that had 100% response from 136 requests for contact information.

We never had anyone unsubscribe because she carefully plans what she's sending out to them. This one young one that just joined us recently, was shocked. He said he was very scared to call people. And I said you are not leaving this office today until you phoned everybody on that list to verify contact information and fill in the blanks of what you're missing. When he finished he said, everyone was so nice and I have an appointment. It's a miracle to talk to people. It doesn't really hurt.

Million Dollar Agent Key Idea #147

"A proper database needs to include all kinds of information - names of spouse and children, physical mailing address, as well other information if possible - like birthdays, anniversaries, mortgage renewal dates."

Phil/Dan: *As simplistic as that sounds, that's pretty amazing.*

Greta: Yeah, it's really amazing. That allows you to connect with them and then you follow that up with a really good marketing piece to them that's valuable, that gives them something that they're looking for, everybody wants to know what's happening in the marketplace. They'll want to know what their home is worth; there are certain things they want from you. So send it out once in a while. Let them know what's happening.

Phil/Dan: *That is so important. In terms of the strategies used by agents that are successful, they're client-focused. They're providing them knowledge and their expertise. They've got a database. They've got their method* *in terms of gathering information and putting it in one place with fol-low-up, which is the opposite of what unfortunately most agents do. Most agents are transactional. They don't do this. As simplistic as it sounds, they often say some of the greatest truths in life are simple. People tend to overcomplicate things. What has changed in the real estate business today from say 20 years ago?*

Greta: The way that the public wants their services delivered. And I think that has changed. Whether or not it sells their home, they want to see the services delivered in a different way. They want to know that you are marketing their home, mass marketing their home online. They want to know that it's being marketed in print. They want to know that it's being marketed in person. So the way that you deliver services today and the level of professionalism that is expected from agents today, is much greater than it once was.

Million Dollar Agent Key Idea #148

"What has changed today is the level of professionalism that is expected from agents that justify the commissions that they make."

They want everything that they want from print materials. Everything on down has to be sleeker. They want to know that they are getting something for the high commissions that are being paid out. It used to be that you put a sign on the lawn and had the broker's company name on it. It didn't even have the agent's name on it. That's what sold real estate. It's very unusual. And things have changed to everything being much more professional in the industry right down to the way that the realtor presents themselves. But it's very, very important for the realtor to have a presentation. In video, in print, in an email format, you have to be able to deliver service in a way that the consumer wants it.

Phil/Dan: That is such a critical point, Greta. The realtors have to portray themselves in a very highly professional way because all they've really got is the relationship they have with people and their expertise, the ability to package that information in ways that create value for people. And I think this is so important that a realtor understands what their value proposition is. And part of that is in their ability to take the information that are out there and present it in a way that assists their clients in making wise deci-sions. Would you agree with that?

Greta: Oh, absolutely. And I think that when you see realtors that dis-miss things, the clients are looking and they say, "Well, that doesn't sell houses," that is not the answer. You have to deliver service in a way that they are looking for it. And it's an interesting thing to me to see these agents that want their own website.

I'm not a big fan of agent websites. I think they're a complete waste of money. All that the consumer wants is to know that they have an online presence. So here, attached to a solid brand that has a very good website and you have an incredibly solid profile page. So one thing that's really nice about that is your listings are up-to-date on there. It's not out-of-date information. You have access to all of the information and all of the services that your brand provides. And if you point your URL into your dot com or your dot ca, the domain name is right. That makes far more sense because the consumer is looking for that.

Link it to your social media. They want to know that you're on social media. They want to know that you have an online presence. That's what they're looking for. And they want up-to-date things.

Phil/Dan: I have often said that a website is simply an online postcard in the absence of a conversion strategy.

Greta: Waste of money.

Million Dollar Agent Key Idea #149

Phil/Dan: *And it's a waste of money because the key issue is how to get people to go there, what happens when they're there, what is*

"In the absence of a conversion strategy, a website is an online postcard that does not necessarily lead to any business."

their useful knowledge and information that adds to their credibility? And then once they're there, how do they capture the lead and then finally how do they convert that person into an actual client. It's part and parcel of a larger, more comprehensive strategy. That's why it's such a small percentage of business that actually comes from a website. Do you need a website? Do you need these things? Yes. With respect to social media, people google an agent's name if an agent meets somebody at an open house. They do their due diligence. They check you out. So the key issue is what content is there? How does this add to your credibility?

Greta: I look at the brands like ours, it's Coldwell Banker, that's where I work. We have an incredible website. It's the number one visited website in our industry in North America. And what I like about it is it has really great information on it. It's got it in video, it's got in print, it's got everything on there, and each agent gets their own little URL attached to their name. I went through it yesterday. I googled the agents at my office that I knew had separate websites or were really robust on our network. And we were always out-ranging their personal website in terms of Google search. That's what you should be focusing on, a site that actually provides the information to your clients. And if they google your name, this is the first thing that pops up.

You don't need to have five different websites.

Million Dollar Agent Key Idea #150
"To be successful, websites and social media in general, must enhance the realtor's credibility."

Phil/Dan: It's not the website that generates business, it's part of the process, it's part of enhancing the realtor's credibility. People use technology to do their due diligence, to check you out and it needs to enhance that. You've been very gracious with respect to your time. And I can't tell you how much I appreciate that. What is the future of real estate?

Greta: Well, my big belief is that's the end of the independent real estate brokerage. I think being aligned with trusted strong brands and being a franchise and part of a larger organization is the only way that a real estate office can deliver service in a way that the consumer, the public now wants it because of the amount of money that it costs to build an infrastructure that supports the needs of today or the desire or the want of the consumer.

The only way you can do that is to have a larger group of people paying into the development of that. And I see it with our own system what we have in terms of interactivity. We have this crazy program now where people can actually log on to the website starting in October, see the listings and interact with their experience of viewing their home. So the homeowner will see firsthand communication from people that are viewing their properties. You can't do that if you're an independent. You can't create an infrastructure that supports all that.

Phil/Dan: So, a sole practitioner or an independent and small, tiny real estate firm cannot provide that in a way that a large national, international franchise can.

Greta: We have our local website with the websites that have the power. It's our national and our global websites. We have somewhere around 11 or 12,000 people moving in a year. We have the newcomers to Canada, moving into Manitoba alone. I hate to think what it was across the country. They are also coming from countries that are part of our network, so they already know who we are.

We're in an office with 18 languages depending on the dialects, and I find it interesting the amount of people that reach out to us from other countries because we are in a global network. And I think to myself how does a local independent realtor or real estate office provide the service that brings the market to the seller like we can?

Phil/Dan: *Do you ever think that technology will replace a real estate agent?*

Greta: That has failed because at the end of the day you still go walk through a home with somebody, still have to have an understanding of the market, you have to have a conversation where you can actually share your insights and you can be intuitive as to what their needs are. A program can't possibly do that.

Phil/Dan: *So, you think there'll be always place for great real estate agents and the future of real estate is a good one?*

Greta: I think the future is a very good one. I think it will change in time. And all things change. I think that the realtors that are coming into this business are coming in at an exciting time if they're joining an office that is helping them to be the very best that they can be, that has a plan in place for their success, not just asking them what their plan is. And I think that is the future of the industry, offices like ours, and working with companies like yours. I'm proud to have a package of Morris marketing materials to provide to each new agent that enters our premises because I know that is going to work hand-in-hand with strategies that I have in place for them and how I want to help them to move forward in their career.

Phil/Dan: *Having said that, Greta, I want to thank you very much for your time. And this has been very insightful.*

Greta: If you have any other questions, do let me know. And thank you again for thinking of me and I hope that I had something of value to say.

Phil/Dan: *I think you had a ton of value. And I think any one of these concepts that you brought, I could write a book on it alone. Thanks, Greta.*

Greta: Thank you.

Million Dollar Agent Key Ideas Summary

$ **Being** accountable for yourself and your actions is so important to creating a successful and consistent real estate business.

$ One of the absolute keys to a realtor's success is not only to acquire the knowledge and skills to be successful but also the self-confidence and self-belief in order to apply the knowledge and skills that they have obtained.

$ Whether you are new to real estate or have been in the business for years, it is very important that you continually learn and grow and challenge yourself. It is very easy to slip into a comfort zone and ultimately the amount of business you have will reflect this.

$ Successful behaviours that lead to positive results begin with a success mindset.

$ Successful realtors never rest on their laurels no matter how well they are doing.

$ Success has a structure and one of the best ways to learn this structure is to model those realtors that are already successful.

$ The top realtors understand that even though they are very busy now, they must still do the key activities they need to ensure they have a steady stream of business in the future.

$ The best and most successful agents are the ones that do the most transactions and actually keep the money in their pockets to create referral business for themselves and build relationships with people.

$ If you don't have enough business, you need to go out and make more friends.

$ People do business with a realtor based on trust and likeability but most importantly based on their knowledge and expertise. Both are essential for a realtor to be successful.

$ To be successful in sales you need to be curious and really like people.

$ A proper database needs to include all kinds of information - names of spouse and children, physical mailing address, as well other information if possible - like birthdays, anniversaries, mortgage renewal dates.

$ What has changed today is the level of professionalism that is expected from agents that justify the commissions that they make.

$ In the absence of a conversion strategy, a website is an online postcard that does not necessarily lead to any business.

$ To be successful, websites and social media in general, must enhance the realtor's credibility.

WADE WEBB:
One No Closer to a Yes

WADE WEBB IS a managing broker/owner in the Okanagan. For the past 20 years, Wade has been honing his real estate skills during a very successful, thirteen-year career as one of the top agents in Penticton and Kelowna. Wade is also a past director of the Okanagan Mainline Real Estate Board.

An international speaker, coach and trainer, his knowledge, experience and marketing expertise plays a key role in the continued development and success of his brokerage. Wade is also a provincial licensing instructor. Wade loves spending time with his family. He also enjoys travelling, golf, music, movies, speaking and training.

IN ADDITION TO being a great managing broker, Wade is a phenomenal mentor, coach, speaker and author whose life story is a true inspiration for anyone wise enough to learn from him. Having discovered his unrelenting desire and passion for sales as a young man he had no choice but to abandon a promising future as a musician to pursue a career in real estate. Initially working with his father, he made a name for himself as a highly successful and well-respected realtor. In building his real estate practice he exchanged wealth for health and he learned the hard way the invaluable lesson of the need to create work-life balance and take back control of his personal and professional life. This experience was the catalyst for Wade not only to reinvent himself and to build one of the most successful brokerages in Western Canada but also to share his knowledge and expertise with other brokers and agents throughout North America.

Phil/Dan: Well, good morning, Wade. We thank you so much for taking the time out of your busy day to do this. We can't thank you enough.

Wade: My pleasure. Thanks for having me.

Phil/Dan: Wade Webb is a true success story, not only in terms of realtors, but brokers. And I've watched Wade as a fan. He has grown his business from a smaller brokerage well over 10, 15 years ago to this dominant force, not only in the Okanagan Valley but throughout Western Canada. If you speak to his agents, he's not only a wonderful broker but also a coach and a mentor. He inspires them. They come from far away to work with Wade and Wade is an author of his own book called "The Lazy Realtor," which is a great book and I often recommend it to realtors who want to learn about the real estate business and be more successful. So, Wade, thank you for doing this. And, Wade, I've got some questions for you.

In doing the interviews for this book, I am fascinated by the backgrounds of people who are in real estate. But, a lot of people come to real estate as a secondary, sometimes, a third profession. What did you do before you entered into real estate? What were you doing?

Wade: My introduction to real estate came through one of the most unorthodox methodologies. I was in university, majoring in piano and minoring in saxophone. I was a kid that received a set of piano books for his fifth birthday instead of a hockey stick, because my mom was a piano teacher.

I ended up taking piano lessons in high school bands, fast lessons. And I'll be honest, I wasn't the best student nor was I scholastically inclined. But thankfully, I had a gift in music that allowed me to get a scholarship and that's how I ended up in college and university, thank goodness, because it wasn't because of my grades. It was because of my gifts and talents in music. But while I was in university, I ran across an ad in the Vancouver Sun that piqued my interest. It said, make seven or ten thousand dollars in the summer as a university student. And so I went to downtown Vancouver, applied for a job, and got it. Little did I know they hired every university student that applied and so I ended up selling encyclopedias door-to-door for Collier's in 1992.

Phil/Dan: *Interesting.*

Wade: They taught us university students a two-and-a-half hour canned sales presentation in five days. So we studied from 9 in the morning till 5 at night; went home, repeated the presentation and scripts with all the visuals, went through all the material and learned all of it in a week's time; memorized it. And then they took a car load of four of us, our field manager and three of us university students in each car. And I proceeded to head on to Saskatchewan. And I sold encyclopedias for June, July and August of 1992 in Saskatchewan for three months.

We would start at 3 o'clock in the afternoon. Our field manager would drive us through the neighborhood. We'd get a feel for the neighborhood and yell at our field manager, "I like this neighborhood, it smells like money; stop the car." And so he would stop the car. He'd let us know that he'd pick us up at a gas station or convenience store or somewhere at a pick-up point and not until 10 p.m. He wouldn't come and get you. So, if you weren't knocking on doors and selling books, you're basically stuck out on the field until 10 p.m. So, 3 o'clock to 10 pm, I proceeded to knock on probably on average 250 to 275 doors a night.

I would have people in Saskatchewan tell me where to go and how to get there more ways than I could shake a stick at. And I proceeded to be one of the top salespeople of that company for that summer and made several thousand dollars and absolutely fell in love with sales and realized that it was something that I can do well.

I'm in Kindersley, Saskatchewan, in a telephone booth. I phoned my dad and told him that I'd fallen in love with sales. "I'm going to quit music. I'm not going to be a high school band teacher. This is what I want to do. I love it." And I'll just give you bit of background, my dad was a salesman from day one. My dad sold ATCO Trailers, he sold carpet, furniture and appliances, televisions you name it. My dad was a salesman of all salesmen and had just gotten into real estate himself finally at 42 years old, and he was two years in the business when I called him.

He basically said you're crazy, finish your degree and don't get into sales. And like any kid, I ignored what my parents said. I told my dad, "You have two options. We can either do, one, work together as partners in real estate or two, we can compete against each other. What do you want to do?" And so, long story short, I had the privilege and the honor in 1993 to join with my dad and be his business partner, his real estate partner in Penticton from 1993 till September 2000.

My dad was my mentor. He taught me everything that I needed to know in sales and from the real estate side of things. But I'll go back to the books. Selling encyclopedias and that whole entire lesson and what I learned about myself was the drive in me, the tenacity, the rejection and objection handling and realizing that when I sold books, I had a vision. I had a belief, and my belief was that I was on a mission from God against illiteracy, that these people in Saskatchewan and their children needed these books, I needed the money but they needed the books more importantly and it was that vision and that belief that drove me to be able to convey that message to compel them to buy books for $1,999.99.

Phil/Dan: Interesting.

Wade: I'm going to just do a quick disclaimer. I had no belief or knowledge that the internet was coming.

Just like book ends and they have a paperweight at home now because of the internet. But truly, I believe that they needed that, they needed these books, they needed to find literacy and they needed the education, they needed the belief to get their kids smarter and wiser and have that resource. And I also realized that every door I went to, I was just one 'no' closer to a 'yes', and it's a number's game. The rejection just started to be like water off a duck's back and just flew off and it didn't really bother me anymore. And I just really believed that they needed this. I needed to make a sale. I love the thrill of the negotiating in that.

And I learned so many lessons in that experience that lead me to believe, I'm just one more 'no' closer to a 'yes' in getting a listing or getting a sale. And that it's okay, no big deal, just keep moving on and that I believe that somebody is going to buy something today, they just don't know it yet and somebody needs my help and needs to sell something or buy something. And I believe that I'm the right person to do it for them and to help them with that real estate transaction.

It was a weird way in which I got to it. And who would have thought door-to-door sales of encyclopedias would have given me this feeling, that I really, really love this and enjoy this. And my wife always jokes that she wishes she was one or two things. She wishes she was a Montreal Canadian or Hab, or she was the real estate deal, because I love both of them so much, I have passion and love for both of them. And I truly believe that real estate is the world's greatest business for us to be able to create an incredible lifestyle and it's an incredible honor to be able to help people with the single largest transaction and experience of their life - buying and selling a home. And we're responsible for that. That's a pretty cool honor to be able to be responsible for such a big thing in people's lives, and we get to do that. I hope that everybody doesn't underestimate that on that privilege that we have, and that responsibility that you have as a real estate professional and never take it for granted.

Phil/Dan: *That is so powerful, Wade. If I can underscore a couple of things that you've said just for the reader, and that is self-belief, belief in your product, belief in the importance of what you're doing because I think that whether it was encyclopedias or homes, you could be selling anything. You could be selling hockey*

Million Dollar Agent Key Idea #151

"To be truly successful in real estate you need to passionately believe in the importance of what you are selling and the fact that people need and want what you are selling."

pucks in Florida, but the bottom line is that belief was the catalyst. And it still carries, and the passion that you have is just so admirable. When you started in your real estate career, what would you say was your greatest challenge?

Wade: It's really simple. I was 21 years old in 1993. The number of agents that age in the industry in Canada I could count with my fingers and toes in 1993. "He's a kid," I remember my broker owner saying to my dad; "I don't like it. He's never owned a house. He's got no experience, life experience. He's young. He is wet behind the ears blah, blah, blah." And I thought, "You know what, I'm going to prove that guy wrong."

So it was great that he had said that and started a criticism. He told my dad, "He's your responsibility so keep him out of trouble, and I'm fine with that." So that was one challenge. The other challenge was that I didn't want anybody to think that I was riding my dad's shirttail. So here's a father-son team and everybody, "Oh, his dad is spoon-feeding him and he's giving him all this business and that." I just needed to make sure that wasn't a challenge that people saw; that it was me that was doing it.

And then the third challenge is that mortgages were more expensive than their houses. And I'm like, "Holy cow. What kind of industry did I sign up with?" Everybody was under water, upside down. So their financing was in excess of what they could actually sell a house for. And I remember telling people, begrudgingly, the best thing is that you should stay.

Imagine your first two years in real estate and you told more people to stay because they were under water than to sell it. How crazy is that? Those were three crazy challenges for someone like myself to get into the industry and to break through it, starting out on my career.

Phil/Dan: *You know what's interesting? For those people who are reading this or listening to this, interest rates were 18, 19% back then. So if I'm not mistaken, the interest rates were through the roof.*

Wade: They were way higher than any interest rate we've seen in the last 10 years, let's just put it that way, absolutely. My recollection was more like 9%. In the '80s, they were 18, 19, 20, 21. They were astronomical. This year it's 2.69 or something like that. So interest rates were definitely more of a challenge than they are today.

Phil/Dan: *I think there was a little bit of a gift in a way because a lot of agents that are starting today probably don't have any perspective.*

Wade: Right, right. I'm so grateful that the market was that way in '93 because I had to learn some incredibly important habits. You have to learn habits and create different habits than you create in a good market. When I first started I thought this was crazy, frustrating, angering. There were so many emotions flying and what am I doing? Second guessing. But today I wouldn't want it any different. Those habits are key to my success and there are things that I learned to implement that you would never implement in a strong, country club market versus one that's a challenge.

Phil/Dan: *And I just want to underscore something that I think this is one of the reasons, having gone through that adversity, that makes you such a great coach, a mentor and a broker today. You have that perspective to share with your agents, especially the ones that are there seeking advice, that's invaluable. Looking back on your career, what has been your greatest challenge over the years?*

Wade: The greatest challenge for me I would think, I know for sure that it is - work-life balance. That's always been a challenge, because when you're passionate about something, being able to control that passion and energy and to just to remind yourself of what is important is probably one of the ongoing challenges for me. I definitely learned some invaluable and valuable lessons and I've learned them through failure. I'm going to be completely transparent and honest that I've learned from a lot of mistakes.

I've made a lot of mistakes in the last 23 years in this business but those mistakes have been a tremendous opportunity for me. The work-life balance challenge has meant maintaining a higher level of health and of my own personal health and mindset has been the challenge. I am a comfort eater and I have always struggled with my weight and my health and so that's been a challenge.

The other challenge in this industry, as a real estate agent, is blaming myself – so relationships. The challenge is that if you do not maintain communication; you do not maintain relationships with people. The ongoing battle is that we all have relationships existing

Million Dollar Agent Key Idea #152

"It is very often beneficial for an agent to start their career in a challenging market, as opposed to a strong vibrant market, as they develop habits and skills that will serve them well throughout their entire career in real estate."

in place and when is the last time you spent any time or added value to those relationships. And that's an ongoing challenge as a broker-manager and as a real estate agent, is that we're so busy recruiting our next agent or hiring our next agent as a broker or we're so busy looking for a new customer, a new lead, a new person. We already have more than enough sitting already in our relationships that we already currently have, that if we just spent more time with them and built more value in them, in their lives that we would have more referrals, more business and more growth than you could shake a stick at. But we're such creatures of habit as brokers, owners, managers, and as agents, that we always spend more time and money looking for new business instead of taking that same time and money and putting it on existing relationships that we already have sitting right there, if we just take the time and be intentional with it.

Phil/Dan: *That's so well put, Wade. I think it's human nature. A lot of agents that I speak to, when they start their careers, it's all about the next deal, the next deal, the next deal. But once they reach a certain modicum of business in relationships if they forget to nurture those and take care of them and provide them value, then they get caught in what I often refer to as the transactional trap. They repeat their same first year business over and over again. It's a constant challenge because we're always looking for the new. I'm sure we'll talk about the value of systems. But the bottom line is it's all about creating value, taking care of people. I truly believe it adds to the enjoyment of what you do and frees you from the commodity-based marketplace. It's something that takes a while to get to for a lot of agents.*

Wade: And it does. You learn, you make a lot of mistakes, you lose a lot of customers, and you lose a lot of relationships because you didn't treat them like they were a first class passenger on your airline. You didn't even treat them like they were in coach. You treat them like they were in the baggage compartment.

You just did the deal and never, ever, ever took the time to deepen the relationship with them. We're all guilty of it. And you can make that shift and really, really understand the value and the importance of taking care of what you already have and it will grow through that. It's powerful, it's very powerful. The other reality is that if I made more money, then my life and my health would be that much better. That was a lesson where I learned that it's the furthest thing from the truth. In 2004, I got in a brokerage, not into broker managing and ownership, not because of the opportunity to make money and do everything else, and not like most people would. It wasn't a business decision at all.

Million Dollar Agent Key Idea #153

"As a realtor you want to avoid the 'transactional trap,' otherwise you end up repeating your first year of business over and over again throughout your career."

My health. I was on pace to do about a million GCI in 2004. I was near 400 pounds in weight. The back of my vehicle was full of more fast food bags than you could shake a stick at.

I remember waking up in the spring of 2004 having chest pains at about 2 o'clock in the morning, rushing to the hospital and my wife dragging me down there, and hooking up to all these EKG monitors and all these devices. And then my wife at the same time letting me know that if I didn't change, she was leaving me, taking my children and my whole entire world was like, "Can you not see that I'm having a heart attack here?"

I'll tell you, the day before that, I thought I was the most successful person in real estate I knew because if I just kept making more money, making more sales, it would just get better, it would get better. And the reality is that I was slowly killing myself physically. I was slowly killing myself emotionally and mentally and not even taking care of the most important people and the most important relationships in my life, and that was my family and my wife and my kids and my friends.

I neglected all of them. I neglected myself, I neglected my friends, I neglected my family and I basically said that I sold my soul to the real estate devil. And that's ironically where I hit a crossroad as salesperson in 2004 and not by chance, but was offered an opportunity to control the beast and get out of sales and move into broker owners and managing, and to be able to just work Monday to Friday, somewhat, and more of a 7:30 in the morning till 6 o'clock at night and control all that.

So I'm happy to say that through a personal trainer and through a nutritionist, I'm physically healthier and stronger and not that guy in 2004. And we just celebrated our 17th wedding anniversary. And my three children – 11, 13 and 25 – are happy and we have an awesome relationship. And, I let all that go and underestimated all of that. Don't fall into that trap as a real estate agent because I see so many people, where we create these monsters in our business where it's work, work, work, make money, make money, make money, you'll be happier, happier and you'll be healthier, and it's the furthest thing from truth.

Don't get caught in that belief that if you just make more money and you spend more time doing what you're doing and work harder that your life is going to get any better, because I know that's not the case and that's my experience. I basically completely lost control and lost balance

Million Dollar Agent Key Idea #154

"Like many businesses real estate can be all consuming and it's extremely important that you avoid trading your health, relationships and other important aspects of your life for wealth."

on that, and that ironically lead me to how I ended up being an owner, a broker and a manager. It's not the prettiest story on how I become a broker, an owner, and a manager but I hope that other people learn, make sure that you don't take the people in your life and your health for granted. Because if you lose your health, you lose your family, you lose friends, there is nothing, no amount of money can replace it, trust me. No amount of money can replace any of that.

Phil/Dan: *If I stopped the interview right now and that's all the reader got from this interview that they could potentially save their lives, that is such valuable advice, Wade. I can't tell you how many realtors have traded wealth for health and traded relationships. So we're all guilty but to a greater or lesser degree.*

Wade: Absolutely. I'm not passionate and not disciplined in my relationships, life and in my health life. So I seek out a coach for training and I seek out an adviser for my marriage and my relationships to keep me on track and hold me accountable because I'm never going to be out of the woods. I have that A-type driver personality that needs to have someone constantly reminding of what I should be eating, looking after my nutrition, looking after my health, and reminding me of my date nights and my family and my relationships.

I didn't just all of sudden fix it and change, I just realized that it's something that I'm not able to control myself. I sought out other people to hold me accountable, to coach and mentor me and keep me on track, and I've had to do that for the last decade. You're just not going to wake up one day and decide that you're going to be a lean mean exercising machine and you're going to eat properly when you're a comfort eater and a comfort drinker. And if you're an A-type driver personality like me, you're just not going to decide that you're going to create a date night and you're just going to be that perfect husband and that perfect father and that perfect friend. You need to find people to hold you accountable and have mentors and coaches and have those people to make sure that you keep yourself on track.

Phil/Dan: *How beautifully said. And again, the accountability factor. The fact that you have consciousness and awareness, and that it's a process, it's a never-ending process.*

It's funny. I've got to tell you, I'm turning 51 this year. I haven't missed a workout in 35 years. And I'm only telling you that just because of the fact that, ironically, when I started working out 35 years ago, I had thought that if I just do one more workout, I would be in shape and realized that I haven't been able to stop. But my point is that it's a constant struggle, even after 35 years I am looking into to getting a personal trainer.

My friends say, "Well, you've been working out for 35 years, why would you need a personal trainer?" Because it's always about keeping on track. Wade, you're in very good shape, you look great, you're not that same guy that was in the hospital that night, you're so admirable. It's just something to admire greatly. How would you describe your lifestyle now versus when you started out in the business? You've realigned your values in such a way that you really have a good sense of what's important.

Wade: If you can avoid having these apocalyptic moments in your life like a EKG machine and a heart attack and on the verge of a divorce and never spending time with your friends, don't be as stupid as me and wait till the last degree until you realize how important it is and have those mindsets. Have that change in your beliefs about what's important.

I never knew how important it was to surround myself with other people that are able to hold me accountable and to remind me of what's important, because I think we all need that. I think we all need somebody in each area in our lives that we struggle with, to be able to have you there and to hold you there and to hold you accountable on that. Because you just can't do it on your own. If I could have done it on my own then I wouldn't have been in property, I would have no one to stay home and spend more time with, my friends and family and my wife.

There's no dress rehearsal in life. And so, you want to make sure that when you're here, the movie that we're making in our lives matters. The one thing for me now is that more importantly, I'm trying to leave a legacy with my children and with my organization and trying to have impact.

And before it was about the money. Now it's more about significance and more about who am I helping, who am I being able to teach and to learn from. What are people going to remember me for? They're never going to remember that you're in a chairman's club or you made a million dollars in a year. There's more to life and there's more things I want to leave that people are going to learn and take away from and be remembered for than just being a big top producer and a high roller and making a bunch of money.

Phil/Dan: You've answered so many of the questions. Wade, what makes you the best at what you do? And I got to say that you're one of the best in the business.

Wade: It's being humble. It's humility and gratitude. It's my humility and being humble about what you do and being grateful for what you do and being grateful for what you have. Those are two incredibly powerful things that you constantly have to focus on and work at and keep yourself humble and keep yourself grounded and keep yourself grateful and thankful for what you do have, and not being focused on what you don't have and what you haven't done.

So humility and gratitude would be probably the two keys to my success. And the other one is, I surround myself with people that are gifted and talented and passionate about the things that I am not, but I know that are truly important. So you're going to talk about systems and things like that.

Million Dollar Agent Key Idea #155
"Humility and gratitude are two very important keys to being successful in real estate and in life in general."

I couldn't organize a five-year-old's birthday party, but I understand the importance of having a well-organized and executed birthday party for my children. So the reality is that I've learned and surrounded myself with people that are able to raise my game. I have to be able to delegate and to be able to systemize and automate because I'm just not going to be that person with all of those gifts and talents and strengths.

Phil Collins has got a great book, get the right people on the bus and make sure the right people are on the right seats on that bus. And if those people aren't the right people in the bus and are not in the right seats then stop the bus and get them off and move the right people onto bus and on to those right seats. I'm learning to let go and to not have to worry about being in control of everything. And that someone else doing something 85% as good as I would do is fantastic because it's not me doing it.

And the last lesson I think that has made me grateful and successful is just giving. I wake up every single day in hopes that I could impact and improve an agent or someone that I cross paths with, personally and professionally every single day. So my faith is reminding me that every single day, I'm here to try and help someone personally and professionally. When I focus on helping others personally and professionally, I get back ten-fold of what I give out. And so I am truly blessed because I bless others on a regular basis, and my goal and what drives me now is to get up and to help others, personally and professionally. My goal honestly is five people a day.

What's cool about this opportunity in this book is that I may have the opportunity to help hundreds or thousands through this book. And so, thank you for my being able to help you impact people personally and professionally through this book.

> **Million Dollar Agent Key Idea #156**
> *"Another great key to success is to be a giver; give of yourself, your knowledge and expertise, your time and this will come back to benefit you in many ways."*

Giving to get, impact, improving people's lives, giving up control and surrounding yourself with people that are gifted in the areas and the strengths that you are not and keeping humble are important. Remembering where you came from, you were just the young 21-year-old kid that never, ever sold a house but had sold encyclopedias door-to-door, and never forget where you came from. And just being so thankful every single day for what you have and forget about what you don't have and constantly be grateful for what you already have and all of what you've been given and blessed with. Those would be things that I think would be the key important secrets to my success.

And I'm humbled and grateful that I never thought a kid from Saskatchewan selling encyclopedias would ever be where I'm at today. And I think that it still blows my mind and it's still amazing, and I never really focused on staying true and humble and being grateful. I never stopped focusing on impacting and helping other people and leaving that impact and leaving that behind because I think that's what it's about, we're here to help others and we can help someone else.

I tend to find that things just keep coming back bigger than what I anticipated and they come back ten-fold. And it is biblical, right? You help other people and you'll get back ten-fold. So, through that belief and that understanding, I think it has helped me become the person and the man and the husband and the father and the leader and the broker and the owner and salesperson that I really want to be. I've never arrived. I always believe that I can do, be more and be better and impact more and impact others more, and I'll never lose that drive to continue to start to just be better and to be more.

Phil/Dan: So well said, Wade.

Million Dollar Agent Key Idea #157
"Never underestimate the power of systems and delegation to free you up to do what you do best and are passionate about."

Wade: I'm just touching the surface of the secrets to my success. Humility, gratitude, sharing and impacting, improving people's lives and helping others and surrounding yourself with people that are gifted and talented and areas that you're not are four incredibly powerful things.

Phil/Dan: There are personality profiles of the most successful and you certainly fit within that, such as having great communication skills, people skills, negotiation skills, relationship skills, but by nature they're not necessarily administrators. And so by surrounding themselves with people who understand systems and have talents that are complementary, it's not that they can't do these things, it's just that they need to be freed up to do what they do best and they get to that understanding and that allows them to express their talents.

Wade: You can't underestimate the importance and the power of systems, delegation and systemization and surrounding yourself with those people that are in the sweet spot, that frees you up to do what you do best. You cannot fail at something that you love to do and you're passionate about, you cannot fail.

Phil/Dan: There are so many nuances in terms of what people do differently but gratitude and appreciation are at the top of the list. One of the things I tell my kids – they asked, are we wealthy? Because they're making mental comparisons between what they have and our family has relative to their friends at school. And I would say over and over again, one who has wealth who appreciates it, and I underline appreciates what they have, because you can have millions and billions of dollars but if you don't appreciate, it ain't worth anything. Appreciation, I always say is, is the ability to create more.

Wade: I saw Ken Blanchard up on stage and he does a Q&A after his speech. And he's in his 80s. An agent said, "Mr. Blanchard, why do you continue to do what you do every single day?" And he stopped and looked at her and the whole place was just packed with hundreds of agents in there and realtors and brokers and owners. "Young lady," he says, "You have the ability to take care of other people." He says, "When you realize that if you help people get what they want and need in their lives, you will get what you want and what you need in your life ten-fold. When you wake up every day and figure out how you can help, how you can serve, how you can get people what they want and they need in their real estate, their real estate needs and wants, and you focus that energy and that attention on helping them get what they want in their lives, you will get what you want ten-fold. And I never stopped being blessed and I never stopped getting more than whatever I anticipated because helping other people get what they want never gets old," he said. And that's what makes me want to continue to do what I do every day and I'm in my mid-80s now.

I think he might have just stopped speaking and teaching and training, maybe about a year ago. He might do few special engagements but to listen

Million Dollar Agent Key Idea #158

"When you help people get what they want and need, all your wants and needs are taken care of."

and to realize, that's all we do as a real estate agents in this business, is we help other people get what they want and they need on a real estate level, on a personal level. And if you do a good job and you're focused on that, not the money, you will be getting back in return ten-fold. And I truly believe in what Mr. Blanchard had to say because it has been true in my life and my career in the last 27 years.

Phil/Dan: How do the best realtors look at the world differently than everyone else?

Wade: The real estate business is the world's greatest business. I can sell anything but I sell homes. And to me, a home is probably one of the greatest products that we ever get to sell. It's people's lives, their hopes, their dreams, their memories, everything, the most important thing about life is in their home. And so what's cool about it is that we could sell anything and be a part of anything in the world of business, but we're on the single most impactful, powerful product to our service in any business, in any sales. And so for me, real estate is home actually and we get to do that, when we get to the sell one of the coolest services and commodities and things in people's lives that you could possibly be a part of.

Phil/Dan: Well said. How do the best realtors think differently?

Wade: I truly believe that the most successful agents in real estate have an incredible and abundance mindset. There is so much out there for so many of us, and there is no competition. Competition is from your right ear to your left ear, which is where competition exists. It's called the little voice in your mind that is telling you can't do this, you're not getting good at this, you shouldn't be able to do this, right, blah, blah, blah, that little voice.

Having an abundance mindset - there is so much out there for so many and that's why I'm so willing to share because there's more than enough business out there, you just have to choose to go get it. And those top people have that abundance mindset and know that there is so much and so little time and they just choose to impact and take action and go get it. And that's the difference between the 20% and the 80% is that they have an abundance mindset and they just choose and act and take action and go get it. And there is and there always will be more than enough for the agents out there.

Million Dollar Agent Key Idea # 159
"One of the key differences between the most successful agents and those that are struggling is the most successful agents have an abundance mindset."

Phil/Dan: I love the quote - we live in an infinite universe; it's only our thinking that is finite. And if we'd only open up our consciousness to have a prosperity abundance mindset to realize how much wealth there is and then take the actions and go get it as you so eloquently said.

Wade: What would you rather choose, speculating on stock options that you're going to die, you're going to get sick? We can sell so many different things but I'm just honored that I get to sell such an awesome product or service as a home. We underestimate the importance and the value of a home, right? It is an incredible honor to be able to work in this industry and it never gets old. It's so much fun to able to serve and help other people with that home and that opportunity to bring them home.

Phil/Dan: What are the key practices that you believe lead most to your success?

Wade: Always start yourself out with the morning routine. The morning routine has always worked for all top producers and all top high-performance people. They all have a morning routine.

Wade: So the routines are usually reflection. They're usually affirmations. They're usually gratitude exercises, where they take time to reflect and have that morning routine to prepare themselves with their emotions and their mindset and everything. Having a routine is definitely a key thing. I'm looking for those five people to help every day and to serve everyday personally and professionally. I know that is a number one thing. Sales is a full contact sport. And so I'm about face-to-face and voice-to-voice in full contact. And if I'm not face-to-face and voice-to-voice with people then I am not doing my job because I am in the relationship business and that is not tweeting, it is not texting, it is not emailing, it is not posting or commenting or liking. Relationship is about the greatest gift and that is our gift of our time to people, and face-to-face and voice-to-voice and adding value to them. And if you don't focus, you're missing the whole entire concept of sales and relationships. Be belly-to-belly giving people the greatest gift that you can give in your time and sitting there and being face-to-face and voice-to-voice.

I think that my focus on impacting, improving full contact and taking that daily morning routine and setting my mindset and choosing to have the right

Million Dollar Agent Key Idea #160

"Sales is a full contact sport that is so much more than simply texting and tweeting."

mindset, the right attitude to believe and be grateful on that. Those are probably the three most important things that I do on a daily basis when I am working and when I'm doing what I'm doing for a profession.

Phil/Dan: *Wow. Your answers provide so much value for those people who are wise enough to pay attention to some of the nuances and that's why I'm so glad I'm documenting them in this book. One of the things I want to highlight is, when you talk about this is a relationship business, when I speak to younger realtors who say to me, "I've got social media and an email strategy," that's all important. But really, real estate being a people business, you can't take people out of the equation, and a face-to-face communication is so critically important. That's why I fly all over North America literally, to meet with people one-on-one because sending someone an email or text or even social media, you can only go so far.*

Wade: I agree. And I think that any other form other than voice-to-voice or face-to-face, what do they say? The words that you say are a percentage. Your body language and your voice inflection, your eye contact and so many other things are far more important on how you connect and how you communicate with other people than the words that you use and the words that you say.

Phil/Dan: *I think the statistic is 7% of human communication is words, 55% is body language or body physiology and only 38% is voice tone. So when you're texting someone, you've eliminated 93% of human communication. What are the best realtors doing consistently better than anyone else?*

Wade: They focus on the people that they already know they can trust. So they have some consistent regular system or process in which they're adding value and they're maintaining communication with their existing relationships.

And that would be key, number one. And they're adding value and they're deepening those relationships constantly with people that they already brought into the fold of their relationship. The second thing is that they know that they need to create and work on new relationships but 30%, 40% of their time is on finding new business and lead generation and prospecting, 60% is already deepening and enhancing and adding value of their existing relationships.

Phil/Dan: *That's interesting because most people have the exact opposite.*

Wade: Right, the exact opposite. So we tend to see that they're flipped backwards most of the time. And I would emphasize that it's 70% on lead generation, prospecting, finding strangers and that 30% on the people that we know we can trust. And we all know the step that we spend six times as much money and time getting them as we do keeping them which is completely crazy and ironic but those top producers have that shifted and they spend 70% of their time on keeping it and their money and efforts on it then finding it and creating it. But you always have to be filling in the funnel, over and above the existing client base that you have now.

And then the other thing that's incredibly important is that they understand. Put a sale together each day. There are four activities that get you paid in real estate - take a new listing, get an existing listing repositioned and priced properly, get a buyer to sign and hire you as their buyer's agent, and write a purchase contract and create a buying opportunity. So, you're not sitting and waiting, you're promoting buying opportunities to your buyers and writing contracts and negotiating.

You are repositioning homes that are getting sales and offers on them and you're getting buyers who want to work with you and buy those buying opportunities, and you're finding people that want to sell. And that's it. These are the four things to focus on daily - take a listing, reposition your price on a property, get a buyer to want to buy and create buying opportunities for those buyers. That's right, that's the key to the things that get you paid on a regular basis and keeping it that simple with those four things.

Focus your time, energy, efforts, and your money on the people that you already have. Don't put all of your time into going and finding people that are looking for the next deal.

Phil/Dan: This is where systems help you to be freed up to do the high-income producing activities.

Wade: They're calling them the high-dollar activity. And their high-dollar activity is talking to people, talking to existing clients looking for new clients,

Million Dollar Agent Key Idea #161

"There are four activities that get you paid in real estate - take a new listing, get an existing listing repositioned and priced properly, get a buyer to sign and hire you as their buyer's agent, and write a purchase contract and create a buying opportunity."

taking a listing, repositioning and properly price-listing, getting a buyer to want to work with you and hire you as their exclusive buyer's agent and creating a buying opportunity and getting people to buy those deals that are in that marketplace that you have, right?

Phil/Dan: Totally. Over your career, what was your dominant revenue stream?

Wade: That's an easy answer. My dominant revenue stream was on face-to-face activities, because my passion, enthusiasm, and my joy for serving others always made me a fortune. So an open house, a kiosk, a floor shift, a pop by, a visit with a client, anything where I could get in front of people physically was my moneymaker, because that's where my gifts and my strengths were, when I was with people. I made a fortune off of my passion, enthusiasm, and they could see and feel and experience that passion, enthusiasm only when I was with them.

Phil/Dan: Right. And so just sending out an unaddressed postcard, no matter how good the picture is, does not convey that.

Wade: Those systems and those postcards did allow me to do what I do best. It opened the door for that appointment to be able to do what I do best, which is exude passion and enthusiasm and be able to get people to want to be a part of what I have.

Phil/Dan: *Well, you answered the next three questions. So with the height of your career, I know you're broker-owned and I'm sure you have clients you serve. Where does the majority of your business come from today?*

Wade: Repeat and referral. When you focus on adding value, deepening relationships and taking care of the people that are most important to you, they will pay you back. They will pay it forward. They will return the favor. Reciprocity is the single most powerful marketing tool in the world: giving with no expectation of return. The belief is that the more you give the more you get back, and it is repeat and referral business. If you focus on reciprocity and adding value and giving, you know that it's going to pay ten-fold, it is true to this day that the single most powerful tool for me is giving. And I tend to get more repeat and referral business because I focus on giving before getting.

Million Dollar Agent Key Idea #162
"Reciprocity is the single most powerful marketing tool in the world - giving with no expectation of return."

Phil/Dan: *When someone believes in that principle and has the face to apply it or belief to apply it, it takes a leap of faith to suspend your need for immediate gratification. When you do that, it doesn't come right away. But when it does, boy, it reinforces.*

Wade: That's a great story. One of my coaching clients had the courage after 10 years to go and see all of his past clients with pies. And I've encouraged him for years and years to do it and he finally had the courage. I don't know why it takes us so long and it takes so much courage. When he had finished, he looked at me and said "My $700 investment of pies I estimate will probably make me $70,000 in referral business. Thank you for pushing me to go have the courage to go see my people and bring them a pie after a decade of being in this business." Really it is that simple. Never underestimate the power of an apple pie, and have the courage to go see somebody and to spend time with them and give them the gift, give your time and give him that apple pie and watch what happens.

Phil/Dan: *It probably had nothing to do with the pies, just the fact that you encouraged him to go out and actually see people, spend time with them, and value them.*

Wade: It took him 10 years to have the courage to go out and see the people.

He said he was just blown away at every single person, they were in awe that he was there and that he had something for them, a pie and the people just invited him in to visit every single time. He was just overwhelmed and blown away at the response and the opportunity of the business that he was going to receive. And he said, I would have never estimated but now I've seen it. He was so excited he went and bought more pies to go give more.

Phil/Dan: *Right. Whoever sold him the pies is probably very happy as well.*

Wade: Absolutely. It can be anything. It doesn't even have to be pie. There's a great book, it's called the "Generosity Factor," by Ken Blanchard. And he said we have three things to give to people: the gift of our time, the gift of our touch, and the gift of our talents. And it has nothing to do with monetary items. It has to do with our talents and our gifts. It has to be just a hug or a kiss or a handshake or a touch and our gift of time. And those are three most powerful things that you have to give to people and to give to the people that are fans of you and your business. And if you give that, you will get. I know it to be true. If I can touch and give time, talent, and touches to others, I'm rewarded handsomely year after year after year in my life.

Phil/Dan: *Wow. And that's so well said, Wade. And that's one of those principles that I think is cross-contextual. It applies to life generally, not just real estate.*

For someone getting into real estate today, what are the things they need to do in order to be successful and prosperous in their business?

Wade: Seek out a mentor. Find someone that has already done this and copy them.

Phil/Dan: *Don't try and reinvent the real estate wheel. Beautifully said. What has changed for those getting into business today?*

Wade: Easy. More distractions, more shiny pennies, more things to distract the real estate agent from the fundamentals of our business. That is the biggest nemesis that has changed in our industry, is that it is the same thing we've been doing over a hundred years in the same way in which you become successful. The challenges with technology and everything out there, just so many shiny pennies, and distractions to pull you away from the core fundamentals of what you should be doing in this business. And the demise, unfortunately, of real estate is that there are just so many other things, all those other shiny little things that are distracting us and pulling us away from those fundamentals. That's the biggest thing I see - distraction.

Phil/Dan: We're living in an ADD world with so many things but I call this the illusive obvious, applying the things that have always worked consistently.

Wade: Yeah, it's so true. And there's just so many different things that we want to try or are being told to try that would do well in real estate, and the reality is that we get distracted from those key things that are right there in front of you.

Phil/Dan: What in your view is the future of the real estate profession?

Wade: I still remember sitting in the real estate office in 1995 when the internet was coming and realizing, "Oh, crap, we have to go back and use my degree because computers and the internet are going to replace the real estate agent." I believed this. This business will always need us, it will always need people, and it will always be. The technology and everything is just a tool and a vehicle for us to communicate and to expedite things but it will always be people-to-people, it will always be business-to-business, it will always need somebody there to be able to negotiate, to be able to handle all the emotions that are involved in this whole entire experience.

And the future of real estate will look completely different especially with the access to the public and wanting the information. But the reality is that if you have relationships in real estate in the next 10, 20, 50, 60, 100 years, you will not fail. If you focus your time and energy and efforts on relationships and people first, I don't care what it looks like in the next 10, 50, 100 years, you will still be a success in real estate, I believe that.

Phil/Dan: On that note, Wade, I want to thank you so much for taking the time to do this. It's been a fabulous interview and I can't wait till we speak next.

Wade: Okay, buddy. You let me know if you need any more information or time, okay? Thank you.

Phil/Dan: Have a great, great weekend.

Million Dollar Agent Key Ideas Summary

$ To be truly successful in real estate you need to passionately believe in the importance of what you are selling and the fact that people need and want what you are selling.

$ It is very often beneficial for an agent to start their career in a challenging market, as opposed to a strong vibrant market, as they develop habits and skills that will serve them well throughout their entire career in real estate.

$ As a realtor you want to avoid the 'transactional trap,' otherwise you end up repeating your first year of business over and over again throughout your career.

$ Like many businesses real estate can be all consuming and it's extremely important that you avoid trading your health, relationships and other important aspects of your life for wealth.

$ Humility and gratitude are two very important keys to being successful in real estate and in life in general.

$ Another great key to success is to be a giver; give of yourself, your knowledge and expertise, your time and this will come back to benefit you in many ways.

$ Never underestimate the power of systems and delegation to free you up to do what you do best and are passionate about.

$ When you help people get what they want and need, all your wants and needs are taken care of.

$ One of the key differences between the most successful agents and those that are struggling is the most successful agents have an abundance mindset.

$ Sales is a full contact sport that is so much more than simply texting and tweeting.

$ There are four activities that get you paid in real estate - take
    a new listing, get an existing listing repositioned and priced
    properly, get a buyer to sign and hire you as their buyer's
    agent, and write a purchase contract and create a buying
    opportunity.

$ Reciprocity is the single most powerful marketing tool in the
    world - giving with no expectation of return.

EPILOGUE

SOMEONE ONCE SAID that a book is never really complete – it is abandoned. For it can always be rewritten, edited, tweaked, and rewritten again, over and over.

Still and all, it is always ultimately up to the author to determine when to call it done.

In the case of this book, this is not a completed work but only a beginning. We say this because while we chose to interview some truly great realtors, managers and brokers and share their stories and document their journeys and valuable lessons of how they became successful and prosperous, there are numerous other absolutely great examples that we wanted to interview and include in this book.

Many other realtors, managers and brokers were not included not because they weren't worthy but rather due mostly to logistical reasons. As such, we are left both inspired and motivated to continue the process of meeting with, learning from, and sharing the valuable lessons from those that we meet and work with as we continue our journey through the ever-changing and always fascinating world of real estate.

PHIL HOLLANDER, M.A., is the Vice President, Business & Professional Development for Morris Real Estate Marketing Group in Toronto, Canada.

For nearly two decades, Phil has spoken at hundreds of real estate gatherings throughout North America. He has shared his insights with thousands of realtors, teaching them how to build their business through incorporating the fundamental principles of referral marketing into their day-to-day business.

In his seminars, Phil shares his expertise on "what really works" in terms of effective real estate marketing and, in the process, provides participants with valuable knowledge about how they can significantly grow their referral business through proven "Systems-Based, High Probability Selling."

Throughout his career Phil has coached, mentored and assisted his clients by providing them with the knowledge, tools and resources so they can take back control of their lives and literally transform their businesses from being transaction-based to creating successful and prosperous systems-based businesses.

Phil is the co-author of *The Referral and Repeat Marketing Book*, as well as the recently published *Choice Points: When You Have to Decide Which Way to Go*.

Morris Real Estate Marketing Group Inc has been in business since 1929. For the past 30 years Morris Real Estate Marketing Group has specialized exclusively in assisting real estate professionals across North America to increase and enhance their business through the *Client Referrals System*. For a comprehensive overview of the *Client Referrals System* please refer to: www.morrismarketinggroup.com.

Phil can be contacted at: phollander@morrismarketinggroup.com or via phone at 1-800-308-6134 ext. 217.